Harold Ogle
Jun 1930.

LORD JOHN RUSSELL

LORD JOHN RUSSELL

(*From the painting by George Hayter, engraved by J. Bromley.*)

LORD JOHN RUSSELL

A STUDY IN CIVIL AND RELIGIOUS LIBERTY

BY

A. WYATT TILBY

WITH EIGHT HALF-TONE PLATES

CASSELL & COMPANY, LTD.

LONDON, TORONTO, MELBOURNE & SYDNEY

127056

First published 1930.

PRINTED IN GREAT BRITAIN

Biography has no dignity. It is
well to have a hero, and a hero with
a good many faults and failings.

Lord John Russell.

PREFACE

FAME is proverbially an irrational quantity, and fame has treated few men more scurvily than Lord John Russell. The world still talks familiarly of Pitt and Peel and Palmerston, but it seems almost to have forgotten the last Whig Prime Minister.

Less than a century ago the hero of the Reform Bill fight was a household word. His name is now recalled— if recalled at all—as the responsible author of the No Popery fiasco.

Many a man lives to see his successes forgotten. Many another dies in the knowledge that his failures are remembered. But not very many are doubly penalized like Russell.

Brougham, it is true, has had an almost worse fate. Everybody remembers that he introduced a famous carriage; but who recalls that he instituted the Judicial Committee of the Privy Council?

With Palmerston, on the other hand, a too grateful country has reversed the process. Lucky in death as in life, that spoilt darling of fate and fame has had his failures forgotten and his successes remembered.

The truth probably is that it is better to fail at the start and succeed later than to score heavily at first and fall behind at the finish. With politicians as with horses, it is the last lap that counts.

But, apart from success or failure, there happen to be special reasons why Lord John Russell's career has a peculiar interest of its own to-day.

He, more perhaps than any other man in English history, was whole-heartedly on the side of liberty against authority, and from first to last he regarded liberty as the solvent of almost every problem. His long public life, in and out of office, touched on practically every political, economic, and ecclesiastical question that confronts society; and the manner in which he treated these refractory matters reveals at once the strength and the weakness of his creed.

Russell, like many another man before and since, regarded the struggle of liberty against authority as equivalent to the march of progress against reaction. The two things are often intimately allied, but they are not in fact the same thing. A community may be free without advancing, and progress in one field often creates the very problems which can only be solved by liberty in another.

It was the progress of transport and industrial invention and medicine which created the problems of population in the new State which Russell and his successors had to solve; and if he sometimes failed, it was at least partly because the foundations on which he had to build were shifting day by day.

The country did progress, and the liberty which Russell insisted on helped it to progress, at a time of extraordinarily rapid change in civil, religious, and scientific outlook. His life coincided almost exactly with a period of not merely physical but mental revolution, and at such a time liberty was even more essential than in the quieter century that had preceded it, when men were only beginning to question the competence of the authority which had seemed to serve them well.

In the main, then, his policy was right for the time, though his methods were sometimes wrong.

But it is clear that Russell regarded liberty as an end in itself, and he did not sufficiently realize that the only end to which men ever put liberty is to build up a new authority which must in time limit—if only by consent— and may in the end subvert the very liberty which has nourished if not actually created it. When, but only when, the new authority falls short of expectations, they turn to liberty again. In other words, men use Liberal doctrine for Conservative purposes, and remedy Conservative defects by Liberal principles. Neither creed is sufficient unless supplemented and corrected by the other.

Russell did not see this, nor Gladstone, nor Morley, because they had not quite thought out their principles to the logical conclusion; with the result that all three showed a sense of frustration and disappointment when the world adopted their theory and then put it to uses they had not foreseen and, because they had not foreseen them, could not approve.

But though they did not realize it, this was in fact liberty in action.

To-day the whole world is again faced with the problem of liberty and authority. It does not, indeed, put it in those terms, because some distrust liberty and others dislike authority, but it is that nevertheless. Once more it is a double problem: the authority of the State to restrict the liberty of its subjects or citizens, and the liberty of the State to assert that authority by an attack upon its neighbours.

(The question of defence, as the size and scope of armaments shows, is really the question of attack. We all know this. It is simply that we do not like admitting it.)

The tendency of the time is everywhere to increase the internal authority of the State and to diminish—at least to attempt to diminish—its external authority; that is to say, to diminish the liberty of the individual in relation to the State, and to diminish the liberty of the State in relation to society as a whole. The former tendency began earlier, and has gone farther, than the latter; with results good and bad. The latter tendency is still in the preliminary stage.

But we are in effect at the beginning of a new period of history, for science will make far greater changes in the social structure, the religious belief, and the traditional morality of civilization in the twentieth century than politics ever contemplated in the nineteenth; with the inevitable consequence that the relations of the individual to the local unit, and of the local unit to the whole fabric of society, will have to be thought out afresh from their foundations.

Unfortunately political thought is now almost as far behind contemporary scientific thought as is religious doctrine, and it falls more in arrear every day; with the natural result that it shows a timidity of approach, an increasing tendency to compromise on major issues, and an increasing lack of precision and certainty in conclusions that make for general contempt. While this prudential cowardice continues, the reputation of politics and political thinking will decline. We cannot expect to find our way out of a wood by shutting our eyes; and we are hardly in a position to throw too many stones at the pugnacious little Whig who was always ready to go to war for liberty.

To-day, it is true, the world talks more about peace and less about liberty. But peace, like liberty, is a means to an end, not the end itself; it is a purely negative ideal, useless until it is used. Men use liberty to establish a new authority, and they use peace to prepare for another war. The only question is whether the new authority is better than the old, and the new war more worth fighting than its predecessor?

The peace that the world needs is not a mere cessation of conflicts between States, but the richer and fuller and more abundant life that would be possible were human energies transferred from their preoccupation with destructive war between societies to the constructive war of society on the hostile elements of nature. A static peace that merely guarantees a continuance of the present social discontents is bound to end in war as the lesser of two evils. A dynamic peace that substitutes a higher ideal of achievement and a larger purpose might well be permanent.

We should not realize it at the time. The citizens of London did not realize that there would be no more plague for forty years after 1665. But it happened.

It is the maladjustment of States to their political environment that produces war. But those maladjustments arise in the main from the poverty and insecurity of society within the State, and those evils could be largely cured by diverting human energy from the conquest of man to the conquest of Nature.

Unfortunately the conception of concerted war on Nature is novel and therefore difficult, whereas the conception of war on one's neighbour is traditional and therefore easy. There is a quality of inertia in man which makes new ways hard; with the result, at once lamentable and ridiculous, that the more it talks about peace, the more it thinks about war.

Now a war to maintain liberty may be bad policy, but it is at least intelligible; whereas a war to maintain peace is simply unintelligible. It is merely an open confession of the failure of States to solve the problem of their mutual relations within the whole body politic.

It is the old problem of liberty and authority on a larger scale, no longer as between individuals but between groups of individuals. These particular questions are not in fact insoluble, for many of them were solved on a smaller scale in the eighteenth and nineteenth centuries. They are simply insoluble by our present methods, which say one thing and mean another, and seem unconscious even of the contradiction. We make an arsenal, and call it peace.

It happens that Lord John Russell was a clear if limited thinker who believed in principle rather than compromise. He made many mistakes, which I have not attempted to disguise; but he said exactly what he meant, and he meant exactly what he said.

I commend this practitioner of a lost art to his successors, who spin words without ceasing, and are caught in the net of their own pacts and phrases.

CONTENTS

Contents

LIST OF ILLUSTRATIONS

LORD JOHN RUSSELL

CHAPTER I

THE WHIG CADET

LORD JOHN RUSSELL was born at Hertford Street, in the Mayfair district of London, on August 18, 1792, a few months after Edmund Burke had published his "Appeal from the New to the Old Whigs," and a few days after the fall of the French Monarchy in Paris. An extremely delicate and undersized child, it seemed unlikely that these or any other public events would ever affect him, and still more unlikely that he would become a great national figure as the last Whig Prime Minister, and die in extreme old age at the very time when the principles he had carried to victory were beginning to decline.

The third son of John, later sixth Duke of Bedford, and a lady who did not live quite long enough to become sixth Duchess, he remained for long a puny infant who survived rather than grew. Even when eleven years old he was only 50 inches high and 56 lb. in weight; and although the next ten years remedied this extreme insignificance, he remained well under the normal size through life.

His mother loved and tended the fragile child with exquisite care, and he never forgot her. More than seventy years later, an old bent man, who had survived almost all his contemporaries, would look back across the storms of State to the early days when he used to call her every morning, and read Plutarch at her knee; and all his life he treasured a letter addressed "To the best of all good little boys, J. R.," in which the invalid lady wrote: "I miss your dear voice when I wake, and I regret you every moment of the day."

This admirable woman was indeed a pattern to all her

sex, for she described her husband as a being who deserved universal reverence. But there was the substance of man behind the god she worshipped, for he married again less than two years after her death, and had ten more children by her successor. This patriarchal disposition did not, however, lead him to neglect his earlier family, and he seems to have taken considerable interest in the careers of his three eldest sons.

When his mother died, in 1801, the delicate little John had already begun the expensive absurdity called a gentle-man's education. An incompetent private school at Sunbury-on-Thames was followed by the traditional bar-barity of a great public school at Westminster. The full rigour of the system was mitigated by the fact that he fagged for his elder brother; it was, in fact, the bad food rather than the doubtful Latin that compelled his removal, and after a few months of tuition at home, he was sent to another private school, kept by a Mr. Smith, a clergyman, near Sandwich. This worthy gentleman, according to Lord John's later account, was "without any remarkable qualities either of character or understanding," but he knew some of the classic authors and as many of the modern aristocracy as he could. The acquaintance can hardly have been unprofitable, for half the Whig dukes of England seem to have entrusted their sons to his select academy.

Dukes or no dukes, the boys were taught their manners. Little John complained that he once dropped some mutton fat under the table, but he was made to sweep it up and eat it, dirt and all. Outside the house, however, the boys were allowed to do much what they liked, and walking, riding, and shooting not only varied the routine of lessons but helped to strengthen the weakly lad's constitution. If he was small, he was tough and plucky, and it began to look as if he might grow up into a man after all.

A visit to Dublin—his father had become Viceroy of Ireland in the short-lived Whig administration of 1806—was followed by a tour through the Lake District and the Highlands to Inverness; and this was preliminary to a trip to Spain with Lord and Lady Holland, when Lord John was sixteen.

2

Foreign travel was a passion that he never lost, but this first flight was doubly memorable from the fact that the Peninsular War had just begun. The party travelled in cavalcade with a retinue of muleteers, soldiers, and litters, as befitted noble and wealthy tourists of that day, but these elaborate arrangements were often disturbed by the campaign. His elders probably cursed their bad luck in crossing Napoleon's star, but the high-spirited lad sniffed the spice of adventure, and liked it so much that after a nine months' visit to the battered country he returned to it at the first opportunity.

No doubt he learnt much more of the world in Spain than the excellent Mr. Smith of Sandwich could teach him. But education of the more formal type had presently to be attended to, and the matter of a university was now debated. The Whig Russells would never, of course, patronize the Tory Oxford, and John naturally looked forward to a year or two at Cambridge. It happened, however, that the Duke of Bedford had no opinion of Cambridge scholarship; but Edinburgh was then at the height of its academic fame under Dugald Stewart and Playfair, and to Edinburgh and a room in Playfair's house Lord John was sent.[1]

He protested at first against his father's idea. "The thing I should most dislike, and least profit by, would be an endeavour to acquire Scotch knowledge in a Scotch town. Political economy may surely be studied in England. As for metaphysics, I cannot even understand the word." These two subjects, in fact, always eluded him, occasionally to his disadvantage in later life; he had little sense of figures, and his philosophy remained elementary. His mind worked to the end in a purely political frame, and the vast speculative range which lent light and shadow to the innumerable activities of Gladstone escaped him. His mind, like his body, was limited, but within those limits it was strong, simple, and direct. Others might hesitate and doubt; John Russell never did.

[1] Curiously enough, Lord John's future colleague and rival, Palmerston, had studied at Edinburgh a few years before, boarding with Stewart instead of Playfair. Unlike Lord John, however, he went on from Edinburgh to Cambridge—which, like the Duke, he found reason to hold in low esteem.

He opposed, then, the idea of Edinburgh, but when the time came, he bowed to his father's wish, and applied himself with sufficient diligence to the arid field of abstract ethics. He joined the Speculative Society as a matter of course, and became an active member; but his contributions to the discussions were on such practical matters as the justice of the war with France and the education of the poor. We may perhaps assume that the cut and thrust of these prentice debates were of greater interest to the budding statesman than the lectures of Dugald Stewart.

But the Continent was soon calling him again. His elder brother, Lord William Russell, was on active service in the Peninsular War, and in September, 1810, John was on his way to the battlefields. The liberated student was kindly received by Wellington, with whom he was to have much to do in later life, and the admiring youth has left us an animated picture of the great man: "his eyes bright and searching as those of an eagle, his countenance full of hope, beaming with intelligence, as he marked with quiet perception every movement of troops and every change of circumstance within the sweep of the horizon. There stood the advanced guard of the conquering legions of France; here was the living barrier of England, Spain, and Portugal prepared to stay the destructive flood, and to preserve from the deluge the liberty and independence of three armed nations. The sight filled me with admiration, with confidence, and with hope"—to such an extent that when he returned to England he wagered Lord Ponsonby a guinea that Wellington would still hold the lines of Torres Vedras a year later.

Lord Grey thought it a foolish bet, and cited chapter and verse from Marshal Villars to prove it so. But twelve months later the guinea changed hands. The youngster had been right.

After this trip the studies at Edinburgh were resumed, with an occasional holiday at Woburn Abbey. It was the time of the Regency, when manners were gay and morals were loose, but these things did not affect the Russells, and a pleasant picture survives of country life at its best in the Bedford home. "The magnificent and well-regulated style of living," wrote an appreciative artist of the time, "the manners of the Duke most amiable and unassuming, and similar to their father are his sons, the Marquess of Tavistock and Lord John Russell. They speak but little, but make themselves agreeable to all persons. The Duchess is very easy and lively, and at the head of her table is very pleasant."

The needs of soul and body were both provided for at Woburn: "At half-past nine every morning, prayers are read by a clergyman in an apartment appropriate for it, at which the servants attend, and always some of the family and some of the guests. About ten o'clock breakfast is ready under the management of the groom of the chambers. Every individual has a teapot, so that each person breakfasts when he pleases and independent of others. Dinner is sat down to at six o'clock, and the gentlemen remain until about half-past eight, when they go to the ladies."[1]

From time to time the other Whig magnates from Bowood and Chatsworth came to Woburn, and the cadets met their future chiefs and colleagues; and at family conclaves politics were discussed, plans were laid, and careers decided. The time was coming for Lord John to take what place he could in the great world—his father was doubtful of his success, not only on account of his size, but because he thought him deficient in judgment—but at these debates it was decided that when a suitable opportunity offered, the lad should have his chance in Parliament. He hated Pitt and worshipped Fox ; what more could the country ask of a Whig cadet?

Meantime the Duchess appears to have thought that John might profitably spend his next holidays nearer home, and the worthy Mr. Playfair was persuaded to take charge of a three weeks' tour through the manufacturing districts of the Midlands and North of England. The professor discharged his task with the utmost gravity and zeal, and the pupil saw something of the new urban industry which was to revolutionize the country in his lifetime. But the

---

[1] There was no afternoon tea in those days. This innovation was first introduced into England by a later Duchess of Bedford about fifty years afterwards.

best of professors is apt to be a little heavy in the hand even with the best of pupils; and although the experiment was successful enough, it was not repeated. In the following summer Lord John left Edinburgh University—it was not considered necessary that he should take a degree—and soon afterwards he was off abroad again, but this time without a professional mentor at his elbow.

He had planned something more ambitious than the ordinary grand tour of gilded youth, and intended to visit Egypt and Syria, as well as Italy and Greece. But Spain lay on the way to all those countries, his brother was still serving there in the now victorious British armies, and to Spain he naturally went first. We may assume that an occasional invitation to the Duke of Wellington's dinner-table was as enjoyable as the academic conversation of the Edinburgh evening tea-parties; but the tour was seriously intended, and Lord John had travelled as far as the Balearic Islands when it became necessary to change his plans.

Opportunity had come sooner than he expected. The member for Tavistock in the House of Commons had recently died. The borough belonged to the Bedfords, and the Duke instructed the thirty-odd free electors of the place to return his third son to Parliament. Lord John was not quite of age, but nice customs curtsey to great owners; the Whig cadet left England a mere boy on a holiday, and returned home to find himself a responsible statesman.

CHAPTER II

UNREFORMED PARLIAMENT

THE activity and perseverance of mankind, remarked the sententious Playfair to his pupil, are continually defeating the folly and caprice of their governors. The perfect apophthegm, like the perfect acrostic, reads as easily backwards as forwards; and it is perhaps an open question whether the folly and caprice of mankind have not as often defeated the activity and perseverance of their governors. The passions and prejudices of the people are not infallibly right. The plans and projects of politicians are not invariably wrong. It is not altogether inconceivable that the heads of the State have a larger horizon than the feet on which it marches; nor is it entirely incredible that progress should come from the leaders, and be resisted by the followers.

These propositions are indeed obvious in the second quarter of the twentieth century, when the incompetence of democracy to solve its own problems, and its tacit refusal to take a serious interest in politics, is causing its decline. But in the first quarter of the nineteenth century the position was precisely the reverse. The benevolent despotisms had collapsed, autocracy had failed to maintain itself, and aristocracy itself was beginning to feel the thrust of the professional and trading middle class. It was therefore natural for the eminent Playfair, who was, after all, a greater authority on mathematics than government, to see all the vices in the rulers, and all the virtues in the ruled.[1]

The truth behind his generalization was that social and

[1] Dickens would have agreed with Playfair. "My faith in the people governing is, upon the whole, infinitesimal; my faith in the people governed is, on the whole, illimitable."

The novelist had seen politics at closer range than the professor. As reporter in the Press Gallery, he heard all the great speakers at the time industrial change was knocking at the door of political constitutions. In England there had been a steady increase of population in the towns for a century past. It peeps out shyly in the pages of Defoe's "Tour" under George I. It attracts the casual attention of Wesley on his interminable gospel rides, fifty years later. It forces itself equally on Lord John when he visits the new manufacturing centres and finds them very good, and on Cobbett, who finds them very bad.

Agriculture had not indeed suffered by the emergence of this new rival and future conqueror; its first consequences had in fact been helpful, for towns must be fed and clothed, and the market for produce had naturally increased. Land had never paid so well, and great palaces and roomy farmhouses were being built on the profits. Owners and tenants were both prosperous, and enclosures combined with rotation and high prices to increase their profits. Bar a little sheep-stealing and rick-burning, the troubles of agriculture were all in the future.

But politically, the position was becoming difficult. The Englishman was accustomed to boast the perfection of Parliament to the intelligent but inferior foreigner, and the boast had been received with due humility by the lesser breeds without the Habeas Corpus. But when the persistent alien pursued his inquiries, it needed some agility to defend a representative system which made Palmerston a member for the Isle of Wight on condition that he never set foot in the constituency, which gave nominee members to dead villages in the south like Old Sarum and Gatton, and which still called Midhurst a parliamentary borough, though all the houses had been pulled down; while at the same time it ignored great cities in the north like Leeds, Bradford, Sheffield, and Manchester. Englishmen are seldom expert in casuistry; but when a property-owner named a waiter at White's as member for one of his boroughs, and the formality or farce of an election had to be gone through again because the

when Lyndhurst and Brougham were in their prime. It gave him a contempt for Parliament, but much of this was probably due to disgust at the mechanical nature of his work.

proposer did not know the man's Christian name, even an expert casuist might have found it difficult to make his logic convincing.

It is true that the latter case was a scandalous exception, and that decency was generally preserved; the House could not otherwise have maintained its high reputation under the Georges. Most of the borough-owners had at least some sense of responsibility, and many of them made a point of selecting young men of ability for their Members. The trouble was not so much that the wrong men were returned to the House of Commons, but that they were returned for the wrong places by the wrong means.

The problem was certainly not beyond the wit of man to solve; apart from the vested interests that had grown up and a possible question of compensation, a simple redistribution of seats would have sufficed. But time and the pressure of events had been against the reformers for fifty years. Liberty Wilkes had agitated, but a disreputable man who happens to be right seldom succeeds when he attacks a reputable institution which happens to be wrong. The voice of the people was the voice of God till the Gordon Riots taught him better; democrat Wilkes fired on the London mob that was wrecking property in the City, and his influence was gone.

The younger Pitt as a Tory had intended to reform Parliament, but the French War side-tracked that and many another project. The new Whigs whom Fox led had also believed in reform, but their power in argument was counteracted by their poverty in numbers, and the whole Whig party was divided and disgruntled by the French Revolution and the French War, which their principle of civil and religious liberty made it difficult either to oppose or support. The Tories, on the other hand, had been stampeded by the Jacobins across Channel into stark Conservatism. The name was not indeed yet coined—it was first used by Croker in the *Quarterly Review* in 1831—but the spirit of reaction was there, and the nation held it to be justified.

In the main, no doubt, the nation was wise for the time being, for the reaction was simply against excesses which shocked the Whig Burke even more than the Tory Dundas; but while the Whigs played with fire, the Tories decided to put it out, and in the thirty years' struggle with revolutionary French Imperialism which followed, a good many other things went out as well as Jacobinism, including the Tory faith in Parliamentary reform.

The Tories governed on the simple but sensible principle of battening down the hatches while the ship was weathering the storm; but when the tempest was over, the victory they deserved had converted a foul-weather expedient into a fair-weather principle. Sixty years of Tory supremacy, said Russell nearly sixty years later, "had placed the country in a position of immense power, enormous debt, and great internal difficulty." The verdict was conspicuously fair,[1] but the method adopted by the Tories of solving their difficulties was to keep the hatches permanently battened. The Tories of the old school, said Stanley—the Rupert of debate—were "sticklers for inveterate abuses under the name of the wisdom of our ancestors." Those who recall the Eldon school of statecraft will hardly challenge the judgment.

Even allowing for the inertia that infects a nation after an exhausting war, it seems at first sight strange that a party which could be so described should have been able to retain power more than fifteen years after the Peace, while hungry Whigs were clamouring for office in the name of Progress. But when the actual position is examined, the reason is clear enough.

It is true that Pitt had been nearly ten years in his grave. But the extraordinary prestige of the Duke of Wellington in the Lords more than made good the lost leader in the Commons. And in the Lower House, Castlereagh, though a far smaller man than Pitt, was always cold, calm, and capable; while many remembered that he had solved a problem that had baffled both the Pitts and Dundas—he had created the expeditionary force that had fed the con-

---

[1] *Cf.* his earlier and more partisan judgment of 1838: "It is difficult to find any political evil which is not to be traced to Pitt. However, one has the satisfaction of thinking that a country which has survived being governed by Pitt must last for ever."

tinental campaigns. If he was hardly a great, he was at least a very effective man; the monstrous caricatures which the Whig historians drew of him after his unhappy death were merely party spite and venom.

Lord Liverpool was of still smaller stature in debate, but he understood the business of administration. No man can be Prime Minister for fourteen years who is entirely incompetent, and even his opponents admitted his personal integrity, his fairness in discussion, his moderation in policy. Moreover, in strong contrast to Castlereagh— a bad speaker whose faults were only redeemed by his sincerity—and Liverpool, who was merely dull, was Canning, the darling of the Commons and, in his day, as great a master of the House as Fox and Sheridan and the giants of the past. George Canning was one of those rare spirits to whom England gives herself both heart and mind—a statesman whose name resounded through Europe, an orator whose lightest word was heard with strained attention by his friends, and a wit whose sallies charmed even while they confounded his enemies.

And on the other side of the House, the Whigs were still in the very trough of the wave of depression. Gone, never to return, were the great days when the fourth Duke of Bedford and the notorious "Bloomsbury Gang" had controlled English politics for a generation; gone, too, were the famous pair who had so long dominated the Opposition, and so often made the mediocre Tory Treasury Bench look contemptible. Burke was now revered in his grave by both parties for the political wisdom which neither would listen to in his life; Fox, the idol of his side with feet of clay, had quietly followed Pitt to the tomb. In their place were leaders who disdained office, and followers who disdained everything else.

The Whig dukes were in the first stages of that slow decline which overtakes all political institutions that withdraw from the struggle for power. Too great to fight their battles in person, the time was coming when the enemy would simply ignore them. Like Richmond Castle in Yorkshire, they were so impregnable as to be neither attacked nor defended, and what had once been a necessary fortress of Government was now gradually decaying into a picturesque survival and ornament.

That time was not yet come; but the rest of the Whig peerage that had once ruled England, exquisite, fastidious, and cultured as it was, was beginning to show signs of that peculiar disease which only attacks the privileged, the anæmia of prosperity. Lansdowne, indeed, who like Pitt had been Chancellor of the Exchequer at twenty-four, was politically active. But Earl Grey, the ideal Whig politician, a man of austere virtue and an aristocrat of aristocrats, loved his native Northumberland so much that he could hardly be persuaded to come to London, and would do almost anything rather than lead his party.

Althorp was hardly in the same class as a statesman, but his character and ability were undoubted; yet he, too, had no stomach for office. "If I had my choice," he said to Russell years afterwards, "I would prefer anything, death not excluded, to sitting on the Treasury Bench"; and Lord John Russell himself was of opinion that while Althorp might possibly intrigue to get out of the Cabinet, he would certainly never intrigue to get in. Perhaps no man who weighs his breakfast carefully before eating it, for fear of the gout, and rushes half-famished from the room rather than risk another ounce of toast, is really equipped to lead in the rough world of politics.

Like the less enterprising angels, the magnates of the party had flung away ambition. But what is a virtue in Paradise is a vice in Parliament; and it was unlikely that an able and ambitious youngster like Russell, who was stamped in the authentic Whig mint and was determined to push his way to the front, would find the path to high office permanently blocked by men so fastidious and afraid of soiling their finger-nails as these. Politics, after all, is the art of the practical, and those who are too proud to fight are generally taken at their own valuation by men who want a career. The former get all the praise, but the latter get all the power.

Russell's real competitors were to be men of another class—men for whom things had not been made so easy that they could afford to stand aside while others snatched the prizes, and therefore men who were ready to toil at the ordinary routine of official duty while the great aristocrat led a life of cultured leisure and dignified ease. Of these competitors there were four who might have disputed with him the supreme place in the State; two definitely succeeded, two failed to stay the course, and Russell the courageous weakling survived them all.

Of these four, Melbourne and Palmerston were close and intimate colleagues for years, and we shall meet them on almost every page of this history. Graham, who was born a Whig and died a Tory, was mentally at least their equal and morally perhaps their superior, but he failed from a timidity and irresolution of character which contrasted oddly with his splendid physique and commanding appearance. Bold in debate, he was fearful and irresolute in action. He described himself as "always shuddering on the brink of the torrent": in every conceivable course he saw great evil, and the course actually adopted usually seemed to him the worst of all. Too much of a Tory for the Whigs and too much of a Whig for the Tories, it seems clear that Graham chose the wrong vocation. He could not trust the people, and he would not distrust the people, and his ineffective virtues would probably have made him an ideal bishop.

Sir James Graham was exactly contemporary with Russell; Palmerston was three years and Melbourne thirteen years his senior. Of the same age as Melbourne, and high above them all in intellect and industry, was the fourth and most formidable of Russell's competitors—the magnificent and meteoric Brougham, the greatest mind since Bacon, the most versatile and restless spirit who has ever entered our politics, who might have left a nobler fame than Fox and a greater name than Gladstone had the second part of his career been even half as splendid as the first.

The astounding range of Brougham's gifts was catalogued with pride by his friends and with despair by his enemies; if this great lawyer had only known a little law, said a jealous wit of the time, he would have known a little of everything. Even Macaulay, who was seldom

13

generous to a competitor till he was dead, had to admit that Brougham did one thing well, before going on to proclaim that he did two or three things indifferently and a hundred detestably.

These spacious interests would indeed have gone for little in an age that worshipped eloquence, had they not been adorned by excellence of speech; but Brougham's rhetoric was by general consent sublime, and his invective like a tornado that beat down everything in its path. It was said that he vowed not to open his mouth for a month after he entered Parliament—the spiteful Creevey declared that once the month was up he never shut it again[1]—but Brougham's effortless mastery of speech was seldom equalled and hardly surpassed even by Plunket in that last wonderful decade of the unreformed House of Commons, when oratory, in Russell's opinion, rose to a height of art it had never touched before and has never since attained.

But these gifts of understanding and eloquence were marred and ultimately rendered useless by fatal defects of character. It was not merely that Brougham was vain, for many men, from Cicero to Morley and Haldane, have been both vain and successful. It was not that his amazing industry led him to sit in court at all hours of the day, and even to hear causes on Good Friday—the first judge to do so, as Lincoln's Inn observed, since Pontius Pilate—but the age was not noted for religious scruples, and the Oxford Movement was still to come. It was certainly not that he was so incessantly active that he had no time to think[2]; for that defect is inevitably common under a parliamentary system which makes men quick rather than deep reasoners, and many politicians build up a great and not undeserved reputation for wisdom in counsel on a very limited mental equipment.

---

[1] Creevey describes Brougham as "this mass of insincere jaw." But Brougham's speeches read as if they were sincere.

[2] He admitted this himself. His whiskers turned grey while his hair remained brown, and he replied that this was "quite natural, because his jaw had been at work for twenty years, while his brain had been in perfect repose."

These things might possibly have prejudiced and handicapped Brougham a little, but they could not have prevented a man of such commanding ability from dominating the political landscape. Yet no man in our time has risen to such a height, and fallen so fast or so far; and the reason is simple.

With all his genius there was one defect, but that one was fatal. His colleagues could not trust him. He could not stand by his friends. He deceived his client the Queen. He could not keep a Government secret.[1] He could not be depended on to tell the truth. And there came a time when his colleagues, even while they recognized that his abilities were far greater than their own, would not have him at any price.

When he was left out of the Government he attacked Melbourne in a speech of devastating brilliance. The Prime Minister replied simply: "My lords, you have heard the eloquent speech of the noble and learned lord—one of the most eloquent he ever delivered in this House—and I leave your lordships to judge what *must be* the nature and strength of the objections which prevent any Government from availing themselves of the services of such a man." The retort was convincing.

Seventy years later another Chancellor sat on the Woolsack. Unlike Brougham, Halsbury's opinions were rigid; unlike Brougham again, his interests were limited, and his mind, though precise, was by comparison mediocre. But his motto was "Never turn your back on a friend or an enemy," and he held that seat for seventeen years, and died respected by friend and enemy at ninety, without being once reproached for infidelity to his maxim. Had Brougham combined Halsbury's sterling straightness of character with his own surpassing genius, he might have ruled England for a generation.

[1] Brougham was told in strict confidence of the dismissal of the 1834 Melbourne Government by the King. The next morning it was in *The Times*, with the addition "The Queen has done it all"—which was untrue. In the divorce affair, it was reported all over the town that he had "sold the Queen." In fact he defended her. But Liverpool as Prime Minister offered a large sum to settle the case, and Brougham concealed the offer from his client.

The interminable Croker once remarked to Brougham, of all men, that Canning had a squint in his mind's eye. As applied to Canning the criticism was unjust, but it was an exact description of Brougham himself. The tolerant Melbourne could forgive anything in a man except letting his friends down, but when even Melbourne excluded Brougham from his Government, the greatest and perhaps the least trustworthy genius of modern politics fell, never to rise again.

And with the fall of Brougham and the conversion of Graham to Toryism the path was clear for Lord John Russell, whenever the Whigs should return to power.

CHAPTER III

PRENTICE FAILURES

IT has been necessary to look ahead a good many years in order to understand the position when Lord John Russell entered Parliament. We must now return to the House of Commons, of which he found himself the youngest member in 1813.

The name of Russell had been so long associated with English liberty, and so many Russells were held in pious memory at Westminster, that no cadet of the house of Bedford could enter Parliament entirely unobserved. But it would have been difficult for any member whose father was completely unknown to have attracted less attention at the start.

Lord John had no intention of being one of those who attempt to take the House by storm ; at barely twenty-one, and with that puny figure, it would have been foolhardy, and indeed almost certain failure, to have risked it. But many a shy young member with a becoming sense of modesty has plucked up courage to stammer a few platitudes in his first session, and been rewarded by the kindly cheers of veteran debaters on both sides, who remember the mingled agonies and hopes of their own maiden speech years before. For six months, however, the young representative of Tavistock did not open his mouth in public.

We may assume, if we please, that he was carefully studying the moods and mannerisms of the assembly he was afterwards to lead for so many years. But it is a belief that rests on very scanty evidence of attendance; and the truth seems to be that the new member of the House, like the new boy at Westminster School across the road a few years before, took more interest in Drury Lane and the other play-houses of the town than in his proper studies.

His first speech, on the union of Norway and Sweden, made little noise and was soon forgotten. In the following year he protested against the renewal of the war with France, on the plea that we had no right to compel any country to adopt a particular form of government. But Napoleon had returned to Paris, and Liberal doctrine of this sort fell on stony ground.

In 1816, when peace was restored, he seconded an amendment condemning the Government, and early in 1817 opposed the suspension of the Habeas Corpus Act. "We talk too much," he declared, "of the wisdom of our ancestors. I wish we could imitate the courage of our ancestors. Anxious as I am for reform, I am still more anxious that the House shall preserve the respect of the people."

For the first time, so far as we can tell—the earlier speeches have not been preserved—he had given a taste of his future quality. But the appeal as yet was in vain, and Russell's attendances at the House, which had always been intermittent, now ceased altogether for a while, and he spoke gloomily to his friends of abandoning political life. No doubt he recalled that Pitt had been Chancellor of the Exchequer at twenty-five, and contrasted the great Tory's early prominence with his own obscure position on the Opposition back benches.

His career, in fact, started rather slowly and not very successfully. But there was no particular reason why the world should pay special attention to him. The spectacle of a young Whig politician who looked little better than a dwarf lecturing a Tory Government that had been in office before he was born on the art of statecraft, can hardly have been impressive. Exactly the same sentiments had been heard from prentice hands any time a hundred years past, perhaps rather better expressed; for Russell was not naturally a good speaker. His voice was thin, and his manner awkward ; and a House of Commons familiar with the finished orators of the day was not likely to give much more than a casual glance at a young fledgling talking the ordinary party stuff.

In any event, his health was still against him, and the

"little white-faced boy" whom Creevey noticed and liked because he was a Russell—"all the Russells are excellent, and there is nothing in the aristocracy to be compared with this family"—was as yet too delicate for the rough and tumble of debate, the late hours, and the vitiated atmosphere of Parliamentary life. Moreoever, he was by no means merely a politician, and for several years to come his interests were scattered over a larger variety of subjects than any man could hope to excel in.

Much of his time was still spent on foreign travel, an expensive luxury in which the Bedford family could afford to indulge, and he was frequently seen in that bizarre Restoration society of Paris of which Balzac has left us so faithful and attractive a figure. But the glimpses we have of Russell in memoirs of the day picture him there rather as observer than participant, and a Frenchman of the time laments that he "shows to so little advantage in society, from his extreme taciturnity, and still more from apparent coldness and indifference to what is said by others."

It might be charitably surmised that Russell, like many another young Englishman abroad, felt ill at ease in another tongue and with another code of manners. But we shall meet the same complaint of coldness and indifference too often in later years from observers nearer home for that explanation to hold.

The facile suggestion has of course been made that he was entirely self-centred and self-satisfied, but that is also untenable. Russell was a man wholly without affectation, extraordinarily loyal to his friends, and full of affectionate abandon among his intimates. But he made friends rather slowly, and there was always a gulf fixed between the select inner circle and the many casual acquaintances of the man about town; and when the latter made unwelcome advances, he seems to have snubbed them more effectually than politely.

It is possible, of course, to write this down as the aloofness of the aristocrat, and Russell certainly never forgot that he came of noble stock. But I think a truer explanation of the shyness and coldness he always showed in general company lies in the defects of his physique.

The little man had no reserves of strength. But ambition made him attempt rather more than the small tough body could properly achieve, and when the day's work was done, there was no small change left over for those polite and superficial contacts with general society on which a man's personal popularity depends. Had Russell been content to dawdle through life, he might easily have found time to be charming. As he intended to make his way, he had no surplus resources for the minor social graces.

At this time, too, he was much preoccupied with another possible path to fame. He had not made so deep an impression on Parliament that he could be sure even of an Under-Secretaryship in the improbable event of the Whigs obtaining office, and speech having yielded little in the way of reputation, he turned naturally to writing.

It is true that authorship goes ill with affairs of State; for politics and letters are both jealous mistresses, and the rival arts of oratory and writing are too akin in their aim, and too different in their appeal, to lie down happily together. But for some years, while Russell was spending more of his time in Paris and Florence than Westminster, he wrote assiduously and published regularly, and a small shelf might easily be filled with his literary remains.

It is not necessary to examine these productions closely. His verse has the smoothness without the spirit of Pope; the Bedford level in poetry is as flat as the native Fens. By an odd coincidence, Lord John Russell had been born within a week or two of another rebellious spirit; but the glorious goddess that lavished her most exquisite gifts on Shelley had nothing but schoolboy rhymes for the future statesman.

His drama has been criticized as the worst tragedy in the English language. "Don Carlos" can claim no such melancholy distinction, but it is very much farther from the best. It was never acted, but it can be looked through, if not with pleasure, at any rate without conscious heroism, at least by those strong souls who have survived Otway. Of his translation of Homer it was cruelly said that if it had been made by another man in another metre it might have passed muster; but the judgment was delivered by a friend, not an enemy, and has not been appealed against.

Of his essays, the best that can be said is that they are readable, in the same sense that food which is neither good nor bad may be described as edible; but they contain nothing that has not been better said by others not in the front rank. If Lord John Russell had done nothing more in literature than this, he would stand as high, but no higher than those familiar aristocratic authors whom the world conspires to praise because they prefer sonnets to stag-shooting, but all the same one would sooner digest their venison than their verse.

But it would be as unjust to assess Russell's literary capacity by his drama and essays as it would be to judge Gladstone by his book on Church and State, or Winston Churchill by his early novel. These things were the recreation of a young man who was feeling his way in life; his more solid work was his "Memoirs of the Affairs of Europe," his "Essay on the French Revolution," and above all his "Constitutional History of England."

It is true that the first has been superseded by time, and the second and third by research. But all three may still be read with profit; not, indeed, for any unusual qualities of style or matter or profundity of thought, but as showing a fresh young mind in contemplation of the problems it was later to deal with in action. These works are, in fact, a confession of the Russell faith; and it was a faith that was to move England, not perhaps to its highest or greatest deeds in the world, but in a steady orbit of practical and common-sense political achievement.

For this, of course, there were special but sufficient reasons. Lord John was to prove the fragile flower of the sturdy Russell stock; and the Russell family was typically English. The Greys were too cold, the Percies too hot, the Lansdownes too mixed, the Cavendishes too heavy, the Churchills too uncertain, and the Cecils too superior in one generation and too inferior in another, to rank as typical English families; in the whole country there was only one stock, and that the Stanleys, who could rival the claim of the Russells to be ordinary intelligent Englishmen of the better sort.

But the Stanleys had never quite known which side to support, and had therefore never quite pulled their weight in the boat unless it was certain to win; whereas the Russells had just that touch of doggedness and decision which the Stanleys had always lacked, and though they liked power and place as well as other mortals, they had never deserted their side. A Tory Russell would have been a freak of nature; they were consistently conservative in their habitual liberalism. As they were born, so they died; if you wanted to convince a Russell, said Sidney Smith, you had to trepan, not argue.

But the Russells had certainly done very well for themselves. The superstitious had always maintained that those who took Church lands at the Reformation were fated to misfortune, but for three centuries no visitation from heaven had descended upon the fortunate owners of Covent Garden and Woburn Abbey. Their vast possessions were prudently managed; there had been no runaway marriages, and no mad spendthrifts among the Russells, such as had brought other great families from a palace to a pawnshop.

They had a steady eye upon the main chance; and when Lord John was a child of eight, Londoners were provided with a conspicuous example of the family foresight. Metropolitan land values were going up as the town extended, and the opportunity was not overlooked by the prudent heads at Woburn Abbey. In the year 1800, Bedford House in Bloomsbury was dismantled, and the pictures and furniture sold on the spot by Christies; and the mansion and grounds were so enormous that Russell Square and Tavistock Square were both laid out on the vacant site, to the great profit of the family.[1]

The Russells used their wealth wisely in draining the countryside, starting model farms and carrying on stock-breeding experiments. They could be generous but never

---

[1] This land-hunger and sense of real estate values existed in Lord John himself, and was once used in the national interest. When he was for a short time Colonial Secretary in the Melbourne Government, the French Ambassador asked him how much of Australia the British claimed. He promptly replied, "The whole."

prodigal, and the family was on the whole nearer to meanness than extravagance.   It was said in town that the fifth
Duke, who was the target of Burke's famous retort,[1] was
close-fisted, and what may have been malignant gossip in
his case was certainly true of the seventh.   Society was
scandalized and amused by stories of the miserly mil-
lionaire; Greville told Clarendon how Lord John's elder
brother had borrowed a pony at Newmarket rather than
bring his own horses; and Clarendon capped it with an
anecdote of the seventh Duke asking people to buy lozenges
for him when he had a cold, in order to save sixpence;
while Lady Eden remembered that he had borrowed her
carriage rather than order one of his own coachmen out.

His meanness with his younger brother was almost
incredible.   Lord John was not extravagant, and he once
confessed that he was never in debt until he was Prime
Minister; but his resources—even allowing for the income
from the Holland estates at Kennington, which the Holland
family willed him for life—were hardly adequate to the
great position he built up for himself.   Yet it was not
until 1857, when Lord John was well over sixty, that the
Duke settled an adequate annuity on his famous brother.

But the Russells were ever as careful guardians of liberty
as of property; indeed, they were almost hereditary stewards
of the national freedom.   In the Short Parliament of 1640
the Bedford of that day had been one of the minority of
twenty-five peers to agree with the Commons that redress
of grievances should precede supply.   A later Russell
lost his head and gained an immortal reputation in the
reign of Charles II.   They had played a leading part in
the Whig Revolution of 1688, and since then the family
had been among the half-dozen chieftains of the Whig
oligarchy that ruled England in the eighteenth century.

[1] The Duke had attacked the grant of a royal pension to Burke in 1796.
He replied that royal pensions to the house of Russell had been "so enormous
as not only to outrage economy, but to stagger credibility.   The Duke is
the leviathan among the creatures of the Crown.   Huge as he is, he is still
a creature: his ribs, his fins, his whalebone, his blubber, the very spiracles
through which he spouts a torrent of brine against his origin, and covers
me all over with the spray—everything of him and about him is from the
throne.   Is it for him to question the dispensation of the royal favour?"

But with all their wealth, they had never, even in a corrupt or casual age, deviated from their love of liberty, they had never tampered with Habeas Corpus, and never failed to support the cause of parliamentary reform.

Like most highly placed Whigs, the Russells were conformists rather than ardent believers in matters of religion. A decent respect for the opinions of mankind made them support the Church as long as it acknowledged the supremacy of the State. But all creeds were much the same so long as they were not enforced, and most doctrines inoffensive so long as they were optional.[1] The important thing was not what one professed to believe, but what one permitted others to believe; and since the strength of the Churches was palpably on the decline through the eighteenth century, it was not only right in theory, but expedient in practice, to support full religious as well as civil liberty.

The fourth Duke was in favour of relaxing those laws against the Roman Catholics which Whigs as well as Tories had approved after the Revolution of 1688; the sixth Duke had practically brought down the short-lived Whig Government of 1806 by advocating emancipation, as Viceroy of Ireland; and John Russell himself always supported freedom of conscience so long as the ecclesiastics refrained from activity. Then, knowing the tyranny of faith, and disliking even the faintest reminder of the smell of burning, he bestirred himself and wrote the famous "No Popery" letter.

That particular episode, with its disconcerting sequel, will concern us later. It is mentioned here simply to indicate that Russell had not thought out his principles quite to their logical conclusion. The only cure for the excesses of liberty, said Macaulay in a famous essay, is more liberty. Russell manifestly considered that the same cure was not necessarily applicable to an autocracy or theo-

[1] Lord John's own attitude is summed up in four sentences: "Christ had told his apostles to preach a religion of love. It had been perverted with a religion of logic. St. John, St. Paul, and Christ himself had called for sympathy. St. Athanasius and St. Thomas Aquinas relied on a syllogism." In two words, No Dogma.

cracy that established itself within a free system, which it used to its own advantage.

The fact is that the Whig philosophy was not quite at the centre of truth. It was nearer the mark, at least at that time, than the rival Tory creed, which was little more than a negation, and might have been summed up in the maxim of Machiavelli that "All history proves it is necessary for the ruler of a republic to presuppose all men to be bad, and bound to act in accordance with their natural malignity on every occasion that gives them opportunity." Men may be bad, but the appeal to history certainly does not prove them to be as bad as that.

The reforming Whig, on the contrary, presupposed nearly all men to be good, and so good that most of them would naturally vote for their Whig benefactors, who would be restored in a reformed England to the place which they had loved long since and lost awhile, while the Tories languished in outer darkness. Men may be good, but the event proved that in the long run they are not so good as that.

Lord John was to take the lead in the agitation for parliamentary reform, and it is on his long record in that campaign that his fame as a statesman chiefly rests. But had he been able to look into the minds of his contemporaries, he would have seen that things were not likely to fall out quite as the Whig reformers hoped. "I am for a reform of some sort," the sturdy Cobbett wrote on November 25, 1822, "but not Lord John's sort. What I want to see is the men changed. I want to see some fresh faces. I am aware that this is not what the great reformers mean. I believe that Sir Francis Burdett has not the smallest idea of an Act of Parliament ever being made without his assistance, that he looks upon a seat in the House as his property, and that the other seat is, and ought to be, held as a sort of leasehold or copyhold under him."

The Whig junta, of which John Morley remarked that a few patricians carried away the great prizes while other men did the work, lasted indeed for many years longer. But even by 1846 Clarendon observed that the vitality of the exclusive aristocratic group was declining; twelve years later Lord Derby considered that the country was tired of the Whig family clique; and after the second Reform Bill of 1867, its influence sank rapidly towards impotence. The benevolent despotism of the old Whigs was swamped by the new Liberals, and the tributaries who had been kept in their places by a smile or a frown soon reversed the traditional position. It was the tribunes who henceforth controlled the citadel, and allotted a few ornamental places as a favour to their old masters for past services rendered or in recognition of an historic name.

Lord John Russell lived to see himself, in a biting phrase of Sir William Harcourt's, the last doge of Whiggism; he did not live to see, and would hardly have believed it had he seen, the later turn of the tide against parliamentary government and constitutional rule in twentieth-century Europe. "It is impossible," he cried in his youth, "that the whisper of a faction shall prevail against the voice of a nation." But he forgot that the people are often indifferent to their rulers, he did not understand that political liberty is not necessarily a solace for economic insecurity, and he could not foresee that the increasing complexity of civilization would require expert scientific knowledge which neither progressive politicians of the old school nor the spreading democracy of the new school could possess or control.

He did his work, and it proved well worth the doing; indeed, much of it was essential to the making of modern England. But perhaps few men would have been more surprised at its ultimate result than he.

CHAPTER IV

A TEN YEARS' STRUGGLE

IN the summer of 1819 public meetings were held in various parts of the country in support of parliamentary reform. The greatest of these was naturally at Manchester, the largest of the new cities which were without representatives in the House of Commons. A foolish and probably frightened magistrate ordered troops to fire on the crowd, and what became known as the Peterloo Massacre ensued.

Meetings to express remonstrance and indignation were properly held in other parts of the country; the Government became alarmed and summoned Parliament. The Ministers had no idea of removing the cause of the complaint by assigning members to the new industrial centres; their proposal was merely to strengthen the law, already strong enough, against dangerous or disorderly expression of opinion.

It was obviously high time for the Whigs, as friends of liberty, to act; and Lord John Russell returned hastily from a foreign tour in which polite letters and a polite flirtation had replaced home politics. Prentice days were almost over; he had now set his hand to the special work that was to give him the leadership of the party and eventually of the country.

Russell had carefully studied the technical as well as the popular case for reform well in advance, and in place of the Tory policy of repression, he asked the House to agree that (*a*) all boroughs in which gross and notorious bribery and corruption should be proved to prevail, should cease to return members to Parliament; (*b*) that the right so taken away should be given to some great town or the largest counties; (*c*) that it was the duty of the House to consider further means to detect and prevent corruption at elections;

and (*d*) that it was expedient that the borough of Grampound should be disfranchised.

The resolutions seem to us a piece of modest common sense. But it is clear from a letter which Russell wrote to his friend the poet Moore on the eve of the motion that he anticipated failure, and a speedy resumption of his private life.

Actually, however, things did not so fall out. The Government would not, of course, accept the motion as a whole, since it would have shattered their whole policy. But the ground of attack had been well chosen—the member who had purchased Grampound had been sentenced to a heavy fine and two years' imprisonment for corruption—and it was impossible for an honest Tory to defend methods of that kind. Lord Castlereagh, therefore, offered to accept the last portion of the Russell motion, if Lord John would withdraw his general proposals.

This was an unexpected success, and Russell at once agreed. The truth was, no doubt, that the Grampound affair was too much for any appetite, but to admit the Russell principle in one case was, in fact, to undermine the whole Government position. Chance, however, favoured the Tories, and parliamentary reform was to be delayed more than ten years longer.

This was, no doubt, a bad thing for the country, and an extremely bad thing for the Whigs as a party. But it was certainly a good thing for Lord John Russell. If the Tories had been less recalcitrant and the fight less severe, he would have had fewer opportunities of distinguishing himself, and making good his claim to promotion against the time when the Whigs came in. But so many of the Whigs were privately lukewarm on the reform question that his eager assistance had long since become indispensable when a Reform Ministry was actually formed.

A few weeks after Russell's little victory over Grampound the old King died, and it became necessary to elect a new Parliament. Before the dissolution, however, Lord John not merely introduced but actually succeeded in carrying through the Commons a Bill to suspend the three corrupt boroughs of Penryn, Camelford, and Grampound; and on the motion of another member, Barnstaple was added to the list. The Bill was sent in due course to the Lords, but in the meantime the Cato Street Conspiracy to murder the Cabinet had been exposed.

It could not, of course, be suggested for a moment that any advocate of constitutional reform was concerned in this horrible business, least of all a Russell. But any stick is good enough to beat a dog with; and in the general revulsion of feeling, Lord Chancellor Eldon had no diffi-culty in persuading the Lords to do what they wished to do. The Bill was rejected, and corruption breathed again.

The old system was hopelessly out of date and logically doomed. But it was strong in possession of the field; and the public mind, which prefers a personal quarrel to an issue of principle, was now distracted and delighted over the Queen's divorce. On this matter the Tories, being in office, had to stand by the King, and the Whigs naturally made what capital they could out of the Queen. Lord John, like the rest of his friends, supported the unhappy if indiscreet lady by a speech—he was ignorant, of course, of the fact that Brougham had dishonestly failed to reveal the Government's offer of settlement to his client—and he compared her, perhaps a little unfortunately, to the irreproachable Catherine of Aragon.[1]

This was merely good party politics—or perhaps bad party politics, for George IV naturally hated the Whigs for defending his injured if doubtfully innocent consort, and the public soon tired of her. The town smiled at the verse:

> Most gracious Queen, we thee implore
> To go away and sin no more;
> But, if that effort be too great,
> To go away at any rate.

But presently it became known that the miserable woman was about to take the advice. "I am going to die, Mr. Brougham," she said quietly to her advocate, "but it does not signify." It did not.

[1] Historical analogues were not Russell's strong point. Later in life he compared Napoleon III to Richard Cromwell.

But some of the driving power behind the reform agitation had necessarily been diverted by this scandalous interruption, and the franchise now proved itself to be like one of those strange variable stars in the heavens, which blaze out brightly from time to time, only to fade again periodically into complete insignificance. There are few more curious instances on record of the instability of the public mind than the almost complete cessation of the demand for reform in the eighteen-twenties, and the phenomenon would be worth investigation by students of popular psychology.[1]

In the New Parliament, as member for another constituency—Lord John had exchanged Tavistock for the county of Huntingdonshire—he pressed the subject forward on every convenient occasion. But the tide had now turned against him, and the life had gone out of reform. Castlereagh died by his own hand in 1822, and although many Tories admitted privately that some measure of reform was necessary, they foolishly thought it wise to postpone the evil day, and Castlereagh's successor, Canning, persistently regarded all reform as revolution. The country itself was becoming completely apathetic, and at the general election of 1826, Lord John found himself at the bottom of his county poll.

Once again he went abroad, and once again he thought of abandoning political life, this time for classical literature. But Russell was a statesman, not a scholar, and while he was wrestling with Greek verbs of which he knew little, the town was beginning to talk of a very different composition, of which he knew much.

In a paper he had written on political bribery, Lord John had drawn a lively picture of the way in which "a gentleman from London goes down to a borough of which he scarcely before knew the existence. The electors do not ask his political opinions. They do not inquire into his private character. They only required to be satisfied of the impurity of his intentions."

[1] The variation of the demand is clearly shown by figures of annual petitions to Parliament for reform. These were : 1821, 19; 1822, 12; 1823, 29; 1824, 0; 1825, 0; 1826, 0; 1827, 0; 1828, 0; 1829, 0; 1830, 14.

The paper was published without his knowledge as a pamphlet and in *The Times*, and it was obvious to his friends that a hand which could put things with such point and force was better occupied with Parliament than Parnassus. It was one of the advantages of an unreformed House of Commons that such little matters as a by-election could be arranged without the candidate's, and almost without the constituency's knowledge; and before the end of the year the Duke of Devonshire wrote to inform Lord John Russell that he had been elected for the Cavendish property of Bandon in Ireland.

The House of Commons to which he returned after a few months' absence was not in appearance or membership very different from the House he had left. But the long period of Tory ascendancy was, in fact, drawing to a close. Early in 1827, after an unbroken premiership of fourteen years, Lord Liverpool died, and Canning was his inevitable successor. But Canning's accession involved a party split; six of his late colleagues resigned rather than serve under him, and their places were filled by mild and inoffensive Whigs.

The combination—it was not a coalition—was an odd one. Lord Lansdowne, one of the new Whig Ministers in the new Tory Cabinet, was described by Lord John as being as honest as the purest virgin, but too yielding for public office. Stanley, better known to a later day as the Rupert of debate, was a dashing speaker and great sportsman, but at heart a timid and ineffective amateur, with his family's fatal readiness to accept high office and shirk responsibility. Tierney, on the other hand, stipulated that he should be free to vote in favour of that very parliamentary reform which the Prime Minister refused even to consider.

Even the genius of Canning could hardly have kept a composition Cabinet without a backbone on its feet for long. But Canning's great career was practically over; after a brief hundred days of office he was dead, and Goderich—the "transient and embarrassed phantom" of Disraeli's contemptuous phrase, who seems to have coveted title rather than power—replaced rather than succeeded

31

him. But in this case the living dog was too conspicuously less than the dead lion, and since the Government obviously could not survive many weeks, the Whigs began to think their turn had come at last.

The gossips even began to discuss the division of the spoils, and it was reported that the masterful Lady Holland had asked the faithful followers in her drawing-room why Lord Holland should not be Secretary of State for Foreign Affairs—to which Lord John replied in his quiet way, "Why, they say, Ma'am, that you open all Lord Holland's letters, and the Foreign Ministers might not like that."

These hopes, however, were deferred. The Goderich Cabinet, like the Canning Cabinet, lasted a hundred odd days, but when it fell, the Duke of Wellington stepped into the breach. The Whig contingent retired once more to the wilderness, and the last Tory Government was formed.

In these manœuvres the Russells, like the rest of the Whigs, had been divided. The disgusted Duke of Bedford had closed his political book, and was content to oppose the Canning Ministry—at Woburn; his sons Tavistock and Lord John preferred to support it at Westminster. There was perfect frankness on both sides, and father and sons agreed amiably enough to differ on a question of expediency. But they can hardly have regretted the return of normal conditions when a Whig was a Whig, and not merely a suspicious and suspect sort of Tory—a creature like a bat in the story, which the birds would not have because it was a beast, and the beasts would not recognize because it was a bird.

Indeed, it seemed likely that it would soon be necessary to close the party ranks, and inject a little vigour into the veins of the more anæmic Whigs, who were unhappy when reform was mentioned, and almost as unhappy when it was not mentioned[1]; for the new Tory Government was less strong than it looked. Wellington compared himself to a dog with a canister tied to its tail, and Peel, who now led

---

[1] The Grenville section of the party had steadily opposed reform, and they could quote Burke in their favour. Cavendish also told Russell that he had never known the subject of reform brought forward without doing the Whigs harm.

the Commons, complained that he had only half a party to fight a party and a half.

The complaint was true. The death of Canning had fatally injured the Tory host. Peel had to contend against the grave sobriety of Graham, always stronger at criticism than construction, the torrential eloquence of Brougham, and the steadily increasing power of Lord John Russell; and he had to do it practically unaided. The industrious Croker could speak, as he could write, on any subject, and at any length, but could inspire on none; and the country gentlemen who were the main strength of the party could vote but could not speak.

The Tories, in fact, had the appearance of power, but the Whigs soon found they had the reality. In 1828, for example, Lord John brought forward the question of the disabilities of the Protestant Dissenters, for whom "a pardon, such as it was, was passed yearly to forgive good men for doing good service to their country." To his great surprise the motion was passed, and a Nonconformist grievance of a century and a half removed for ever.

It was his first substantive success; and in the following year he turned again to the question he had taken up even earlier, the removal of the disabilities of the Roman Catholics. But the Tories were now disintegrating almost to the point of dissolution; and his desire to raise an agitation on the subject—which the more cautious Whigs discountenanced—was rendered unnecessary by the capitulation of the Government.

The Duke gave way, Peel gave way, and last of all the King gave way. The Tories could not survive what the ordinary party man regarded as a betrayal of principle; in another year the Government itself had given way, and the Whigs were in.

CHAPTER V

REFORM

LORD JOHN RUSSELL was now thirty-eight, and in the ten years that had passed between the affair of outposts over Grampound and the fall of the Tories, he had thoroughly learnt his trade of politics.

Casual visitors to the Strangers' Gallery might still be startled by his physical insignificance when he rose to address Mr. Speaker, and they were not always favourably impressed by a voice which could not compare with that of Peel, and an eloquence which could not compete with that of Brougham. But older hands could tell them that there were moments when that small icicle would emit words of fire, and that the dwarf-like form had the heart of a lion; for Russell's fellow-members had begun to recognize that the little fellow was as full of pluck as an egg is of meat, and when he spoke to a motion it was always wise to put up a big gun to reply.

Russell was the sound and straight party man who hated all Tories except the Duke, and loved all Whigs except the lukewarm and Laodiceans who were willing to let others do the work so long as they had the privilege of criticism. But he had now definitely emerged from the rank and file whose place it was to sit and cheer from the back benches. He was not yet, it is true, one of the acknowledged leaders of the party. But he was already recognized as belonging to that selected and approved raw material out of which future leaders are made. So much had the delay over reform done for him.

The advance in his position is evidenced by the fact that when Lord Grey announced the composition of the first Whig Government for a quarter of a century in November, 1830, the Tapers and Tadpoles of the time were surprised to find that Lord John was not in the Cabinet;

34

he was merely Paymaster. The real explanation lay in the post being a sinecure.

There was not in those easy days any reluctance to give young men of promise high executive office on the score of inexperience; Cabinet Ministers learnt the job of administration as they went along. But even Cabinet Ministers had to do some routine work; and about this time one begins to hear the first faint whisper, that was presently to swell into a roar, against the tyranny of the desk. The rest of the world has never taken the laments of its governors over the severity of their labours very seriously, but there does seem to have been some fear at the time that Lord John's health would not be equal to daily attendance as head of a department.

It is possible, too, that a mishap at the general election of 1830 had not helped him. He chose to stand for Bedford, where the Russell family influence can hardly have been negligible, but Bedford rejected him by one vote.[1] A small misfortune of that kind was still easily repaired, and the Duke of Bedford's frontier garrison at Tavistock at once accepted what the citadel had refused. But Lord John seemed to have a facility for losing seats; and although Lord Grey was the last man to keep his ears close to the ground, wise Prime Ministers do not promote such dangerous candidates too rapidly, lest worse things befall them.

The actual office was, however, of small importance. The Grey Government was a Reform Government, and Lord John Russell had become known to the country as one of the foremost champions of parliamentary reform. He took a large part in the preparation of a measure which two-thirds of England was awaiting with enthusiasm, and the other third with something near despair, and he was properly given the distinction of introducing the first Reform Bill, on March 1, 1831.

The usual Westminster crowd followed the statesmen charged with the measure as they walked the short distance

---

[1] He attributed defeat to the Wesleyan vote going against him, on account of some remark about prayer. But the Wesleyans were traditionally inclined towards Toryism. (Gregory, "Sidelights on the Conflicts of Methodism".)

from Downing Street to Palace Yard on the famous day;
but an eye-witness of the scene records that as far as he
could judge, there was more interest in Lord Althorp than
in Lord John on the way down Parliament Street. The
same observer remarks that Russell looked pale and subdued, but it does not appear that he was more nervous or
embarrassed by the responsibility that lay ahead than any
man in such a position must necessarily be.

By general consent, however, the speech in which he
introduced and recommended the measure to the consideration of Parliament was below the standard of oratory
which had been anticipated for so important an occasion.
Its contents, indeed, astonished the expectant members,
but after a statement of two hours he sat down in profound
and ominous silence. The carefully prepared peroration,
it was said, stamped him as a statesman, an orator and a
patriot; but it failed to draw a single cheer.

For this, indeed, there were sufficient reasons; silence
was almost a greater tribute than applause. The preliminary discussions in Cabinet had been held in profound
secrecy. The Opposition knew nothing of the proposals
in advance; indeed, only a few days before the Bill was
introduced, Peel had predicted that it would occasion
disappointment by the meagreness of its proportions and
the trifling nature of the changes recommended. But as
he sat listening on the Front Opposition Bench, his face
turned crimson with surprise and mortification, and towards
the end of Russell's speech he buried his head in his hands,
wrapped in a grief he no longer troubled to conceal. Peel
was a great statesman, but he lacked the supreme gift of
political foresight, and it seemed to him then and for long
afterwards that the Bill foretold the ruin of the Tory party.

The actual reading of the schedules was necessarily a
dull affair, more particularly to an age which preferred resounding rhetoric to dreary details of business; but as the
full scope of the scheme was unfolded, contempt changed
quickly to astonishment, and astonishment to unmeasured
alarm. Derisive cheers from the Tory benches greeted
the lists of suppressed and substituted boroughs, but when
the House had recovered from its amazement, an influen-

tial member observed quietly that the Bill was an honour to the age, but only an Oliver Cromwell could carry it.

A moderate Whig, of the type that Russell detested—the same Laodicean variety that was to congregate thirty years later to his undoing in the Cave of Adullam—told Graham that he supposed the Government would resign the next morning; and it was in fact well known that some of the members of the Cabinet were by no means enthusiastic over the scheme. Lord Grey, indeed, was convinced, and rightly convinced, that reform was the alternative to revolution. But Lord Lansdowne was timid, Lord Holland tepid, Lord Melbourne merely tolerant, and Lord Palmerston frankly bored by the whole business.

The Radicals alone were delighted, and ready to vote that black was white in order to carry the Bill. In this the Radicals represented the mind of the nation at that moment probably better than either official Whig or Opposition Tory: it was not so much that this particular Bill was popular as that any genuine measure of reform was bound to be popular. Their support was clamant and vociferous, and Lord John now tasted for the first time that potent and dangerous drug, the loud applause of the crowd. Like others before and since, this shy cold man of the aristocracy enjoyed it so much that he was not quite above playing to the gallery more than once in the later part of his career.

These things, however, were still in the future, but the Radicals, after all, were only a small minority in the House, and almost as dangerous allies to a Whig Minister as Hengist and Horsa to the distressed Britons. The Bill survived for a time, but it was easy for those who did not want any reform at all to show that it was inconsistent with its own professions, since many small boroughs were still represented and many large towns still unrepresented. These criticisms could not be logically answered, and although the zealous Brougham raised the clarion cry of "The Bill, the whole Bill, and nothing but the Bill," it passed the second reading by only one vote, and the point that it actually reduced the number of members for England and Wales killed it shortly afterwards. England, as Rosebery said sixty years later, was the predominant partner in wealth and population, and the Whigs had forgotten what was, after all, a relevant fact of the problem they had professed to solve.

A dissolution inevitably followed, and Lord John now found himself the hero of the hour. The greatest counties, the most important boroughs, appealed to him to do them the honour of becoming their member; it was even suggested that he should raid the Tories in their own particular stronghold in Buckinghamshire. The offer was tempting, for he had the wind and tide of popular favour behind him. But the Russells were seldom reckless, and Lord John chose Devon, where family connexions made certain what the public homage promised.

Delay was not in this case dangerous; indeed, the fact that the Tories still fought reform with the dogged courage of despair naturally helped the Whigs in the constituencies. The Government returned to Westminster stronger than before, and the new Reform Bill, which Lord John introduced to the new House of Commons in June, 1831, was largely a repetition of that predecessor which the country had so emphatically approved.

The Whigs and Radicals were now solid; the Tories were desperate, and reduced to futile delaying tactics which irritated the country to the point of madness. Hopes and fears were rising as the decisive moment approached; and the Duke of Gloucester told his brother the King that if the Bill passed he would lose his Crown. "Very well, very well," replied the testy monarch. "But, sir, your Majesty's head may be in it," persisted the unhappy Prince.

Such talk was common in Tory circles. The Duke of Wellington spoke gloomily of revolution and ruin ahead. Peel surveyed with despair the rioting and rick-burning which broke out from Yorkshire to Sussex. Even Arnold of Rugby maintained that no human power could save the Church; while Wordsworth, forgetting his youthful hopes, talked nonsense about another Reign of Terror. Croker foretold a republic but, since one must still dine out though Church and State fall, still went out to dinner, and on one occasion when attending a banquet at the Duchess of Kent's at which four dukes and three duchesses were present, he noted with interest a child of twelve. "The little princess," he reported to his patron, "ceases to be little. She grows tall, is very good-looking, but not, I think, strong; yet she may live to be plain Miss Guelph." She lived, in fact, to be Queen Victoria.

The Whigs kept their heads and their tempers better, as was to be expected of the men in possession. But for weeks the fight went on in the Commons, and night after night till nearly dawn Lord John Russell replied to his critics with suavity and strength. Althorp, indeed, assisted him, having overcome his reluctance to office at the prospect of a fight, but the main brunt of the battle fell on the little statesman who had not been considered strong enough for administrative work. His patience in face of obstruction was as amazing as his courage in face of criticism; and in that long summer, while cholera was raging in the slums of Westminster immediately without the precincts of the House, and prejudice was raging within, the legend of his physical weakness finally vanished.

The second edition of the Reform Bill passed the Commons practically intact, but in the Lords it was doomed even before it was introduced. Grey supported it with the cold chiselled eloquence that had first been heard at the trial of Warren Hastings, and Brougham—now Lord Chancellor —defended it with his accustomed heat. Neither moved the peers an inch from their purpose, and within a fortnight the Bill was dead.

There followed a short breathing-space and some manœuvres, in which it seemed momentarily possible that the Tories would replace the Whigs on condition of carrying out the Whig policy; but this came to nothing, and on December 12, 1831, Lord John rose again in his place in the Commons to introduce the third edition of the Reform Bill. This time it passed the Lower House with less, but still with some difficulty; but it was still uncertain whether the Upper House would give way when the Bill was reported to them again.

The House of Lords, however, proved less susceptible

39

to argument than force; but here, as in the debates on the Parliament Act eighty years later, it was only the threat to the dignity of their own order, entailed by the prospect of a wholesale creation of peers, that led them to abstain in sufficient numbers for the Bill to pass.

Once the Act was through, the rioting in the country subsided almost as quickly as it rose. But there had been a week during these proceedings in the Lords when it seemed probable that the Grey Government would be wrecked almost in sight of port, and the Duke of Wellington have to carry reform at the head of an anti-reform Cabinet.

It was known that he was ready, from a sense of public duty, to repeat the part he had played over Catholic Emancipation, but these betrayals and surrenders are not to be done, even from the highest motives, more often than necessary. Luckily the occasion was avoided, but it was a moment of real peril. Lord John was not directly concerned in the affair, but looking back as an old man on his past career, he remarked that it was the only time in his life when he had been uneasy as to the result.

It is impossible for us, a century afterwards, to understand the excitement, the exaggerated hopes, the ridiculous fears, the absurd predictions of disaster, that preceded and accompanied this famous Bill; it was difficult even for Gladstone, who lived through the period and was present as a Tory spectator at the last of the debates, to recall the lost atmosphere of what seemed in retrospect a relatively small readjustment rather than a social cataclysm. Commenting on the change fifty years later, he remarked quietly that, "in 1832 there was passed what was considered a Magna Charta of British liberty; but that Magna Charta added, according to the previous estimate of Lord John Russell, five hundred thousand, while according to the results, considerably less than five hundred thousand voters were added to the entire constituency of the three countries."

Gladstone's figures, like Russell's, were an over-statement. The actual electorate in 1832 was 435,391; the Reform Bill added 217,386 voters to the roll. The electorate in 1867 was 1,056,659; the second Reform Act added another 938,427 names. The Act of 1884 added 1,762,087; the Act of 1918, when women over 30 were enfranchised, another thirteen millions; and the Act of 1928, when women over 21 were enfranchised, another five millions.

These things make Lord John Russell's great campaign look small; and in one sense it is true that it was certainly not a revolution, hardly a reform, merely a redistribution. But Napoleon's armies would also have looked small beside those of 1914; and in another and a deeper sense it is true that the Reform Act of 1832 was much more than a redistribution, more than a reform, and in effect a revolution. For it was the first and most significant stage in the process that marked the passing of power from the country to the town, from the old territorial aristocracy to the new and practically landless middle classes, from those who controlled fixed capital and practically fixed labour to those who controlled fluid capital and operated through fluid labour.

That change was not a small one; it had, as we shall see, many unexpected ramifications and consequences, and its ultimate results are not yet visible.

But for the time being little enough happened. "We shall never again see a Government in England," mused the Duke of Wellington; but that practical statesman soon resumed his entertainments, which had not been seriously interrupted by the crisis. The ponderous Peel continued building his new country house, which had also not been interrupted by the crisis. And the perplexed Croker, hourly anticipating the proclamation of a republic, was surprised to receive instead a prospectus informing him of the project to establish the Carlton Club.

CHAPTER VI

LEADING THE COMMONS

MOST Governments, like most men, take things very much as they come; but the Whig Government which held office, with one brief intermission, from 1830 till 1841, was more than a little inclined to postpone things as they came. The Reform Act once passed, Grey was again anxious to retire to his books and children in remote Northumberland; and since those who insist on playing the part of Cincinnatus at least make room for others on the stage, Melbourne stepped easily into the vacant place.

"There is nothing approaching this damned fellow in the kingdom when he gets on his high horse," Creevey had confessed of Grey in 1820. That mean skunk, who bore unwilling tribute to the cold patrician, could hardly have said the same of Melbourne. Grey's virtue, both in public and in private, was upright and austere to the point of the puritanical; and the gossips who reported that he had once been seen drunk in his youth told the story, as gossips of a later date spoke of the fifth Lord Lansdowne's undergraduate collection of Oxford door-knockers, with a smile and a shrug and a *credo quia impossibile*.

Melbourne, on the contrary, loved both love and laughter, and so long as they came, was not too particular whence they came. If his wife had been involved in a famous amour with Byron, Melbourne himself had been implicated in two matrimonial suits; and his own friends, in a not very censorious age, agreed that he was lucky to escape censure. His attitude in these matters, indeed, was indicated by his reply to Queen Victoria, when that blushing young lady remarked that her future husband never paid any attention to any other woman. "No, that sort

42

of thing is apt to come later," said the Prime Minister, musing over his own adventurous past.[1]

But in two of the most important attributes of a Prime Minister Melbourne was admittedly perfect; he was entirely loyal both to the Crown he served and the colleagues he worked with. For the rest, he was a tolerant and kindly man, except when the importunate became indecent— "Confound it, does he want a Garter for his other leg?" he asked of one whose mouth was larger than his merits— but the Melbournes of this world are constitutionally averse to over-exertion.

Most of the other Whigs in the Cabinet were inclined to agree with him; liberty had had its fling in the Reform Act, and it was now time that property should hold the stage. It is not always pleasant to be called a revolutionary by one's enemies. Some of one's friends are apt to believe it.

They remained to carry the abolition of slavery in 1833; this was a matter of fundamental principle, and in any case, compensation was paid to vested interests. But when the question of tithe and the surplus revenues of the Church came up, the great Whig houses trembled a little, as if a bleak north-easter had struck them unexpectedly on a summer day, and territorial magnates began to shake their heads. This was, after all, not a question of liberty but property, and property that had been unchallenged for centuries had prescriptive rights. Probably there were abuses, and certainly there were sinecures, but one must have a Church, and in any case there were younger sons and even bishoprics to be thought of. Whichever way one looked at it, to abolish ten Irish bishoprics at a sitting was to throw ten sinecures into the gutter. It was well to do something, if only to placate the Radicals who hung

---

[1] Morality runs in cycles, and the dissipated Earl of Egremont remarked to Melbourne as an old man, "William, I have lived long enough to see the hand (of the clock) go round. In the first quarter of my time the world was nothing but profligate. In the next there came a great revival of puritanism. Then came another spell of luxury and licence, and now you have a revival of religion once more." The first was probably Directoire, the second Evangelical, the third Regency, the fourth the Oxford Movement.

43

on to respectable Whig coat-tails. But perhaps it was better to do as little as possible.

Lord John, however, was firm. He had clearly thought the thing out for himself, and he had laid down a guiding rule. "I set out on a principle that a clergy ought to teach religion. It follows that when there neither are nor will be any, or more than an infinitely small fraction, of Protestants of the Established Church (of Ireland), it is not necessary or useful to have a clergyman of that Church."

So Russell in 1832; and on this *per capita* basis for the cure of souls, the Irish Church was doomed. The problem was postponed for a while, but he remained insistent, and in 1834 he "considered that the revenues of the Church of Ireland were larger than necessary for the religious and moral instruction of the persons belonging to that Church, and for the stability of the Church itself; and at whatever cost and sacrifice, he should do what he considered his bounden duty, namely, justice to Ireland."

It was too much. Justice may be done though the heavens fall, but should justice be done when it may make a Whig Government fall? Stanley scribbled: "Johnny has upset the coach," and passed the note to Graham; and the Duke of Richmond and Lord Ripon followed them both from office to opposition.

From that day Graham waited gloomily for "the inevitable grand blow-up" of society which, like the prophecies of the end of the world, was always postponed at the last moment. Stanley, with better judgment, seems to have assumed that so long as Woburn Abbey survived, Knowsley was reasonably safe; but to make assurance doubly sure, he joined his fellow-Lancastrians, Peel and Gladstone, on the Tory benches.

The split had important consequences. Melbourne had hitherto regarded Stanley as the next Whig Premier, and had told a friend that he might last as long as Walpole, who had ruled England twenty years running, a century before. Lord John seems rather to have agreed with this estimate, which proved strangely wide of the mark; but with Stanley gone, Althorp still weighing his breakfast by

VISCOUNT MELBOURNE

(*From the painting by John Partridge. Copyright National Portrait Gallery.*)

the ounce at home and presently expiating his political
sins—the phrase was his own—as Lord Spencer in the
House of Lords, the way was clear, or very nearly clear,
for Russell to lead the Commons. Johnny had upset the
coach, but it was the passengers who got out, and the
driver who remained.

Luckily for him, but perhaps unluckily for his party,
new passengers were necessary, and the Radicals who now
joined the lumbering Whig vehicle wanted it to go farther
and travel faster than official dignity required. Russell
condescended in words—he told a delighted audience that
the early Christians were the reformers of their time, while
Nero was a Conservative—but he refused to palter with
principle; the Reform Bill was a final settlement, and that
was the end of it.

Consistently with his creed, he treated the Chartists
with indulgent contempt; he could not foresee that in a
few years he would be introducing another Reform Bill
and yet another, and that in his old age the Tory Gladstone
would advocate a larger suffrage as a Liberal, and the
young Tory Disraeli—who was now sneering at "Lord
John Straw" in the *Letters of Runnymede*—would out-
bid them both. So much for final principle in politics.

It became necessary, however, to call in another and
ultimately more difficult ally than the English Radicals.
As leader of the Liberal party in the Commons, said Russell
in later years, "I had no smooth path before me," and he
therefore arranged a working agreement with O'Connell
and the Irish members. "Compact there was none, but
an alliance on honourable terms of mutual co-operation
undoubtedly existed. The Whigs remained, as before,
the firm defenders of the Union; O'Connell remained, as
before, the ardent advocate of repeal; but upon inter-
mediate measures, on which the two parties could agree
consistently with their principles, there was no want of
cordiality. Nor did I ever see cause to complain of
O'Connell's conduct." Thus was laid the basis of that
alliance which led Gladstone insensibly towards Home
Rule: sixty years later the Liberals were no longer firm
defenders of the Union, while the Irish remained, as before,

45

the ardent advocates of repeal. So much for alliances which are not compacts in politics.

But the situation of 1834, as it chanced, was more perilous for the party than the country, and not the most confirmed gambler at Brooks's or White's would have risked a guinea on the reconstructed Melbourne Government lasting well into another reign. Disraeli acidly compared the Cabinet to a troupe of performing horses: when one died, it was replaced by a mule; when another bolted, it was replaced by a donkey, until at last nobody knew which was horse and which was donkey, but it was still advertised as the best circus in the world. That the Whig Government, after a brief Tory interlude under Peel, survived even till the death of William IV, was far more the work of Russell than Melbourne, but there were one or two ugly mishaps.

At the general election of 1835, Devon rejected the Whigs after a lively campaign, which is now only remembered for the fact that it was reported for a London newspaper by an obscure journalist named Charles Dickens. When "Pickwick" took the town by storm, a year or so later, the world debited Eatanswill to East Anglia; but it is more probable that the election rowdies—"Shout with the largest mob"—the famous indignation of Mr. Pott, and the notorious love-affair of Mr. Winkle, were reminiscent of Russell's last great battle in the West. Sudbury, in Suffolk, has usually been identified as the local habitation of the campaign, but Sudbury is hardly big enough, whereas Exeter is.

However that may be, Russell was once again without a seat, and a constituency had to be found for the leader of the House of Commons at Stroud; and at the very end of the Whig Government's life, in 1841, when the City of London invited him to stand—a compliment it was practically impossible to refuse—he had the mortification of finding himself the last of the four successful candidates. The City was frankly Liberal, but the worthy aldermen may have thought there was just a trifle too much radicalism in their bantam champion.

The Mansion House was hardly the final authority on

English Literature. But even Lord Mayors have leisure moments between banquets, and more than one of those who had passed the chair might have chuckled over the poet's description of the Whig Government:

> To save the Church, and serve the Crown
> By letting others pull them down;
> To promise, pause, prepare, postpone,
> And end by letting things alone.

Bishop-baiting is assuredly excellent fun. But if bishops are abolished as anachronisms, the Court of Aldermen might be the next on the list, and prudent merchants take few chances.[1]

But despite the weakness of the Government, the six years that followed the schism of the Whigs were marked by perhaps the greatest amount of progressive and beneficent legislation the country had ever seen. All the reforms that had been advocated in vain during the long period of Tory rule were now carried through: the Poor Law was reformed; the Corporations were reformed; the tithe was commuted and the disabilities of Nonconformists were removed; London University was established, and the foundations of popular education were laid; the penny post was instituted, and the harsh penal laws were modified.

These things belong to history, not biography; they were the first fruits of the new Liberalism of which Russell was becoming more and more the recognized leader. He was not, of course, directly responsible for all these reforms, but he was actively concerned as the chief instrument in passing them through the Commons; and it must be added that without him they would not only not have been carried, but the Government could not have survived at all.

Melbourne was easy-going and tolerant of mediocrity and even incompetence—he would have suffered the feeble Glenelg to remain at the Colonial Office had not Russell, the most loyal of colleagues, at last protested against his

---

[1] From that time, however, Russell's electoral vicissitudes ceased. In his first twenty-eight years in the House of Commons he had sat for six constituencies, and contested seven. In his last twenty years the City of London was consistently faithful, with one narrow squeak after the Crimean War.

gross incapacity, and taken the post himself for a time—and the rest of the Cabinet was little more than a cipher.

But Lord John, in his own pigmy person, seemed to make good all their deficiencies, and this was on the whole the happiest and most fruitful period of his life. Ten years before he had been merely a politician of promise; now men began to speak seriously of him as the next Prime Minister.

The time, however, had not yet come. The Government was worn out, and the saying of the day was that the Whigs ruled nothing but Downing Street; in spite—or perhaps because of—reform and progress, the hands of the clock had gone round, and the hour of the Tories had come again.

When the end of the Melbourne Government came at last in 1841, Gladstone, who had been watching Russell closely for years, from the opposite side of the House, pronounced a judicial verdict: "He has risen with adversity. He seemed rather below par as a leader in 1835, when he had a clear majority, and the ball nearly at his feet: in each successive year the strength of his Government has fallen and his own has risen."

CHAPTER VII

RUSSELL *VERSUS* PEEL

"IT is impossible that the whisper of a faction should prevail against the voice of a nation." History probably contains more factions that have prevailed over nations than nations that have controlled factions; but the phrase, which was coined by Lord John Russell in the heat of the Reform Bill controversy, and published in a letter that became famous, was intended for a piece of current political polemic, not a scientific statement of ascertained fact.

The pungent sentence achieved rather more than its purpose. It delighted the nation, at any rate that part of the nation which was opposed to the Tory faction, but it annoyed the King. Lord John wrote a laborious apology that retracted nothing, and the first of several conflicts with the Crown was smoothed over. But the episode was not forgotten at Windsor; and three years later, when Melbourne had succeeded Grey as Prime Minister, and advised that Lord John should lead the Commons, he found that William IV "could not bear" the man, and "stated without reserve his opinion that Lord John had not the abilities nor the influence which qualified him for the task, and observed that he would make a wretched figure when opposed by Sir Robert Peel and Mr. Stanley."

The King thereupon dismissed his Ministers, to their public indignation and private content; Peel was sent for, and came hot-foot from Rome to form the short-lived Government of 1834; and Russell, baulked for the time of the leadership of one side of the House of Commons, found himself automatically leader of the other. From that day until Peel's death, sixteen years later, the two men whom William IV had contrasted were not merely political antagonists but personal rivals.

E

It seemed almost as though Nature itself had taken a hand in emphasizing the difference between them. Russell was physically insignificant, Peel had a handsome presence and commanding figure. His intimates said he was naturally hot-tempered, but he so controlled his emotions that he appeared cold and calm, even under merciless attack; whereas Russell was often openly impatient, and, though not naturally irritable, was easily nettled—he "wriggles round, plays with his hat, and seems unable to dispose of his hands or feet," said an observer, who added in compensation that although his voice was small and thin, five hundred members would hush to catch his smallest accents.

Russell's mind was quick, lively, and naturally active; Peel's was slow, heavy, and secretive. Russell's oratory was of that expansive kind which constantly exposed a good deal of surface, and put forward general propositions that were neither necessary to the particular occasion nor always easily defensible; Peel's oratory was more closely confined to the matter in hand. Russell was naturally venturesome, Peel naturally cautious. Russell therefore gave the impression of enjoying every minute of the day, while Peel seemed to regard life as a duty to be got through.

It followed that Russell was sometimes liked even by those who disagreed with him, whereas Peel was never more than respected even by those who agreed with him. The young Queen, for example, "got on famously" with Russell in these early days of her reign, whereas "Peel is such a cold, odd man, she can't make out what he means" —which we may take as a feminine equivalent of Melbourne's estimate that Peel was "a bad horse to go up to in the stable." Once the ice was broken, and "languid Johnny glowed to glorious John," the little Whig had charm and gaiety even when he was wrong, but Peel was grave and unsympathetic even when he was right.

As if to put a sharper point on these inborn differences of temperament, and at the same time to explain them, the two men came of different social stock. Russell was of the old aristocracy whose position was assured, Peel of the new middle-class who had to feel their way towards power. Russell could lead Radicals as well as Whigs without loss of caste, Peel was always a little uneasy with the old nobility and the mob. Russell's love of applause often led him to tickle the groundlings and play the demagogue; Peel's solid and even stolid respectability could stoop to no such monkey tricks. He sometimes failed his followers, he never flattered them.

Russell could easily bend, but he never broke; first, last, and all the time he was the good party man—usually a little ahead, occasionally a little behind, but always in touch with the main Whig army. Peel, on the other hand, could no more bend than he could unbend; but twice at least he seemed much more likely to break. It is significant, however, of the hidden strength of the man that in the last resort it was the party, not Peel, that broke, and that it was he who helped to rebuild it.

Russell's life seems filled with bustle and achievement that made him, at least at this period of his career, and in spite of coldness to his followers, the darling of his party and often of his country; whereas Peel was cursed in every Tory club for betraying his friends, for splitting his party, and undermining his country. How then does it come that Peel, for all his unpopularity, left a deeper mark on history than Russell?

Part at least of the truth is revealed by the contrast of their attitude towards life. The Whig Cabinets could work hard, and Lord John could apply himself long and steadily to the difficult business of getting a controversial or complicated Bill through the House. But it is impossible to resist the conclusion that the later Whig Governments, for all their brilliance, were often casual; a band of happy amateurs in charge of a number of departments which sometimes went well and sometimes went ill, but never by any chance went together. Their strength in legislation was balanced by their weakness in administration.

The Tory Governments, on the other hand, which were at best weak and at worst merely obstructive over matters of reform, had inherited a long tradition of administrative efficiency. The Tory mind, which has its own excellencies and defects, is naturally more inclined than the Liberal to

order, and therefore to organization and administration:
Lord Liverpool made the machine of State work steadily
and well, and he taught Palmerston as well as Peel their
business. They never forgot the lesson, and Peel applied
it in practical fashion. He opposed reform until the last
moment, but at once accepted the accomplished fact; and
while the absurd Croker refused to sit in the new House
of Commons on the ridiculous ground that it was an illegal
and unconstitutional assembly, Peel not only sat, but
helped to make the experiment work. "It is right," he
said, "that we should do this, but I must say that it was
expecting more than human institutions, intended to govern
the unruly passions and corrupt natures of human beings,
ought to calculate upon."[1]

Peel not only helped to make the Reform Act work in
the House, but while other Tories were sulking in country
houses, he built up a new Conservative organization in
the constituencies which soon began to make itself felt.
Reform is often excellent, and the electors listened with
enthusiasm to the noble speeches in which Lord John
Russell expounded Liberal principles, and reminded them
that Luther and Galileo were reformers, while the popes
were obviously Conservatives. But the hard-headed men
who applauded his sentiments must sometimes have wished
that the Budgets of the Melbourne Government did not
always show a deficit, and when the time came it was for
Peel, not Russell, that they voted.

In the same practical fashion Peel attacked the problem
of government when he came to form the great administration of 1841. There was less talk of progress, but a great
deal more application to the matters in hand. It was a

---

[1] The last sentence is not mere Tory pessimism. It was the period of
Eatanswill, and in almost the first letter which Lord John Russell wrote to
Queen Victoria, in 1837, he "is sorry to add that bribery, intimidation,
and drunkenness have been very prevalent at the late elections, and that
in many cases the disposition to riot has only been checked by the appearance of the military, who have in all cases conducted themselves with great
temper and judgment."

His belief in Playfair's theory of the activity and perseverance of mankind
continually defeating the folly and caprice of their governors seems momentarily to have worn a little thin.

weakness of the Whigs that while they preached peace they were frequently on the verge of war, and a misfortune that while they praised economy they were in fact extravagant. This defect arose, in Peel's view, because the Melbourne Cabinet was "a mere government of departments without a centre of unity": under the Peel system the departments were all subordinate to the Prime Minister.

Peel was no shirker, but he sometimes complained of the increasing amount of work entailed by public office, and he frankly resented the time wasted in listening to parliamentary debates. "The mere attendance on the House of Commons, eight and nine hours every day," he wrote in 1843, "almost precludes the proper performance of his real duties by a minister. Just conceive what I ought to do, and what I must continue to do in some way or other during the remainder of the day."[1] His heart, in fact, was in Whitehall, where policy was administered, rather than in Westminster, where it was discussed.

Russell would hardly have understood this language. To him the main work of a statesman was to attend the House of Commons, and the business of a department, though admittedly important, was in fact secondary. He was always perfectly happy in the House, and although he would not have maintained that debate was more important than office work, he would certainly have claimed that legislation was more interesting than administration.

It happened that the current of affairs favoured the Peel rather than the Russell method; for the routine business of administration was steadily increasing as civilization became more complex at home, and the Empire grew year by year overseas.[2] But the results of the two systems speak for themselves. Many years afterwards Gladstone,

[1] Peel at first agreed with Canning that the Prime Minister should be in the House of Commons, but changed his opinion after 1846. He then confessed that the burden was too great for human strength.

[2] This applied not only to the State. I have heard that an Archbishop of Canterbury at that time sometimes asked the butler at Lambeth to see if there were any letters by the afternoon post. A century later Archbishop Davidson had to keep three chaplains to deal with correspondence, and often, after returning from some public function late in the evening, worked two or three hours into the night to clear off pressing business.

who had more experience of office and administration than any man then alive, told John Morley that Peel's Government was the best of the century for purity and singleness of devotion to the public interest. He did not add—perhaps he did not fully realize—that it was the first of a new model. The old leisurely methods of an aristocratic age were going out; the new business methods of quick despatch were coming in.

Here again it is impossible to avoid the direct contrast between Peel and Russell. It is true that Peel never actually served in the cotton counting-house at Bury. It is true, too, that Russell was never actually a great landowner at Woburn. But the fact remains that the outlook of the one, for all his Conservatism, was mercantile, and the outlook of the other, for all his Liberalism, was territorial.

It is significant that Peel's successes—Currency and Corn Law—were in the sphere of economics, whereas his failures, as in his despair over franchise reform, were in the sphere of politics.[1] It is equally significant that Russell's successes were in the sphere of politics, whereas his failures were in the sphere of economics.

He once introduced a Budget as Prime Minister, but it was so badly received that it was withdrawn; he frankly admitted to Graham that he was no hand at figures, and he never really conquered his youthful feeling that "political economy is an awful thing." A century before, even half a century before, this would have been common form among statesmen, but in the days when economics were coming more and more to the front, the limitation operated as a distinct handicap. The truth is that Peel thought of politics ultimately in terms of economics, Russell thought of economics ultimately in terms of politics; and by the irony of affairs, the one completed the work of the other.

---

[1] Oddly enough, when Louis Philippe fell, in 1848, Peel's comment was: "This comes of trying to govern the country through a narrow representation in Parliament, without regarding the wishes of those outside. It is what the party behind me wanted me to do in the matter of the Corn Laws, and I would not do it." But it was precisely what he wanted to do in the matter of the Reform Bill.

If Lord John was the chief instrument in passing the Reform Act of 1832, which transferred political power from the country to the towns, it was Peel who felt his way slowly to its logical conclusion in repealing the Corn Laws, in 1846, which transferred the economic control from the land to the cities.

CHAPTER VIII

THE EDINBURGH LETTER

MUCH, if not most, of the controversy over the repeal of the Corn Laws arises from the tacit presumption that statesmen control events. In fact they often modify but seldom control events; and this for the simple reason that politics deals only with a limited part of the whole field of human activities.

The bulk of individual and social affairs are and must always be conducted outside the cognizance of the State, and only come within its purview indirectly on particular occasions, and even then only from certain special angles. Obviously no statesman can control a process which began in some religious vision or some industrial invention long before he was born, and whose end is not yet in sight; the most he can do is to modify that particular section of the event which happens to impinge on the general public interests of the time.

Clearly this was so in the matter of the Corn Laws. In the early eighteenth century Britain had exported grain, but as manufactures increased and population grew in the towns, she began to import; first spasmodically, then regularly, then increasingly year by year. When William IV came to the throne in 1830, the English countryside still fed the English people; but when he died seven years later, the silent but epochal day had passed when the population had outgrown its resources. From 1835 onwards, the country depended on its sailors to supplement its farmers.

Agriculture still developed and prospered at home, but the nation could no longer feed itself, and the balance of economic, as of political power, shifted decisively from the country districts to the towns. Long before the days of Adam Smith politicians might be Free Traders or Protectionists in theory, but in practice they remained protectionists, and it was under a protective fiscal system that the great new British industries and the new urban population had grown up. In 1832, however, the Reform Act recognized the gravitation of political force towards the towns, and the recognition of its economic implications quickly followed. In 1800, even in 1820, no responsible politician advocated repeal of the Corn Laws. By 1860 no responsible politician advocated their restoration, and it was not until the decline of agriculture was a menace to national security nearly fifty years later that the subject again became a political issue.[1]

The political difficulties which this change of policy provoked are necessarily trivial in comparison with the economic revolution it entailed, or rather recognized. But the personal consequences to the statesmen and parties directly concerned were by no means trivial in parliamentary history; and although Peel was the chief actor, Russell made two brief but, as it happened, not ineffectual appearances on this particular stage.

Once again, and almost for the last time, Peel and Russell appeared as opponents; but the technical antagonisms of party hardly concealed their actual agreement on policy. The inevitability of fiscal change may be judged by the fact that the two men approached the problem with different political preconceptions, and from different personal angles, but both showed a close coincidence in the remedy to be applied.

There is, indeed, an element of piquancy in the contrast between their positions in this decisive struggle for ascendancy between urban and rural polity. Russell, for all his love of the theatre and the social round of Town, came of a family whose roots were deep in the country; Peel, for all his interest in the turrets and battlements and other

---

[1] "It is quite clear that (twenty years ago) no party contemplated Free Trade in the sense in which it is now spoken of, and least of all Free Trade in corn. Whig Governments fell, and the Conservative Party was formed, upon questions affecting the maintenance of the Established Church, and the integrity of the institutions of the country, the House of Lords included." Lord Stanley to Croker, 1847.

sham mediævalisms of his modern country house, came of a family whose fortune was made in one of the new industrial towns. Russell, however, though one of the old landed aristocracy, led a party which was becoming more and more dependent on the new liberalism of the towns; whereas Peel, as one of the new plutocracy, led a party which was still mainly dependent on the conservatism of the country squires. Both were, therefore, to some extent awkwardly placed for dealing with an economic revolution, and both betrayed the fact by the hesitation and diffidence which led them to postpone action long after they had realized that the old economic system was doomed.

Peel, being in office, was of course much the more awkwardly placed of the two. As a young man he had accepted the existence of agricultural protection as one of the permanent institutions of the country. But he had accepted it in much the same sense that most of us accept the rotation of the earth or the law of gravitation; that is to say, as a thing beyond dispute, but without any special inquiry into the causes or consequences of the doctrine. The Oxford in which he was winning his famous double first was interested in anything but economics, and the Liverpool Government in which he served his political apprenticeship was far more likely to suspend the Habeas Corpus than the Corn Laws.

Since then twenty years had passed in office and opposition, and during the last two or three years prior to 1845 there is evidence from his correspondence that his attention was increasingly occupied with the problem of Free Trade. There are no indications that he was specially influenced by the propaganda of the Anti-Corn Law League, although its leader, John Bright, was after all a fellow-Lancastrian and a fellow mill-owner.[1] But there are very definite indications that his mind gradually came round independently to the Free Trade standpoint, while his body remained a hostage in the Protectionist camp.

---

[1] Disraeli accused Peel of having a dangerous sympathy with other people's ideas. But Disraeli is the last person one would take as evidence against Peel. And Peel is almost the last person one would accuse of excessive sympathy.

His mind, it is true, always worked rather slowly, but at last the process of conversion was complete. For a space he remained in the Protectionist camp, as for a space, almost at the same time, Newman remained in the Anglican Church; but in both cases the creed had shrunk to a symbol, the allegiance had worn to a thread, and only a step remained between private conviction and public confession.

Meantime Russell had also been reflecting on the position, but in his case the process was devoid of the perplexities and anxieties and even the agonies that distracted Peel. His mind being Whig, he was naturally more inclined to favour anything that smacked of freedom than a Conservative Prime Minister. He was in opposition; he had no reluctant and rebellious party to carry with him, but the sweet applause of rejoicing Radicals over the repentant Whig sinner to gain. Cobden and Bright had been denouncing the landed interest for years, and they would assuredly praise Russell as a brand plucked from the burning, a modern Daniel come to judgment.

He had, it is true, supported the fixed duty as against the prevalent sliding scale on corn in the past. But he had had something more than a flirtation with Free Trade in the Melbourne Government, and as early as 1839 had practically joined the camp of unbelievers. Melbourne, however, was perfectly well aware that a Government which was by that time hardly strong enough to walk across Downing Street was in no position to face a serious economic issue. "Why can't you leave it alone?" had been his constant refrain, and he was as reluctant to give the ardent Lord John his head over corn as over the ballot. "It does not matter much what we say, but we had better all say the same thing," had been his tolerant summary of the discussion in Cabinet which left things very much as they were. That opportunity passed, but it is clear that the distance from Protection to Free Trade was shorter, and the road smoother, for Russell than for Peel; and it was in these circumstances that he wrote while at Edinburgh the famous letter of November 22, 1845, in which he announced his complete conversion.

I confess (he said in the two salient paragraphs) that my views have in the course of twenty years undergone a great alteration. I used to be of opinion that corn was an exception to the general rules of political economy; but observation and experience have convinced me that we ought to abstain from all interference with the supply of food.

Neither a Government nor a legislature can ever regulate the corn market with the beneficial effects which the entire freedom of sale and purchase are sure of themselves to produce. . . . Let us, then, unite to put an end to a system which has been proved to be the blight of commerce, the bane of agriculture, the source of bitter divisions among classes, the cause of penury, fever, mortality, and crime, among the people.

The over-emphasis of the last sentence betrays the familiar hand of the political propagandist more than the reasoned argument of the economist. But it was extraordinarily effective; perhaps no manifesto has ever produced quicker and more far-reaching results. John Bright had been saying the same thing for years, but Bright was only a private member, Lord John was leader of the Opposition; and Bright told Russell that the Edinburgh Letter had made the immediate and total repeal of the Corn Laws inevitable.

Bright was right, but its first effect was to precipitate a political crisis.

Peel, alarmed at the failure of the Irish potato crop, had wished to suspend the Corn Laws by proclamation three weeks before, but had been overruled by his Cabinet; and a distracted and divided Government was faced by three alternatives—to modify, suspend, or maintain unaltered the Corn Laws. Like all Cabinets in a dilemma, they postponed decision; and then suddenly found themselves forestalled by Lord John.

The Edinburgh Letter aggravated their difficulties, and Peel confessed himself piqued that his rival had stepped in where the Cabinet feared to tread. Some of his colleagues at length gave a reluctant assent to his views, but he felt they were not really with him, and quite properly resigned.

It does not appear that Russell had been aware of these agonies of indecision; indeed, he could not have been, for he was travelling about the country at the time, and hardly in a position to know the immediate political as distinct from the general economic aspect of the problem. It was said, and no doubt truly, that he took occasion by the hand to forward personal ambition—what statesman does not act from mixed motives?—but there can be no doubt that he was sincerely convinced that the time for change had come. He believed that Free Trade would help the towns without detriment to rural industry; and so far as his generation was concerned he was right. It is true that he exaggerated the case in his manifesto. But we can hardly blame him for his failure to see a century ahead.

He was, as Granville said many years afterwards, a compound of a giant and a little child, and in his actions —which were often condemned as impulsive—he showed the simplicity and directness characteristic of both. It might have been better for him at times to have had a little subtlety in his nature, but his idea of strategy was a direct statement and a frontal attack, and through the whole of a long life he never wavered from that conception. His successes and his failures alike spring from the fact that he was simply the plain man come to judgment; those who, like Aberdeen in later years, declared him to be unfathomable, looked for something that was not there.

In any event, he could hardly foresee that the Edinburgh Letter would force Peel to resign at once. More probably he looked forward to a debate in the ensuing session, a joint attack on the Tory host by official Whig, unofficial Radical, and their useful Irish allies. This might cause a split in the Government, and perhaps their eventual defeat, and—since Melbourne was now a sick man past work—a summons for Russell himself to Windsor and the commission to form a Whig Government on a Free Trade basis.

The upshot, as things fell out, was less fortunate.

On Peel's resignation, the Queen at once sent for Russell, and without any interval for discussion and preparation, the delicate business of negotiation with those difficult dignitaries, the Whig oligarchy, began.

The Edinburgh Letter had been written on his own responsibility, and taken by itself, as Lord John afterwards remarked, it "justified the conclusion that the Whig party was prepared to unite with the Anti-Corn Law League" in demanding the total repeal of the Corn Laws. But the Whig party was certainly not prepared to share the sweets of office with the allies whom it had helped to victory. Policy is one thing, loaves and fishes are another. The Radicals might rage, but they imagined a vain thing if they thought that the "bitter divisions among classes" indicated any weakening of the old exclusiveness in government. Free Trade in corn was all very well, but in the Cabinet there was nothing like monopoly.

The Whig tide was not yet, however, at the full, and a most unfortunate hitch occurred. The great Lord Grey, of the Reform Act, had died six months before, but a Whig Government without a Grey would have seemed like Paradise without Peter at the gate. His son, who was then more familiar to politics as Howick and has since become famous as the most unpopular Colonial Secretary that ever lived, was therefore invited to join the embryo Cabinet. But it was discovered that he would not serve with Palmerston as Foreign Secretary, and Russell considered it "impossible to go on unless I had both."

Russell's own subsequent difficulties with Palmerston show that there was more in Grey's refusal than the mere pernicketiness of a proverbially stiff-necked politician; but the ambition of the expectant Prime Minister was cruelly mortified. He was too generous a man to bear open malice for long, but many years later he told Lord Granville that the great disappointment of his life was Grey's refusal to join his Government in 1845, which had prevented his name going down in history as the repealer of the Corn Laws.

The refusal made no difference whatever to English economic history, but it complicated political history with a question of ethics long passionately debated, and even now occasionally revived. Peel resumed office, the now hated leader of a sullen and mutinous party, and the Corn Laws were repealed. "The field was lost," said Disraeli, "but at any rate there should be retribution"; and on the same night that the Repeal Bill was passed by the Lords, the Conservative Government was defeated in the Commons.

Peel had broken his party, and his party in revenge had broken Peel. He never held office again, and even had he lived forty years instead of four years longer it is doubtful whether he would ever have held office again.

The little group of colleagues who had shared his successes and anxieties of the past five years indeed remained true to him, and we shall meet the Peelites again—the rising Gladstone, the sunny Herbert, the melancholy Graham, and the peaceful Aberdeen. But the ordinary party man had done with him.

It was held that Peel had betrayed his party, and for treachery there is no forgiveness even in politics, where most things are sooner or later forgiven. Macaulay loudly denounced him, and if Macaulay was too bitter an opponent to be quite fair evidence, it must be added that even the usually tolerant Melbourne complained to the Queen, "Ma'am, it's a damned dishonest act." The short straight-forward view of the average blunt Englishman was admirably put by Lord Cottenham. "Either Peel foresaw the necessity of giving up his opposition to the repeal of the Corn Laws, or he did not. If he foresaw it, he was wanting in honesty when he persevered in his opposition. If he did not foresee it, he was wanting in wisdom, and is not fit to be entrusted with the supreme direction of this great Empire."

But the judgment, as it happens, will not do. It makes no allowance for the slow but steady change in the economic position of the country which had become more and more marked year by year since Pitt had first had the idea of Free Trade as a Tory measure half a century before. It makes no allowance for the gradual erosion of a loosely accepted personal opinion in favour of one fiscal expedient to a definite conviction in favour of another fiscal expedient.

63

It makes no allowance for the possibility that if the sudden crisis of the potato disease and autumn rains had not taken the Government unawares, Peel might have completed his official term as a nominal Protectionist, resigned the leadership, and announced his conversion as a private member. Above all, it makes no allowance for the facts that he resigned, that Russell failed to form a Government, and that Grey's refusal practically compelled the Conservative Cabinet to resume office. In the words of the Duke of Wellington: "We may and do wish that the Corn Laws could be maintained, but we know that none of us could form a Government in order to maintain them; nor indeed could any other individual that we know of."

Nor should it be forgotten that in a previous crisis of the same kind on the Reform Bill the Duke had declared that, if he had refused to assist in the formation of a Government, he would have been ashamed to show his face in the streets; whereas Peel declared in the Commons that if he had accepted the task proposed to him, he could not have walked upright into that house. It is clear, therefore, that Peel was not willing to sacrifice principle for power. But it is equally clear that he was willing to sacrifice party for principle.

We cannot wonder that posterity has learned to respect this cold but upright figure. But perhaps we cannot wonder that his party never forgave him.

CHAPTER IX

THE HUMAN BACKGROUND

ON June 27, 1846, the Peel Government resigned, having been beaten in the Commons the same night that the Corn Bill was passed by the Lords. On the following day the Queen, who was staying at Osborne, sent for Lord John Russell to form a Government. He accepted the task with alacrity; and a few weeks before reaching his fifty-fourth birthday "the best of all good little boys," as his mother had called him nearly half a century before, was Prime Minister of the United Kingdom.

I

If to become Prime Minister is to achieve greatness—and at least it is a position that men do not casually drift into—then John Russell was now a great man; the recognized head of what was admittedly the leading political power of the world.

At any rate, he had achieved his ambition; for he was too honest to pretend he did not want to get to the top, and too sensible to talk the common cant, which nobody ever believes, about preferring the peaceful ease of a country squire to the toils and vexations of public life. Russell, like Palmerston and Gladstone, always admitted frankly that he preferred office to opposition, and for the best of reasons: all three had that noble self-esteem which makes men feel that their services are worth giving, and that power in their hands is an instrument for good to their country.

But if Russell had achieved his ambition, it was against extraordinary physical odds.

The devil's advocate will say at once that he had the decisive advantage of birth and class against such tribunes of the people as Bright and Cobden. That is true; but although it is important, it is not all-important; and the fact is that the House of Commons which Russell entered in 1813 was so largely recruited from men of gentle birth, and so largely a preserve of family and class, that the internal competition of the aristocratic cadets was still severe; and perhaps more severe on the Whig than on the Tory side, since the Whig aristocrats generally produced their own leaders, whereas the dumb Tory squires paid reluctant homage to middle-class brains.

But against this advantage of birth, Russell was handicapped with disadvantages that must have seemed equally decisive. Few men have faced and conquered greater difficulties: his rise was a triumph of pluck, persistence, and push, in the face of sheer physical disabilities that seemed overwhelming.

His body was far too small, his figure far too insignificant, his voice far too thin, to give him any assistance towards mastering an assembly that delighted in physical grace, in excellence of speech, and in splendour of diction. He learned in time to speak, and to speak well; but he had never the noble eloquence of Pitt, the impressive phraseology of Peel, or the peculiarly patriotic note which was to exalt his rival Palmerston above him in years to come.

What he achieved was achieved by sheer sincerity and force of character. He never spoke a word he did not believe, and there were few things he believed in that he did not have sooner or later to speak about. These are not common qualities, in politics or anywhere else; and thirty years of devoted service in this kind had given him the first place in his party, while the collapse of the Conservatives had now made him, in the very prime of political life, the first man in the country.

Young enough to enjoy success, and not too old for political life to be a burden, he could reasonably look forward to fifteen or twenty years of supreme power in the greatest Parliament in the world. This was not to be, from causes that will presently appear; but when we ask how it came about that so much had been achieved by so little, we have to look first to the private life of the man, the inner reserves of his stock, his surroundings, and his personal habits, for the answer.

2

"This damned morality will undo us all," said Melbourne of the early Victorian court, with a wistful backward glance at the easier manners of the Regency. The junior colleague who was destined to succeed him as leader of the Whigs would have disagreed; immorality was not in the Bedford tradition, and Lord John's idolatry of William III and Charles James Fox stopped short this side of their mistresses.

Some female philosopher has said that most men can expect a good mother and a good wife, but no woman can expect both a good father and a good husband. The dictum hits men hard, but whether true or not of the mass, the Russell clan were notably good sons, good fathers, and good husbands.

Lord John, like his father the sixth Duke, tempted fortune by marrying twice, and like his father's, both marriages were successful. These things may be merely coincidence, but it is at least a plausible presumption that some exceptional qualities of heart as well as head conjoin to make such records.

Some men show their best front to the world: colleagues find them easy to work with, but wives confess with a sigh or a smile that they are difficult to live with. Others are the reverse: easy at home, but difficult abroad. Russell belonged to the latter category. The private memoirs of the time show that his colleagues and allies sometimes found him difficult to work with, but there is ample testimony that he was easy and even delightful to live with.

He was occasionally in debt—the fault was his brother's, rather than his own—but he had one of those happy natures that does not bother about money, and his servants, like his family, adored him. That fact alone goes some little way to explain his success. Politics were occasionally a desert, but his home was always an oasis in which to restore his strength.

The first marriage, however, was a surprise. Lord John

was turned forty, and apparently a confirmed bachelor, when he astonished Woburn Abbey by the announcement that he intended to marry the widow of the second Lord Ribblesdale. The leader of the House of Commons was still technically a younger son, and his cautious father asked for details of the marriage settlements before he sent congratulations. These prudent apprehensions were happily relieved; the marriage took place, and little Lord John was presently dubbed the Widow's Mite by the wits. But the bride soon learned the penalty of marrying a public man.

It chanced that Peel resigned his minority premiership of 1835 three days before the marriage, and the honeymoon was cut short after forty-eight hours by the strident call of a hotly-contested election. There followed three years of perfect contentment—"he was so attached to her, I don't believe two people were ever happier together," wrote the Queen—and then Lady John died tragically in childbirth.

She had never been a strong woman, but the blow was so utterly unexpected that Russell was completely prostrated. He hid himself from society, and for a time even thought of retiring altogether from public life. But colleagues and friends assured him that work was the best antidote to grief, and the oak was too tough to snap.

After a while he reappeared in the House of Commons, which received him with the generous sympathy it always extends to a man sorely stricken by Fate; but it was noticed that from that time he went out less, and that the two children of the marriage were almost always with him. If they were separated from him for a few days he wrote to them regularly; and though his letters have been lost, their childish replies were treasured by the bereaved father with as much care as if they had been State papers.

For nearly three years he remained a widower; and then, at forty-nine, he took the hazardous step of marrying a girl of twenty. But the Lady Frances Elliot, a younger daughter of the second Lord Minto, came of a family hardly less remarkable in Scotland than the Russells in England, and his young wife had been educated in that atmosphere of aristocratic Whiggery which took life seriously as a political duty.

To the Whig female mind of this type the State was only secure when a father or a husband was in the Cabinet, but the Lady Frances was doubly happy, for within five years of her marriage both the father whom she revered and the husband whom she worshipped were in the same Government. Envious outsiders, it is true, sneered at what was destined to be the last Whig Cabinet as a family dinner-party, but the faithful wife and daughter would probably have retorted that the two best families in the kingdom must needs make the best government for the country.

This second marriage was to last thirty-seven years, and to prove ideally happy.[1] It seems to have been said in the small circle of political intimates that Lady John was the better man of the two, and that the Prime Minister was under petticoat government. But these things are often said of public men, and the charge is more easily made than disproved.

There is, indeed, one piece of positive evidence in its favour. When Russell was Prime Minister, he suggested his father-in-law as Foreign Secretary, and the Queen, we are told, was a little startled at the idea. The second Lord Minto had played a useful part in public life, but there was nothing to show that he was the equal either in character or capacity to his father—who had assisted at the trial of Warren Hastings and been a successful Governor General of India—and it is difficult to believe that Russell would have preferred him to Clarendon, that best of colleagues and most charming of men, had his wife not urged the suit.

But the strongest of husbands may consent to do one job at a good wife's persuasion, and the rest of the tittle-tattle would not hang a cat. It was said that Lady John urged her husband to press his claims against Aberdeen, in 1852–54. But Lord John's own consistent character shows that he needed no urging; he felt he was the better

[1] Lady Russell (of whom a memoir has been written) survived her husband twenty years, and died in 1898.

man of the two, and made no secret that it was his own desire to be Prime Minister again.

It was said, too, that she persuaded him not to take the double office of Foreign Secretary and leader of the Commons. But he himself felt that the task was beyond his strength at sixty; and if a wife is to be blamed for urging her husband not to kill himself, then few men escape being ruled by their wives.

The truth seems to be that Lord John Russell made his political career by his own courage and ability before he had a wife at all, and that his second wife's interference was no more than a proper care for the preservation of his health. Without her it is difficult to see that he would have been more successful, but it is easy to see that he might not have lived happy and content to extreme old age. If we are to blame her for that, then let us be consistent, and say that no wife should venture to have an opinion of her own.

3

It is the fact, however, that she modified his method of living.

As a boy he had had a passion for the play—with the fine omnivorous taste of youth he had seen *Macbeth* and *Raising the Wind* on the same day, in the short Westminster School period—and even the more exciting drama of the House of Commons on a great night had never quite supplanted the earlier taste.

As a young man, too, of good family and rising fame, all the great houses, at least on his own side of politics, were open to him, and he had dined out regularly, and supped at Grillions and the clubs.

It was an age of high feeding and generous drinking, when King William expected his Ministers to manage two bottles a man at dinner, and every respectable statesman of fifty confessed to the gout. Russell, as it happens, was always singularly temperate at table, and although no sportsman, he took plenty of fresh air and exercise in mitigation of late hours and those small excesses which one can only avoid at the cost of being considered a crank.

Even so, it is the dinners, not the debates, that kill; and Lady John, like a wise woman, knew that the pleasures were also the perils of the table, and took steps accordingly.

Russell had built himself a new house in Chesham Place, then a new quarter not far from the fashionable centre of the town. But in order to give fresh air to the children he sometimes rented a villa seven miles out, at Wimbledon—he pulled up there for a romp and a game of ball with them on the way from Osborne to London when forming his 1846 Government—and the Court, knowing something of this, offered him Pembroke Lodge at Richmond for life. It was gratefully accepted by the Russells, and they made it a custom to sleep there on Saturdays, Sundays, and Wednesdays—when the House of Commons rose early—and during the entire week when Parliament was not sitting.

Lady John always claimed that the arrangement prolonged her husband's life by several years, and there is no reason to doubt her. In those days of horse-travelling, however, residence in what was still practically a country town for half the week at the height of the London season involved the refusal of a good many social engagements; and people naturally drew damaging comparisons between the dinners and crushes at the Palmerstons' in Carlton Gardens and the empty dining-room and deserted drawing-room at Chesham Place.

There were, it is true, many jolly week-end parties at Pembroke Lodge, when Russell was full of fun and good stories. But others who penetrated unexpectedly to the wilds of Richmond Park brought back strange tales of the Prime Minister and his wife reading aloud to each other of an evening, and that most dismal of all domestic pastimes emphasized still further the homely background of the statesman's life. One could hardly imagine wicked old Q. reading aloud the latest volume of Prescott or Macaulay to the favourite divinity of the hour.

These things made some smile and others sneer, and did him harm in the small fashionable set which then made up London society. They certainly handicapped him in his long rivalry with Palmerston, and were not entirely without effect in the later days when Gladstone, in Carlton House Terrace, was becoming the rising hope of the Liberals. But they have to be considered in connexion with the physical frailty of the man himself.

Palmerston, Peel, and Gladstone were men who could dine out every evening and go back to the foul atmosphere of the House until the small hours of the morning four nights a week without turning a hair. Russell at fifty would have collapsed in a session without a peaceful home. What there was of him was tough, but there were no reserves of strength; it was indeed a standing miracle that the "ninth part of a tailor," as Carlyle contemptuously called the little fellow, should lead the House at all.

4

There are, of course, many more laborious occupations than politics, which has the singular advantage—or is it a disadvantage?—that those who fail to rise can think but not act, while those who succeed can act but have no time to think. But there are few occupations which involve such constant nervous wear and tear. In no other profession do men of outstanding ability fail so completely because circumstance is against them; in no other walk of life are the prizes so few, or the chances of missing them so many. In no other trade is it so difficult to rise and so easy to fall; in no other walk is loyalty so rare, desertion so frequent, and disappointment so great. The politician, said Gladstone, suspects everybody; and he might have added that everybody suspects him.

Russell chose his hazardous calling, and the event proved him right, for he got to the top. Not only that: there is nothing in his life to suggest that he would ever have got to the top in any other direction.

It was said of him by Sidney Smith that he would have taken command of the Channel Fleet, or rebuilt St. Paul's, at ten minutes' notice. He smilingly disclaimed any such absurdity; his *métier* was to be a politician, and he knew nothing of any other profession.

As a literary man the best we can say of him is that as an amateur not all of his performances are contemptible.

But not even the name of Russell and the fame of a double Premiership could give a single verse, or even a single sentence of his written prose, the feeblest flicker of immortality.   He was friendly with men of letters, but his acquaintances were in the second rank—Thomas Moore, Leigh Hunt, and the banker-poet Rogers.   He knew Macaulay as a colleague, and admired the "Essays" and the great "History" as sound Whiggery come to judgment.   But there is nothing to indicate that he ever cared for Shelley or Keats, and it is significant of his literary limitations that in discussing the appointment of a Poet Laureate to succeed Wordsworth he mentioned "three or four authors of nearly equal merit—Henry Taylor, Sheridan Knowles, Professor Wilson, and Mr. Tennyson."   The order does not suggest a nice discrimination of the higher values.

Of science he knew little, and to call his mathematics elementary would be to over-praise him.   He had none of those hankerings after the mysteries of religion which made men say of Gladstone that if he had not been Prime Minister he would have made a great Archbishop of Canterbury; Russell was merely a sound Protestant who wished the Pope at the devil.

No man ever had a less metaphysical mind.   He knew, as we all know, that there are hidden mysteries, but he knew that these grave matters were not for him.   He had a religion, but it was extraordinarily simple—he summed up all statecraft once, in a letter to Queen Victoria, as the golden rule[1]—and he would have no dogma.   He thought the talk of sacraments mere superstition, and the apostolic succession was to him, as to most laymen, as great an absurdity as that other exploded doctrine, the divine right of kings.   Like a good Whig, he believed in religious toleration, and even thought that the Church might some

---

[1] The statement is so obviously sincere that it is worth quoting.   "The grand rule of doing to others as we wish that they should do unto us is more applicable than any other system of political science.   The honour of England does not consist in defending every English officer or English subject, right or wrong, but in taking care that she does not infringe the rules of justice, and that they are not infringed against her."

Palmerston, of course, would have ridiculed this.

day believe in it too, till Pio Nono undeceived him; but the strife of synods and sermons was not for him. "It conduces much to piety not to go to church sometimes," he said placidly as an old man, weary of the theological controversies of the time; and the remark reveals the simplicity of the pre-Tractarian rather than the scepticism of the post-Darwinian age. It is not of such stuff that great ecclesiastics are made.

If he was no theologian, he distrusted the subtlety of lawyers, and his simple and straightforward mind would have found itself even more handicapped at diplomacy than the Bar. It is said of some men—strangely enough in depreciation, not compliment—that they could not deceive a child. Russell would have scorned to do such a thing; but it is doubtful if he could have deceived anybody.

His whole nature was essentially open, and he practised no reserves; like Pitt—though he would have hated the comparison—everything that was in his mind had to come out. It is this that explains his peculiar horror at the economy of truth recommended by the Tractarians; the spectacle of Newman trying to crack the wind of the Thirty-Nine Articles seems to have made him feel almost physically sick.

No man was ever more utterly devoid of casuistry; he could not stoop, like Disraeli, to flatter the Queen, but wrote to her quite simply as man to man. He was often distrusted by continental statesmen when he was at the Foreign Office, but it was because they disliked his policy and methods of action, never because they thought he was not speaking the truth.

Russell would never, like Bismarck, have doctored the Ems telegram; and had it been necessary for him to play the part of a Cavour, and lie for the good of his country, he would have failed miserably. In the world as it unfortunately is, these deceptions have to be practised, and they are practised for ends that we recognize to be good by men whom we admit to be good. But truth is, after all, a substantive virtue, not a vice, even in politics, and those who use it are not necessarily to be condemned because occasionally it produces unfortunate results.

Russell, in fact, had the utter simplicity and directness of the man who has no doubts and is sure he is always right because he always speaks the truth as he sees it. It is a type that, for obvious reasons, often goes with the persecuting mind, and he detested any form of persecution. But toleration does not, as the rigid dogmatists suppose, necessarily imply mental flabbiness; it may simply mean a tacit faith in the innate superiority of truth over error. This belief is itself true, but it has to be corrected in practice by the recognition that truth is apt to be a slow-motion picture.

In general it may be said of Russell, as Goldsmith said of Burke, that he was too fond of the right to practise the expedient. It must be admitted, however, that Lord John was lacking in the scope and grasp which made Burke not merely the orator of a party, but the exponent of a political philosophy with something of value to all parties. As a practical statesman he was far ahead of Burke, who was simply a tool for the venomous Francis against Warren Hastings; but as a thinker he was equally far behind. One always feels that for Russell the world was created in 1688, and only so long as the Whigs were in office was Providence likely to regard it as being very good. Unluckily for the theory, man's first disobedience was a lapse from Toryism.

These limitations sometimes hampered and sometimes helped him; for if he was a good Whig and a good Liberal, other Whigs and other Liberals before and since have had a broader and a deeper view. His conception both of the State and the Church could easily be challenged as inadequate, and both his domestic and his foreign policy—as we shall see—were open to criticism; but in one field he was supreme.

The question of reform he made his own, and though others wanted to go farther and still others not so far, he was for nearly fifty years the acknowledged public leader of all who believed in constitutional government, free national parliaments, and an open franchise. On that he spoke with unchallenged authority, on that he staked his influence and risked his popularity, and it is for that he will be remembered in history.

75

Liberty, to Lord John Russell, was an end, not a means; the supreme good, not simply the road by which it may be reached. If we hold, as we must, that in the last analysis this is untrue, we must also admit that in practice it is so near the truth that many great spheres of human activity would be crippled by its denial. If Russell was wrong, he was at any rate nobly wrong; for men do not love liberty so much that we can afford to forget its champions, or even criticize them too nicely for their mistakes. These were very great services, and it is right that we should hold the man in honour who did them.

5

He succeeded, then, in his trade of politics, where lesser and perhaps greater men have failed; but the strain was none the less heavy. Birth and family influence no doubt counted for much at the start, but Russell was not the only cadet of a great house in the pre-Reform parliament, and we shall never properly understand the greatness of his achievement unless we recognize not only that he had many strong competitors, but that the influence of the class from which he came was steadily declining through the whole of his political life.

It was a tradition of the Russells, as of the Lowthers, the Cavendishes, the Stanleys and the two dozen or so other great landowning families who made up the government of eighteenth-century England, to have a son or cadet in the Commons, while the head of the House adorned the Lords. This excellent system enabled the youngster to learn the ropes and have his fling among the plebs while middle-aged wisdom (or at least gravity) sat in state among the patricians.

More important, the rough-and-tumble of debate in the Commons taught the rising aristocrat the eternal lesson that mortal clay is all alike, in a manner that could never be obtruded in the Lords, where even spiritual peers differ in dignity, and one Archbishop claims to rule by divine providence, the other only by divine permission. The accidental lack of this training, as the Lansdowne of the Salisbury-Balfour Government confessed, puts a man out of touch with popular sympathy, and acts as a handicap to a political career. But more important still, when the peers began to weigh less in the constitutional scale than the Commons, it enabled the aristocracy to retain their hold on the political machine for at least another generation.

The decline of the House of Lords was due to two separate causes—the increased importance of finance in the modern State, and the monopoly of taxation by the Commons. Its origin can probably be dated from the beginning of Walpole's long premiership in 1720, but it first became evident in the days when Pitt and Fox, Burke and Sheridan, gave an oratorical glory to the Commons which the peers could never rival. The first quarter of the nineteenth century continued what the latter half of the eighteenth had begun, and in 1818 the Duke of Wellington admitted in his blunt honest way, "Nobody cares a damn for the House of Lords, the House of Commons is everything in England."[1]

But the process was still incomplete in Russell's time; the House of Lords might be slowly decaying, but it was still nominally equal to the Commons in everything but taxation until the Parliament Act of 1911, and for half a century after the first Reform Act the Government of England in effect remained aristocratic.

But the influence of the upper class was all the time visibly on the decline. It is true that Gladstone remarked that no Cabinet could have been more aristocratic than the Aberdeen Cabinet of 1852: "I myself was the only one of fifteen noblemen and gentlemen who composed it who could not fairly be said to belong to that class." But the Tories under Pitt and Peel had always been more democratic in practice than the Whigs with their ducal oligarchy, and the days of the oligarchy were numbered.

In Gladstone's first Government of 1868, the Whig aristocracy had still in his opinion more than their fair share of office and policy. But in his last Government of 1892, their influence had become negligible, and with the begin-

[1] After the Reform Bill the Duke told Peel it was difficult to make men who were lately of such great weight, and were still possessed of peerage and property, understand that they were of no importance in the country.

ning of the twentieth century the old pillars of the State were hardly even ornamental columns of a party. Politically the aristocracy were swamped.

Lord John Russell was peculiarly placed, in that he led the Commons at the time when that House was steadily increasing in power, whereas the influence of his own class was as steadily diminishing. He believed in the people, but he was himself an aristocrat of the aristocrats, and he was never quite on easy terms with the new middle class that sent Radical bankers like Grote and Radical manufacturers like Bright into the House of Commons. His principles and his personality were here in conflict, and he never entirely reconciled the two.

It is nothing to the point, indeed, that he was haughty and distant with his party followers; in that he merely followed the tradition sanctified by the Pitts and carried on by Peel and Gladstone to Salisbury and Asquith. None of these was popular with the rank and file on the back benches. But these leaders were content with keeping followers in their place, and so long as the hacks voted straight and asked no questions, the great man would occasionally condescend to a nod and a smile or more rarely a perfunctory compliment.

Russell, on the other hand, had no such arts. When Creevey damned him as "a conceited young puppy," we remember, indeed, that Creevey was a hungry hyena of politics whose only use for principles was a place. But when a dozen other men complained of his icy-cold manners; when the great Delane—who was on easy terms with Palmerston and often the only commoner at Dunrobin and other ducal houses—found intimacy impossible; above all, when Russell's own father warned him that the *haut-en-bas* manner would not do in politics, we are justified in assuming that there was something more at fault than the normal aloofness of the head towards the herd.

In part, no doubt, this was due to the feeling that the ground was slipping from the aristocracy; whispers, and something more than whispers, must have reached Russell that he was regarded as the last of the Whigs, and if the unregenerate Tories could be led by cotton-spinners and shipowners and Jew adventurers, the friends of humanity could not always put up with a junta of great landlords. But in greater part, perhaps, we must seek the cause in Russell's own physical fraility.

A man with no reserve of strength must husband his resources. When he has put in several hours in his department, persuaded or driven a dissenting Cabinet in the way they should go, and made a great speech in the Commons at an hour when ordinary men are asleep, he can do no more; the deft flattery in the receptive ear, the meaning squeeze of the proffered hand, the contrived but casual greeting of the pompous, the insignificant, and the climber are too much. He can face the enemy and rend them; he cannot stoop to tickle the groundlings.

This was Russell's failing, and for this, in the end, he had to pay; "I had no notion how unpopular he was," wrote Dasent to Delane, when the time came for the second Premiership in 1865.

CHAPTER X

PRIME MINISTER

THE man whom William IV had prophesied would cut a wretched figure against Peel, ten years before, was now Prime Minister, and the prospects for his Government in Parliament were rosy.

Lord John had been bitterly disappointed at the failure of his Edinburgh Letter to place him in Downing Street a few months previously, but in the long run the failure of that manifesto had served him better than success. Had he succeeded Peel in January instead of June he would, indeed, have gone down to history as the repealer of the Corn Laws. But the Conservative Party which Peel had built up from the wreck of the pre-Reform Tories would not have split, or if it had, would have split in opposition instead of office, and without the bitterness and the charges of treachery and desertion which kept the two sections sullen and suspicious of each other for the best part of thirty years.

Russell had not, indeed, a majority in the House of Commons. But that mattered little in the circumstances of the time; for the cohesion of the Conservatives was now smashed and broken. The leaders remained, but they no longer led. The followers remained, but they no longer followed.

Peel sat, silent and often solitary, on the opposition bench, covered with the dust of his own achievement. With him was a small knot of personal and official associates in the late Government, men who were ready to bear witness to his sincerity of purpose and integrity of mind, and who agreed generally with his economic action. But for the time being they were of little account.

Graham's timid wisdom had followed his master Peel into the wilderness, a foil to the sunny disposition of that loyal and beautiful soul, the great gentleman Sidney Herbert. With these sat Gladstone, whose future was still obscure, and whose incessantly busy mind was already turning back from the intricacies of the State to the troubles of the Church, entirely unaware that in time to come he was to reach the supreme height and—such are the ironies of party politics—to succeed Lord John Russell in the leadership of the party which he now opposed.

Over against these lost leaders sat the mutinous followers, that solid army of country gentlemen and country squires who have always been the brawn and backbone rather than the brain of the Tory party. These trusty but tongue-tied troops had seldom cut much figure in debate, but now, by one of the strange chances of life, the upheaval threw them an unexpected leader.

Lord George Bentinck was a famous sportsman of the day, who was more familiar with the odds at Tattersall's than the division lists of the House of Commons. Politics had been, at most, the amusement of his leisure hours, and there are few more curious episodes in English parliamentary history than the sudden emergence of this "virtually uneducated man"—the description is his own—as the leader of the Protectionist Tory group.

The race-horses were sold, the field-sports abandoned for the harsh study of statistics of imports and exports of pig-iron and grain and cotton. But his arguments were shrewd and his vision clear; perhaps there are worse schools of economics than the fresh air of Newmarket Heath.

During two eventful sessions his burning sincerity rallied the lost legions and revived the losing cause; and then one morning he went out walking at Welbeck, and was seen no more alive. He was found lying face forward in the grass, as if sudden death had taken him unawares; and the leadership of the Protectionist group passed incongruously to Disraeli, a townsman among countrymen, an author and rhetorician among men who could hardly write an election address or frame a dozen consecutive sentences on their legs, a Christianized Jew at the head of men who had lately revolted against Bentinck's advocacy of civil liberties for the Jews. What, if anything, Disraeli sin-

cerely believed in beyond himself is a problem happily
beyond the scope of this book; at any rate, he had to wait
long and patiently before the stricken Conservative camp
again gathered heart and hope and followed him to victory.

For many sessions to come, then, it was evident that
Peelites and Protectionists would be more anxious to attack
each other than to make common cause against the traditional enemy; the very stars in their courses appeared to be
fighting for Lord John Russell at this time. But in fact
the position was less strong than it seemed, and the Prince
Consort noticed at once that the new Cabinet was anything
but united.

A Whig Government without a Grey and a Lansdowne
and their respective followers would hardly have seemed
like a Whig Government at all, and Lord John invited
them both to join.[1] Lansdowne was an old personal friend
and intimate associate, and accepted at once; but it needed
some generosity to ask Lord Grey. Six months earlier his
objection to Palmerston had killed the embryo Russell
Cabinet before it was born, and Lord John had then decided
to have nothing more to do with him. The expectant Prime
Minister had now, however, recovered from his disappointment, and Grey was again approached. He had, it
appeared, no longer any qualms over Palmerston, but there
were some scruples about Russell's attitude to the Irish
Church which needed soothing. The necessary assurances were given, and a conditional acceptance was at
length forthcoming.

But whether in office or out of office, the third Earl
Grey was equally difficult. He had ability—Merivale
remarked to Manning that his mind was remarkable alike
for great force and great minuteness, and compared it with

[1] Melbourne was not asked. He admitted that he was too ill to serve,
but he was mortified that Russell had not paid him the compliment of offering
him office.

Twenty-two years later much the same situation was repeated, but Gladstone was more tactful in asking Russell to advise, but without office. Gladstone frankly recognized the inherent difficulty of supersession on another
occasion: "The next most difficult thing to admitting a man into the Cabinet
is to leave a man out who has once been in." He admitted that the only
thing was to be ruthless, and play the butcher.

the trunk of an elephant, equally able to pick up a pin and pull up a tree—but he was certainly not the man his father had been, and even with the artificial prestige of that great name, he was hardly worth his place in the Government. In the previous Whig Cabinet Glenelg, his predecessor at the Colonial Office, had been feeble and fussy; Grey was merely cold and critical.

The truth is, he had no sympathy and was useless for team-work. At best his pride made him an angular colleague; at worst, the Northumbrian Whig was jealous of the Wiltshire Whig, and the Grey clique spoke openly in clubs and drawing-rooms of the Lansdowne group as a set of old women. The Lansdowne supporters not unnaturally responded with the frozen courtesy that makes common action difficult and confidence impossible.

Almost within a week of its formation, the Queen expressed herself dubious whether her new Prime Minister possessed the talent of keeping his colleagues together. The doubt was not quite accurately phrased, for they had never really come together as an administrative unit at all. Lord John was able, indeed, to keep the Government in being for four and a half difficult years; and since this was four years longer than the Queen expected, we must regard it as a real testimony to his capacity for leadership.

But like Melbourne's Cabinet and unlike Peel's, it was a Government of departments which literally obeyed the scriptural admonition that the right hand should not know what the left hand was doing. Herein lay its continual and increasing weakness, and hereon was built the continual and increasing strength of Russell's most forceful colleague and future chief, Lord Palmerston.

But Palmerston played too great a part in the life of Lord John Russell and the history of the times to be dealt with as summarily as the Greys and Lansdownes of the Cabinet.

The Prime Minister's other colleagues were often too dignified to be effective. Palmerston was sometimes too effective to be dignified. But there can be no doubt that he was extraordinarily effective. Unlike the other Ministers, who seldom exerted themselves unduly in their depart-

ments, work was a passion with Palmerston. Thirty-two
years out of the sixty-four he had lived had been spent in
office, and in every department where he was employed he
had shown unremitting industry. But it was not simply
that he was a hard worker where the others were a little
inclined to let things slide; he had the strength which comes
to a man who makes himself master of one subject and
leaves the rest alone.

Palmerston was by instinct a Free Trader before Bright
and Cobden stumped the country, but he played no part in
the fiscal controversy. He was by nature an Erastian; his
ideal Church of England was something like a branch of
the Home Office, and he regarded with contemptuous
amusement the ecclesiastical controversies of the time.[1]
Franchise politics frankly bored him; he had supported the
first Reform Bill without enthusiasm, but like Russell, he
regarded it as a final settlement. Unlike Russell, he did
not change his mind, and while he lived there was no extension of the suffrage.

But these matters Palmerston willingly resigned to
those of his colleagues who cared for such things; his own
interest was centred on foreign affairs, and here his knowledge was wide, his attention unremitting, and his decision
prompt and sure. Eight years senior to Russell, he was
old enough to have been trained under Canning as a Tory,
and although he now ranked as a Whig, Canning still
remained his ideal Foreign Minister. In fact his policy
was neither Whig nor Tory, but national; and the nation
sensing this, took him to its heart. It trusted Wellington.
It respected Peel. It admired and applauded Russell.
But it loved Palmerston.

For Palmerston had given the nation good measure, and
made the voice of England heard in every court and chan-
cellory of Europe. Under the Melbourne Government it
was his act that had created an independent Belgium.
Under the same Government it was he who had opposed
and defeated the French schemes in Egypt, on the broad

[1] A bishop's diocesan duties, he once remarked, "are enough to occupy
all his time, and the less he engages in theological disputes the better. Much
mischief has been done by theological bishops."

ground that "the mistress of India could not permit France to be mistress, directly or indirectly, of the road to her Indian dominions."

But he had not merely defended the interests of England; he had denounced tyranny and misgovernment wherever it was found on the Continent. If his attitude towards petty autocrats made him detested abroad—Palmerston "gives them all the stomach-ache," wrote Russell's brother from the little Court at Stuttgart—it brought him unbounded popularity at home.

A foreign king might say that so long as Palmerston was at the Foreign Office, it was certain that England could not procure a single ally in Europe. It was no matter. England did not need allies, and she could afford to pick and choose her friends when and where she wanted them. Meanwhile, the man who could inform the French that "our desire for peace would never lead us to submit to affront either in language or in act," was the man for England.

It was magnificent, but it was hardly diplomacy. Like Carteret, a century before, others might concern themselves with the minor commerce of making judges and bishops, while his business lay with kings and emperors; but Palmerston treated these potentates with the tolerance of an equal, if not with the easy nonchalance of a superior. It was galling for a Habsburg or a Bourbon to be told by a small English landowner that he was wrong, perhaps still more galling to be assured from time to time that he was right. But it was frankly intolerable to be admonished like a small boy by a headmaster on the advantages of parliaments and constitutional governments, and taught that the better way to spell Revolution was Reform.

The nation at home loved it, because it was an implied tribute to the superiority of British institutions, and therefore to the superiority of the British people; political wisdom had been born with us, and those who wanted to learn the art of government had better go to school at Westminster. But it must remain doubtful in retrospect whether Palmerston's incessant interference and advertisement of the advantages of liberty really profited the cause of constitutional government in the long run. The dynasts fumed or trembled, but the storm of revolution passed, and the absolutists returned. They did lip-service to the cause of freedom, but the rising tide of nationalism in Europe used the liberal doctrine for its own purpose, and then turned against it.

It is difficult to love your neighbour as yourself, but much more difficult to reform your neighbour as yourself. And the truth is that Palmerston was living on the political capital and prestige accumulated in the past; Pitt had backed opinion by force, but Palmerston was only able to back advice by argument. He irritated the impotent, but the time came when his bluff was called by Bismarck, and in the memorable sneer of Disraeli, he proved to be ginger-beer and not champagne after all.

But nearly twenty years were to elapse before the nation sensed the difference. During those years Palmerston was in effect supreme; and he was as happy in death as in life, for in the end he died before his countrymen found him out.

CHAPTER XI

IRISH FAMINE AND AFTER

THE Russell Government which took the oath on July 5, 1846, had not long to wait for trouble.

The repeal of the Corn Laws might prove as beneficial in the long run as Peel and Russell both believed. But there was no denying that it was an economic revolution which must be felt far and wide in town and country, and whose effects no man could predict.

The nation, however, was in one of those moods of absurd optimism—less common among English people than our equally absurd pessimism—caused by the rapid spread of the railway system. The mania for speculation presently reached a height it had hardly touched since the South Sea Bubble, more than a century before, and it needed no prophet to foresee that the boom must soon collapse, to be followed by heavy loss and probably a financial panic.

The panic duly arrived. Values fell, banks shut, mercantile houses closed their doors. But underneath the froth and bubble of the speculators the financial structure was fundamentally sound, and after a few weeks of hectic uncertainty the normal course of commerce was resumed.

But a deeper and graver crisis had to be faced than the difficulties of people who had to some extent brought trouble on themselves. The Peel Government had, in effect, gone out on an Irish famine; the Russell Cabinet came in with the Irish famine still to deal with, and the position of that unfortunate country was growing steadily worse from day to day.

The potato blight had first appeared in America in 1844. The following year it crossed the Atlantic, broke out in northern Europe, and attacked Ireland with particular severity. A great part of the potato crop had failed in

1845. But in 1846 the failure was almost complete, and the disease spread north to western Scotland and the Hebrides.

It soon became clear, in the language of Lord John Russell, that "a famine of the thirteenth had fallen on the nineteenth century"; and what had at first been merely pitiful distress soon developed into national disaster. A whole unhappy people was stricken, as it were, by the hand of God upon their crops; and thousands of men, women, and little children, weakened by privation and suffering, simply laid themselves down to die.

No more pitiful story has ever been told than this slow starvation of a great country. This was no sudden visitation of plague, like the Black Death or the cholera, which killed strong men in a night; it was a steady and remorseless pinch of hunger which drove men from roots to grass, from grass to bark, and from bark to bitter death. The mortality was terrible. In the Skibbereen district ten thousand persons out of a hundred thousand died in a few weeks; in the whole of Ireland the deaths mounted abruptly from an average of seventy-seven thousand in an ordinary year to the appalling figure of a quarter of a million.

Nor was this all. The curse of heaven seemed to have descended on the afflicted country, and many of those who had clung faithfully to its green pastures were now moved to abandon their homes and farms and friends. The more prosperous, the more fortunate, and the more enterprising sold their possessions for what they would fetch, and made their way sorrowfully overland to Limerick or Galway to book their passage across the Atlantic. From smiling Wicklow to bleak and melancholy Connemara deserted houses and cold hearths bore mute witness to the ruin that had overtaken Ireland, and the nation was thus doubly stricken. Thousands of those who could go left for America, and thousands of those who could not go starved; and there was no longer any strength in the land, only suffering.

A calamity like this could not but move the heart of England. Estranged as the two countries had been for centuries by race, religion, and politics, wholesale disaster

overleaps all differences of creed and culture. Lord John
Russell did not think it necessary to summon Parliament
to meet that dismal autumn, but prompt steps were taken
to mitigate the worst features of the disaster. Vast quan-
tities of maize were imported from America and distributed
free to the hungry peasants, the relief measures which Peel
had introduced the previous year were extended, and two
million pounds advanced by the Treasury to meet distress.
Large additional contributions were made by private
benevolence, and soon more than half a million people
were living on the funds of the State or individual charity.

Even then the position was ghastly, and the future
precarious. There were inevitable abuses attendant on
hastily improvised schemes: it was discovered that the men
working on the public roads were paid more than those in
private employment, so that the State itself to some extent
aggravated the trouble it had tried to cure. It was found,
too, that when the meal was distributed, some of the people
sold it for money. It was then cooked before distribution
to stop this scandal—and "they throw away the cooked
food, these starving people," wrote Russell in the bitterness of his heart. Truly a famine is not an easy matter
to deal with, nor does the struggle for survival in its cruder
form bring out the best side of human nature. Benevolence, after all, is largely a matter of surplus value.

Yet the disaster was, in fact, also a great opportunity.
Could the Government have risen fully to the occasion, it
is possible that good might in the end have come out of
evil, and the two countries have been reconciled by sympathy and statesmanship. But it was not to be. The
famine came in an unhappy hour for England as well as
for Ireland.

It was not that the price of grain rose to unprecedented
heights, and in any event if Ireland was poor, England
was rich. It was not that the right course was not put
forward and pleaded with passionate energy and conviction
in the House of Commons. It was simply that the rigid
principles of current economic theory had paralysed the
political vision, as diphtheria sometimes paralyses the
physical vision.

A crisis so unparalleled demanded large constructive measures, and the time offered opportunity for development work of a national character, which would have given hope to men who had lost heart and faith and often home, have rescued Ireland from the slough of despond into which it was sinking, and have employed men on productive enterprises that would have been of permanent benefit when the famine was past. Lord George Bentinck now put forward a carefully worked out scheme for the construction of railways in Ireland, to be built by a Government grant of sixteen millions sterling.

There could be no doubt that railways were required in Ireland as in England, and there could be no doubt that they would add to the convenience of life and the prosperity of the country. Unfortunately there could also be no doubt that at that time of stress no commercial corporation could raise the funds to undertake so great and costly a work; only the State could do so.

Englishmen on the whole object to State action. Irishmen on the whole do not. But these things are not matters of eternal principle but of political expediency, and Ireland's need was England's opportunity to carry through a bold policy on lines that Ireland would have understood.

The Cabinet, however, held that railways were a matter for private enterprise, although this was tantamount to saying that for the time being Ireland must do without railways. When principles produce absurd consequences, it is usually wise to consider whether there is not something wrong with the principle. But this was not done.[1]

Not all the blame, it is true, rests upon the Government. Sir Robert Peel and the Manchester School supported the Government in rejecting the Irish railway scheme, and the Bentinck proposal was lost by 204, in a House of 440. But if the Prime Minister had been a man of greater vision, and had supported the Protectionists' scheme in a speech that rose above party and immediate business considerations he might have succeeded. At least he would have left the

[1] The same question arose in Australia. Had railway construction there not been undertaken by the State, the country would have been kept back many years.

memory of a gallant failure, and fewer Irish famine juries would have brought in a verdict of wilful murder against Lord John Russell.[1]

Principle was thus vindicated though the people perished. The money was saved. The opportunity passed. The moment of reconciliation vanished.

John Russell was personally one of the kindest and—within his limited means—most generous of men. Appeals to his private purse, by beggars of high and low degree, were seldom made in vain. But in this grave public matter he failed to show the generosity of purpose and the breadth of sympathy which would have characterized him in private. He could seize a political chance quickly when it offered, as the Edinburgh Letter a year before had proved, and the notorious Durham Letter was to show a second time four years hence, but he could hardly rise from a party to a national policy in an emergency. Perhaps the inherited caution of the Russell ancestry was too strong; in any event, he could not understand that if the disaster was great, the opening for constructive statecraft was not less great.

The Irish problem was at bottom at least as much agrarian as political, and here was an opportunity, such as had never occurred before and might never occur again, for recasting the whole of that accursed land system which was by common consent the worst in Europe. It would certainly have been wise, even in 1846, to deal with the Irish problem by land purchase, and to have left on one side the relatively insignificant matters of Church reform, Disestablishment, and Maynooth, which were the preoccupation and despair of every Whig Government. But Russell did not do it, and even in 1870 Gladstone "could lend no countenance to such plans." Probably the influence of the great Whig landowners in Ireland was too strong.[2]

[1] The verdict, of course, was absurd. But desperate men are often absurd. And it was put about that Russell, as member for the City of London, was influenced by the grain merchants.

[2] Lansdowne and Hartington both opposed reform of Irish land tenure; "property of all kinds was at stake," remarked Hartington. The figures of falling rent-roll on the Lansdowne estates in Ireland hardly suggest that the negative attitude was economically sound.

A greater man would have seized the occasion to reform, a still greater man would have profited by the position to reconcile the country with its neighbour. But Russell merely rebuked it.

He told the people as he fed them that they should have more self-reliance, and work out their own salvation by their own exertions. The words were true, even a truism; we all know that heaven helps those who help themselves. But in this case heaven seemed to have cursed those who had at least sown their own crops; and it is ill work preaching morality to men who are dying on the roadside. This kind of charity leaves bitterness of heart.

It is true that Russell was not master of the House of Commons. But party allegiance sat loosely at the moment, and the support of the Bentinck Tories would have offset the defection of the urban Radicals. The Liberals would have grumbled, and Manchester have protested that this was not sound economics as understood at Manchester. But they would hardly have put the new Government out on Irish famine.

But there are, unfortunately, no indications that even if Russell had been master of the House he would have adopted the Bentinck policy, or anything like it.[1] He had amazing political ability. He had astonishing personal ambition. But he was lacking in that vision of national development which had characterized his ancestor who had set about draining the Fens, and given his name to the Bedford Level; and the supreme statesmanship, that rare combination of sympathetic insight with the daring leadership that can turn misfortune itself into better fortune, was not his. He could not, like Peel, get outside his party skin; and while the Whig-Liberal creed affirmed the doctrine of full civil and religious liberty, it was rigidly determinist in economics.

The famine presently died down. The population

---

[1] Some months later, indeed, the Government brought in a Bill to advance £600,000 to Irish railway companies. It thus tacitly admitted the Bentinck policy was not ill-founded, and the Bill was passed, despite the opposition of Peel. But the measure was too small, and too late.

continued to fall by emigration.[1]   It was said indeed by some optimists and apologists for things as they are that Ireland had previously been over-populated, and was stronger and healthier after the disaster than before.   But it is difficult to find any justification for that view; the country was behind, not ahead of the time before the famine, and under a better agrarian and political system could have supported more rather than fewer people.

In any event, it was now too late.   A blight had settled, not only on the crops, but on the very spirit of the country; and for once the superstitious and the enterprising were in agreement, and what had been cursed by God was abandoned by man.

Ireland never recovered from the famine, and a settled melancholy brooded over the land that had lost nearly half its population.[2]   But for those that remained, the bitterness of the historic past had been increased and deepened by the recent hunger; and now began again that dismal round of agitation and coercion, rebellion and repression, which makes up the political annals of Ireland in the nineteenth century.

The Whigs had naturally criticized the Tories when in office for their methods of controlling the country, and the Peel Government had suffered its final defeat on a Coercion Bill; but one of the first acts of the Whig Viceroy, Lord Bessborough, was to insist on an Arms Bill which, if it was not technically coercion, was at least constraint.   Lord John reluctantly agreed, but the Bill was eventually withdrawn on account of Liberal opposition.

After the famine, however, it was quite impossible to ignore the fact that the situation was steadily going from bad to worse.   Clarendon, who had succeeded Bessborough as Viceroy, reported that armed mobs were intimidating life and threatening property; and by the

[1] Russell, who was always interested in colonial affairs, proposed a scheme for emigrating destitute Irish to Canada in 1849.   It might have been useful, but it was opposed in Cabinet, and abandoned.

[2] In 1841 the census enumerated 8,175,124.   By 1851 it had sunk to 6½ million, and it fell with each successive census; in 1901 it was less than 4½ million.

autumn of 1847 landlords and landlords' agents were being murdered almost every day.

Actually, the diagnosis of the disease was simple, and Russell made it clear in a paragraph: "It is quite true that landlords in England would not like to be shot like hares and partridges by miscreants banded for murderous purposes. But neither does any landlord in England turn out fifty persons at once, and burn their houses over their heads, giving them no provision for the future. The murders are atrocious; so are the ejectments. The truth is that a civil war between landlords and tenants has been raging for eighty years, marked by barbarity on both sides."

The disease was accurately diagnosed. But there was no remedy in the party pharmacy. It was necessary, of course, to take action to restore order—the Whig diarist Greville remarked that if the Government had met Parliament and proposed nothing it would have been swept away in a whirlwind of indignation—and a Coercion Bill was passed in the autumn of 1847. The Whigs, after all, prescribed the Tory medicine.

Lord John, however, adhered to the Whig ideal—sometimes successful and often misunderstood—of sugaring the pill by accompanying coercion with conciliation, and early the next session an Act facilitating the sale of Encumbered Estates was passed, while a further Bill compensating tenants for improvements was introduced.

This last was a mere piece of natural equity; less an affirmation of justice than a denial of injustice. But its reception was so hostile as almost to suggest that equity is too dangerous to be easily tolerated in human society.

The Bill was stubbornly opposed by vested interests, and was finally shelved by being referred to a select committee. If it be admitted that Lord John was not equal to the problems raised by the Irish famine, it must be added that in this matter of justice between landlord and tenant he was many years in advance of the time.

The position at length improved, or at least seemed to improve, if only through exhaustion. In 1849 Russell wrote hopefully that "agitation is extinct, repeal is forgotten, the seditious associations are closed, the priests are frightened and the people tranquil." One can only regret that he did not in the following year take occasion by the hand to reform what only appeared to be pacified; for repeal was not really forgotten, and the Fenian troubles that soon followed were to furnish a frightful commentary on the assertion that agitation was extinct.

It would have been difficult, no doubt, to save Ireland. It was much easier to lecture the Pope. But sometimes the difficult things are better worth doing, even at the risk of failure, than the easy things which only seem to promise success. Lord John Russell would have left a greater name had he thought more of Ireland and less of Italy; the real tragedy of history is in these silent days of missed opportunity.

But by 1849 things were at any rate outwardly somewhat better, and the Prime Minister wisely advised a Royal visit to Ireland. The Queen went, a little reluctantly, and was well received. But she disliked Ireland, a country which she thought nobody would visit for pleasure, and hardly troubled to understand it; and she steadily opposed at a later date Gladstone's advice that a royal residence should be equipped and occupied in Ireland.[1]

The expedient would not, of course, have cured the economic troubles of Ireland. It would not have solved, though it might possibly have eased, the political difficulty. But it would at least have removed the settled impression that Ireland was avoided, abandoned, and accursed.

[1] The Prince of Wales (afterwards Edward VII) also disliked the idea; and as heir to the throne his proper place was London. The Queen tentatively suggested the Duke of Connaught as Lord-Lieutenant; an admirable idea. Unfortunately it was not carried through.

CHAPTER XII

THE HAMPDEN AFFAIR

THE greatest saints, it is said, are sometimes uneasily conscious of the secular foreground that obtrudes incongruously on the field of piety. Lord John Russell would have laughed at any ascription of sanctity, but he was often aware of an ecclesiastical background that coloured and to some extent influenced the proper field of politics. More than once his dealings with the Church provoked something like a crisis; and towards the close of his first Premiership an attempt on his part to turn an ecclesiastical crisis which he had not provoked to his own political profit miscarried, and heralded the beginning of that long decline in public esteem from which he never fully recovered.

Russell was a true Whig, and the attitude of the Whigs towards religion was simplicity itself. The Church was a good servant but a bad master of the State. Whether or not it was actually a branch of the State might be matter for curious constitutional argument; but in practice, so long as it was guided and controlled by the State like some superior Department of Woods and Forests, it was capable of producing useful and indeed necessary fruit in the sphere of public morals and family piety. If, however, it was left without that sober political guidance and unobtrusive secular control, experience showed that religion might provoke dangerous delusions and disturbances, engender troubles that would affect the civil power, and lead to conflicts that could only damage State as well as Church.

The dissenters from the national system of faith could be freely tolerated and encouraged, partly because they had the good sense to support the Whigs against the Tories, and partly because they were not sufficiently important to affect the larger affairs of government. But the Estab-

THE PUSEYITE MOTH AND ROMAN CANDLE

"Fly away *Silly* Moth"

(*By kind permission of the proprietors of "Punch."*)

lished Church, being a great unit, must be persuaded by judicious preferment and promotion, to follow rather than attempt to lead the secular hierarchy.

The State, in short, was the loving and prudent husband, the Church the lovely but obedient wife. Or, to vary the image, the wild flowers produced by nonconformity could be free, because they were only wild flowers. But the greater flora of that ancient and beautiful garden, the Church of England, must be selected and pruned to produce the greater profit.

The theory was not quite a complete statement of the religious aspirations of humanity, for in the last analysis things temporal and secular can only be part of things eternal and spiritual. But perhaps there is no final solution of the relations of Church and State, merely a reasonably satisfactory approximation; and in practice the Whig method had worked out reasonably well.

The Whig system had been in force through the whole of the eighteenth century, and that period had at least avoided the turbulent controversies of its predecessors. In the sixteenth century the more active bishops were banished or burnt. In the seventeenth they were deprived or decapitated. In the eighteenth they were merely promoted to be Primates.

Nor had the Church, when considered apart from its clergy, lost more than it gained at first. The Whigs had not abused their power under the first two Georges, and if the Non-Jurors were left to die out as impractical idealists, the presence of great names like Butler and Berkeley on the episcopal roll showed that the mere sycophant was not unduly rewarded.

Curiously enough it was under the Tory friends of the Church in the second half of the eighteenth century, rather than under the Whigs in the first, that the Establishment began to decline. It was not that their appointments were worse than the Whigs; the root of the trouble was that the population was growing, and neither the machinery nor the endowments of the Church were equipped nor enlarged to cope with the new industrial urbanization. The historic dissenting sects did something to serve this growing class,

H

and the new Methodism of the Wesleys attracted many godly souls whose spiritual needs the Church failed to supply. The Evangelical revival within the Establishment under Wilberforce and Simeon showed that the bones were not yet dry, but as time went on a general feeling of pessimism, almost of despair, set in.

The Church of England, said Gladstone in 1864, "is much more likely to part with her faith than her funds." The verdict of one who was all his life a devoted Churchman would have been nearer the mark in 1820; for while the clergy had ranged themselves as one man against the Jacobin doctrines that had plundered the Gallican Church, they had become remiss in religious teaching, parish and diocese were often neglected by pluralist parson or absentee bishop, and the standard of duty, as of doctrine, was generally low.

The story of the Oxford Movement which revitalized the Church, with its mingled success and failure, its alternate agonies and exaltations, belongs to English history; certainly not to a life of Lord John Russell. He never understood it; probably he never even tried to understand its deep appeal to Christian unity and order, its loving backward glance to medieval practice, its pathetic suspicion of the new scientific spirit which was slowly sapping ecclesiastical authority.[1]

But he knew a Tory when he saw one, and all the Tractarians except Pusey were Tories. It was something more than a coincidence that Keble—a strong Tory—had preached the famous sermon on national apostasy, which all recognized as the real starting-point of the Oxford Movement, so soon after the Reform Bill had become law; for the Church had taken the Reform Bill as foreshadowing its own doom. Out of Oxford had come something new, but this Newmania—the pun pleased the contemporary small fry of piety and politics—was to Russell no more than a new kind of Toryism, and he dealt with it accordingly.

[1] When honorary degrees were conferred on men of science at the first meeting of the British Association at Oxford, in 1832, Keble objected to "this hodge podge of philosophers." The hodge podge were Faraday, Dalton, and Brewster.

He recognized the appeal to Laud and the Non-Jurors as the traditional danger signals of the school. It seemed odd to him that in order to get to Canterbury they should go so near to Rome and yet stop short of the last lap[1]; but with this ecclesiastical geography Russell had nothing to do. Instinctively he recognized an old enemy in a new uniform, and prepared to oppose him.

Very broadly speaking, he was right. The new movement appealed to authority and distrusted liberty, and that was the essential mark of Toryism through the ages. True, it did not quite know where authority lay, but it was reasonably certain it did not lie in the hands of a Whig Prime Minister. Its leaders might revere and revive the curious doctrine of apostolic succession, which had practically fallen into desuetude; but even they, who were reported to believe many strange things, could not believe in Lord Melbourne as the Vicar of Christ. And if they were still uncertain whether authority lay, as Newman thought, in the individual bishop or, as Pusey held, in the whole body of the Church, these things were mere matter of detail; what was certain was that they were opposed to liberty and liberalism root and branch as the doctrine, in Newman's words, "that there is no positive truth in religion, but that one creed is as good as another."

On that matter, as it happened, Copernicus and the Pope who condemned his opinion had both written an unwitting comment more than two centuries before. If ecclesiastical authority was wrong about the physical universe, it might easily be wrong about the spiritual universe; its incompetence to interpret the less was no proof, but rather the reverse, of its competence to decide the greater.

Newman, however, like Keble, was disdainful of science and its methods. By one of the chance coincidences of history, he was interpreting the mystery and variation of Christian doctrine in terms of spiritual evolution during the very years that the young Charles Darwin was interpreting the mystery and variation of animal structure in

[1] In the words of Keble, "We agree with Rome about our major premises; our differences are about the minor."

terms of physical evolution. But while the scientist sought enlightenment in Galapagos and the Antipodes, the theologian was immersed in the Monophysite and Donatist heresies that had vexed the ancient world.

Few, even of those who least relish the conclusion of the voyage, can read that noble spiritual Odyssey without emotion; for in these forbidding and fuliginous controversies, as the shadow of a hand upon the wall, Newman first caught a glimpse of what seemed the positive truth he sought. It vanished like a ghost and returned anon; the heavens opened and closed again for the lonely pilgrim. But when at last he saw his way, it led from the Oxford he had once loved to the Rome he had once hated. There liberalism could have no place; there authority was supreme. *Securus judicat orbis terrarum* were the decisive words that ran in Newman's ears; perhaps it is strange he did not see that the ancient authority to which he appealed was after all no more than the rule of the majority.

A collision was inevitable, sooner or later, between men who thought only of authority and men who thought only of liberty, for the difference was fundamental to any conception of society; but the actual outbreak was accidental.

Early in 1836, and long before Newman had begun to doubt the soundness of the Anglican position, the Regius Professorship of Divinity fell vacant at Oxford. Lord Melbourne, as Prime Minister, took the advice of the Archbishop of Canterbury and of Archbishop Whately as to filling it. The list which the Archbishop of Canterbury submitted included the names of Pusey, Keble, and Newman, as well as Dr. Hampden, Principal of St. Mary's Hall; and had Whately chosen one of the first three instead of the fourth, English Church history might have followed a very different course. It seems, however, that Whately and Hampden were personal friends, and the Archbishop not unnaturally recommended him.

The actual qualification of Dr. Hampden was the fact that he had delivered the Bampton Lectures in 1832. But it seemed to the High Churchmen at Oxford more likely that he owed his promotion to the fact that in 1833 he had written a pamphlet supporting the Government's proposals to admit Dissenters to the University.

The suspicion was unjust, but the Government had, after all, just abolished ten Irish bishoprics and done a good turn to the English Dissenters, and Lord John had talked airily of more to follow.[1]   In any case, Oxford thought the Church was in danger, and the moment the appointment was announced a storm of passion swept through College and Hall.

Seventy-three tutors signed a protest.   Nine heads of Houses followed suit.   The Hebdomadal Board declared that they had no confidence in Dr. Hampden's opinions, and an exhilarating heresy-hunt was soon in full cry.

It has not seemed necessary to this biographer to disturb the dust on the forgotten speculations of Dr. Hampden, nor would he know whether they were in fact heretical. Suffice it that Tait, a future Archbishop, found the theology "frigid and shallow and uninspiring," but not heretical; that Wilberforce, as Bishop of Oxford, was of opinion that the lectures were unsound but not heretical; and that Newman admitted that the extracts he made to prove his case were unfair.

But the furious dons nearly carried the position by assault.   Hampden appears to have come to the conclusion that the kicks were not worth the halfpence, and offered the Prime Minister to withdraw.   But Melbourne was tolerant of everything but intolerance, and refused, on the ground that freedom of inquiry would thereby be prejudiced.   Thus encouraged, the fainting divine stood firm; the storm in a theological teacup subsided, and within a year or two the tables were turned.   It was no longer the orthodoxy of Hampden but of his accusers that was suspect at Oxford.

Eleven eventful years passed.   Newman found in Rome the authority he craved.   The Oxford Movement, broken by his secession, rallied under Pusey; and Pusey had meanwhile been transformed from the heresy-hunter into the

[1] On the other hand, if Russell had helped to reduce the Irish episcopate, he wanted to increase the English.   Objections were raised, and the scheme fell through, but Manchester was added under his Premiership.

hunted. But Hampden's divinity lectures went on, and they might have gone on till he died had it not been for Lord John Russell.

It happened in 1847 that the bishopric of Hereford was vacant; and Lord John, remembering the brief notoriety of the Bampton Lecturer under his old chief, nominated him for the see. He appears to have thought he was doing the Protestant party in the Church a service by the appointment. But inquiry at Oxford would have informed him that Protestants had for once made common cause with Tractarians in the previous hue and cry; the crime of Dr. Hampden was that he was neither High nor Low, but Broad.

Had Russell really desired a staunch Protestant for Hereford he could easily have found one; for they grew on every college bush, and were to be picked for the asking. It is a little difficult to resist the conclusion that the appointment was an intentional piece of spectacular provocation.

Whether that was the case or not, the lion was provoked in his lair, and the hubbub of 1836 was nothing to the outcry of 1847. Thirteen bishops out of twenty-six protested against their new colleague. On the other hand, fifteen out of twenty-two heads of Oxford Houses supported him.

The general feeling of the day was certainly against the appointment, but this time Hampden did not offer to resign. Indeed, when Wilberforce, Bishop of Oxford—the famous "Soapy Sam"—rather officiously suggested he should withdraw the notorious Bampton Lectures in order to prove his orthodoxy, he rightly repelled the suggestion as an insult. It is clear that he now felt himself on stronger ground.

That might well be, for the Prime Minister had handled the thirteen bishops rather roughly in his reply to their remonstrance. "Several months," he wrote, "before I named Dr. Hampden to the Queen for the see of Hereford, I signified my intention to the Archbishop of Canterbury, and did not receive from him any discouragement. In these circumstances it appears to me that, should I withdraw my recommendation from Dr. Hampden, which has been sanctioned by the Queen, I should virtually assent to the doctrine that a decree of the University of Oxford is a perpetual bar of exclusion against a clergyman of eminent learning and unimpeachable life, and that, in fact, the supremacy, which is now by law vested in the Crown, is to be transferred to a majority of the members of one of our Universities. Nor should it be forgotten that many of the most prominent among that majority have since joined the communion of the see of Rome."

The sting of the reply is in the tail; it is the first faint whiff of No Popery. The language was stiff, but not, as it happens, less stiff than that held by the Queen. She had not always approved of Lord John's appointments— only a few months before she had hinted that he was rather inclined to give the sinecures of the Church to his political friends, and that it would be well to promote clergy of scientific attainments. But in the Hampden case she wrote to her Prime Minister that the Bishops were behaving extremely ill, and hinted that the Bishop of Exeter might be prosecuted. The fact is, the bellicose Dr. Phillpotts, who occupied that see, had ventured to criticize the Royal Supremacy.

The matter, however, was not quite at an end. The protesting bishops indeed desisted. Wilberforce of Oxford, aware that Canterbury would soon be vacant, revoked, and took the side of Hampden. But it was now the turn of the Dean of Hereford.

There is a meaningless ceremony of election before a Bishop is admitted by the Dean and Chapter; an absurd survival, because the business is purely formal. The Dean wrote that he would refuse, and Lord John replied curtly: "Sir,—I have had the honour to receive your letter of the 22nd inst., in which you intimate to me your intention of violating the law."

The Dean remained recalcitrant, but the Chapter obeyed; and once Dr. Hampden was installed, the storm subsided. It remains to add that the prelate enjoyed the fruits of victory for twenty years; but that when *Essays and Reviews* was published in 1860, the hero of two such narrow escapes forgot his past, and advised his episcopal brethren to prosecute the authors for heresy. So easily may promotion change principle.

The Hampden affair blew over, and in another few months, when thrones began to totter in the year of revolution, men had other things to think about than the disputed faith of a particular bishop. But the controversy did not help Russell's reputation. It was not that the appointment made the Tories blaspheme; it was the business of Whigs to make Tories blaspheme. But it made the Whigs begin to doubt their leader a little.

The typical Whig was a Low Churchman, but he found that Low Churchmen objected to Dr. Hampden as much as High—indeed it was the one subject on which the two schools could forget for a moment their common differences. If Lord John, therefore, thought Hampden would be welcomed by the Protestant party, he was wrong; and if he thought the appointment would check the conversions to Catholicism he was wrong again; it rather increased them, by exposing the sore point of the Royal Supremacy. A wise statesman does not seek unnecessarily to embitter the difficult relations of Church and State; the head of a minority Government does not in any event seek to expose too much surface, or to alienate possible allies.

Russell's mind, on this and other matters, was simple and direct; he thought Hampden a good man, the appointment was likely to annoy the Tories, and he promoted him. There are manifest advantages in simplicity and directness. But minds so constituted often fail to grasp the subtleties and imponderables of a difficult issue; and there are times when the subtleties and imponderables are the major elements of political diagnosis, when one speaks with the enemy in the gate in order to disarm rather than provoke him.

The ordinary Whig was not particularly interested in the troubles of the Church, which he regarded as a Tory corporation, and he followed Russell's lead without hesitation. But the wiser Whigs of the inner circle had inherited the traditional party belief in tact and the art of management, and they began to doubt a little. They may not have fully understood the issue, which they probably regarded as not very important; Hereford, after all, was not one of the great prizes of the Church. But they noted that Lord John Russell's course provoked more opposition than it gained support, on a matter on which it was not necessary to provoke the enemy at all.

They continued to stand by him in public. But at the back of their minds they docketed this first doubt of his leadership; and the time came when their doubts were verified by events.

CHAPTER XIII

THE YEAR OF REVOLUTION

"OH, he's a foolish fellow," said Palmerston, with a laugh to Shaftesbury about Russell; "but we shall go on very well now." The tone suggests that the Foreign Secretary did not take his Prime Minister very seriously; he had done pretty much as he liked under Melbourne, and there was no reason why little Johnny should rule the roost more than Melbourne.

The Whigs, as that shrewd Liverpool Tory, the elder Mr. Gladstone, advised his fledgling son William, could talk without stopping, but they were not men of business; and when it came to governing, it was the hard-headed Tories like Pitt and Liverpool and Peel who cracked the whip and drove their Cabinet as a team and really got the work done. There was a deal of truth in the diagnosis, but Palmerston, as usual, contrived to make the best of both worlds.

Trained for twenty years in the Tory school of Liverpool and Canning, he never tired of the desk; and he had been his own master for so long in the Whig Cabinet of Melbourne that nothing was now likely to change him. The next five years are, from one point of view, a study of a Queen Regnant, a Prince Consort, and a Prime Minister all trying to control a Foreign Secretary, and this minor note recurs continuously among the graver discords of the time.

I

The first clash came over the Spanish marriage question. Husbands had to be found for the young Queen and the Princess of Spain, and the Chancelleries of Europe united in declaring their high impartiality and their particular desire not to forward a candidate who could by any chance be suspected of influencing Spanish policy in favour of their own dynasty. Unfortunately no Chancellery trusted the word of any other.

The French Court had pledged itself to Windsor not to press a French Prince on the Spanish ladies. But Palmerston unluckily dropped a hint of a Coburg bachelor. There appears to have been no desire in Buckingham Palace, and there certainly was none in Downing Street, to urge the candidature. But Louis Philippe remembered that one Coburg had already married the Crown of Britain, another the Crown of Portugal, and a third was King of the Belgians. The family in his opinion was going too fast and too far, and there were too many Coburgs in the field.

The opinion was not on the face of it unreasonable. But unluckily he held that this absolved him from his pledge to Windsor. His minister, Guizot, was weakly acquiescent, and the announcement of the Spanish nuptials followed. The Queen was to be married to an unattractive Spanish cousin, whose chief recommendation was rumoured to be his physical impotence. The Infanta was to marry a son of Louis Philippe, whose grandchildren would thus occupy the throne of Spain.

The world was shocked, possibly even surprised, at the breach of faith. Metternich was no stickler for absolute rigidity of faith, and he had little use for public opinion, but he remarked quietly that there was a point beyond which public opinion must not be violated—and prepared to take his profit.

The affair had important consequences. The entente between Britain and France being ruptured, the three Eastern Powers seized the opportunity to bring Polish independence definitely to an end. Public morals were now at a heavy discount. Constituted authority was weakened, and one of those periodic waves of revolutionary fervour which tell of the maladjustments of society and government presently showed signs of sweeping over Europe. The year of revolution was at hand.

2

There had been trouble in Portugal in 1847. In the following year a minor outbreak occurred in Paris. It could easily have been suppressed, but the wretched Guizot collapsed, the miserable Louis Philippe fled, and the second French Revolution was over.

The weakness of one Government being exposed, the others were soon challenged; Hungary rebelled, the Emperor of Austria was compelled to abdicate, and Metternich took refuge abroad. Germany was speedily in an uproar, and the Prince of Prussia escaped in disguise. The world now saw, without understanding, the first confused movements of what afterwards became the Italian Nationalist uprising. Indeed, for the time being Italy did not understand them herself; she had yet to find her Cavour. Sicily rebelled against the abominable despotism of Naples. Milan and Venice rose against the moderate administration of Austria. And the Pope, to the astonishment of all good Tractarians and Tories in England, suddenly amazed the world by coming out as a Liberal, and preparing to declare war on Austria.

Lord John Russell was a good Protestant, who hated the Pope and all his works. But he was also, what is not necessarily the same thing, a good Christian; and he was naturally moved at the spectacle of a repentant sinner at the Vatican. When the Scarlet Woman began to talk about civil and religious liberty, the Whig heaven must surely be at hand.

He was soon brought into closer contact with the surprising phenomenon. The new Pope was looking round for support for his policy, and he naturally pitched on the chief Liberal Power of the day. England, it is true, was Protestant, but there had been some Catholic conversions and might be more; and there was a Whig-Liberal Government in Downing Street.

Bishop Wiseman, a rising young English Catholic, was therefore despatched from Rome, in 1847, with a list of projected Papal Reforms, and he called at the Foreign Office with his message. Palmerston and Russell acted quickly, and within a week Russell had sent his father-in-law, Lord Minto, on a special mission to the Vatican to encourage this brand plucked from the burning.

Unfortunately for his hopes, the Liberalism of Pio Nono

lasted no longer than a profligate's penance—a fact which can hardly have diminished the joy with which Lord John hastened to attack the same Holy Father in the notorious Durham Letter, three years later.

3

"My God, they want to make a Napoleon of me, who am only a poor country parson," Pio Nono had exclaimed at his election, two years before. He was not that, but he left a deeper mark on Europe and the world than any ecclesiastic since the Middle Ages.

The Pope soon discovered that whatever Liberalism might promise for the State, it was not for the Church. If he appointed laymen to govern the Papal States, he declared, they would soon cease to be Papal States; so the ecclesiastics remained another few years. He discovered, too, when his minister Rossi was assassinated and he himself was thrown out of the Quirinal, that the postulate of human goodness and intelligence on which Liberalism relies is not universally true. The Italians, he said, were a dissatisfied, interfering, turbulent and intriguing race; they loved revolution and could never learn how to govern themselves, because they did not know what they wanted.

In other words, he determined to defend his patrimony as best he could; recovered it from Mazzini and eventually lost it to Cavour. The temporal power fell at last, and Liberalism scored a point; but the infallibility of the Pope was proclaimed, and Liberalism lost in the spiritual field what it had gained in the secular.

But in 1848 these things were still far in the future, and the Pope was in exile under Neapolitan protection. By the time he had returned to the Quirinal with a French army behind him, he had decided that progress was an evil which the Church must resist at all costs; and the stage was now fairly set for another contest between authority and liberty.

The time soon came when Russell and the Pope stood before Europe as representatives of opposite principles; and the contrast for us is heightened by the odd coincidences of their lives. The two men were born within three months of each other, in the revolutionary year 1792. The one became Pope in the same year that the other became Prime Minister. Both lived far beyond the normal span; and they died within three months of each other, in 1878, with the great battle still undecided.

4

But this was a mere incident of the great year of revolution. Belgium stood firm, but Ireland rose in revolution, and there were some indications of approaching trouble in England.

The now venerable Croker anticipated the speedy dissolution of society, and the melancholy Graham expectantly awaited the immediate "grand blow-up" he had predicted as inevitable several years before. Fortunately Russell kept his head better than anybody except the Duke of Wellington; and the boy who had followed the Duke nearly forty years before through the Peninsular War now took counsel as Prime Minister with the aged Field-Marshal as to the best means of dealing with the Chartists, assembled on Kennington Common and threatening to march on London.

Chartism was a force that might easily be turned to good or evil. It had the pathetic faith of the time in political action as the source of all progress; but it was not at heart revolutionary. It merely desired another amendment and extension of the constitution which had recently been amended and extended.

Russell was inclined to be a little contemptuous of the Chartists, and this was perhaps unwise. But it was far less unwise than being afraid of them, like Croker and Graham. It was claimed that they desired to do nothing more than present their petition to the Government, and this seems in fact to have been true. Russell himself would have let them cross the Thames bridges; but the Commissioner of Police, who knew that the disreputable follow in the train of respectable demonstrators, and was naturally apprehensive of riot and looting, agreed with the Duke of Wellington that the procession should be stopped on the south side of the river.

Lord John concurred; and on the appointed day twelve

to fifteen thousand people assembled in good order and good humour near the spot which has since seen far greater crowds assemble for a cricket match. The leader of the Chartists was told that the meeting was permitted but the march prohibited; he agreed that the Government was right, and the people dispersed while the famous petition went off to the Home Office in a cab.

The Government had taken the ideal way of dealing with a situation that was not in itself dangerous but might easily have become so, had the crowd been either provoked or allowed to get out of hand. The hopes and fears of English revolution subsided peacefully in a four-wheeler; not a life was lost, not a nose blooded, but within a few years most of the points of the Charter were incorporated in the Constitution.

Russell had himself sympathized with some of their demands—in 1837 he had advocated the ballot against Melbourne's opposition—and there is little doubt that the Chartist affair turned his thoughts back to the familiar subject of franchise reform, which he had supposed finally settled. Within three years of the famous Kennington meeting he had reopened the whole question himself as an active political issue.

5

The Government were naturally less successful abroad, and that not merely because they had no jurisdiction on the Continent, but because they were at cross-purposes among themselves. The Queen was liberally inclined, and believed in constitutional methods, but no Crown can really enjoy seeing other crowns in the gutter; and the Cabinet was uncertain whether to support the rebels, condemn the bloodshed, or do nothing at all.

The cabbalistic word "self-determination" was not yet coined, but the idea already existed as an integral part of Whig policy. It was not easy, however, to decide in practice how to apply it; and while Russell and Palmerston both sympathized with Italy, and more particularly with Piedmont—which had set up a constitution—the Queen's family connexions naturally made her more interested in the unity of Germany, where she also saw hopes of the liberal and constitutional movement.

On the tangled German politics of the time, however, she could not carry her Government with her. Russell had no prejudice against Germany; he was not, according to Bunsen, misinformed, but merely uninformed. With Palmerston there was more active opposition. He made no secret of the fact that he thought the Queen was under the influence of the Prince Consort, and suggested a little tartly that she wished her Foreign Secretary to become "minister for the German Confederation."

The reproach was ill-founded. But it proved a plausible and popular idea that affected many persons and policies during the next ten years, and it marks the definite beginning of that antagonism between Palmerston and the Court which led to the former's temporary downfall and the latter's temporary unpopularity.

On German politics there was no moving the Cabinet, but when Russell and Palmerston showed a disposition to support Italy against Austria, the Queen was on stronger ground. She asked how England would appear before the world when she was at the same moment defending rebellion south of the Alps, and struggling to maintain her own supremacy in Ireland.

There could be no answer to her logic, and the contradiction between theory and practice was to trouble good English Liberals for many a year to come. We shall meet it again later in Russell's career, but for the moment the difficulty subsided.

The difference of policy between Court and Cabinet was more or less smoothed over by the common impotence of both. Victoria, after all, could only welcome the jetsam of foreign royalty when it was cast up on our shores, and Palmerston could only signal to the flotsam of rebellion when he saw it on the wave. Moreover, the tide of rebellion presently began to fall. Constituted authority reasserted itself. Russia put down the Hungarian insurrection. Austria defeated the Italians at Novara. Mazzini and Karl Marx took refuge in London. Monarchy was restored, a little shaken, but only for the moment, by the earthquake; and the year of revolution was definitely over.

In retrospect, the more significant thing was not that Europe rose against its rulers in 1848, but that it fell back again in 1849. Pio Nono might be wrong in think-ing that people did not know what they wanted, but the majority seemed reasonably inclined to accept what they were given in the way of government. It looked as if there might be rather more in the new Pope's second thoughts on politics than Lord John Russell had supposed.

CHAPTER XIV

NO POPERY

EUROPE'S year of revolution passed into history; the constitutions and the kings returned, a little battered and bloody, from the struggle. At home the Prince Consort planned the Great Exhibition; and with the strange dichotomy of history, another crisis in the Church followed the late crisis in the State.

In a quiet vicarage in the West of England was preparing the trouble that led to the Gorham Judgment, which shook the Church of England to its foundation; and far away in the Vatican was preparing the Restoration of the Hierarchy—Protestants called it the Papal Aggression—which put all England in a rage, and contributed both directly and indirectly to the fall of Lord John Russell.

I

The Gorham case is, for our particular purpose, little more than the voice of a prologue spoken off-stage.

Mr. Gorham was an obscure country clergyman who held doubtful views on the difficult doctrine of Baptismal Regeneration; a subject which will certainly not be discussed here. His bishop—the same fiery Phillpotts whose prosecution had been suggested by the Queen in the Hampden affair—refused to institute him to a benefice in the diocese of Exeter; and the ecclesiastical tribunal known as the Court of Arches decided against Mr. Gorham. He appealed, however, as he was entitled to do, from the Church to the State; and the Judicial Committee of the Privy Council, sitting with the two archbishops as assessors, reversed the decision of the inferior court.[1]

The flood-gates of wrath were now opened. The

---

[1] The Judicial Committee had been established by Brougham, in 1834. It was therefore still something of a legal novelty.

enraged bishop, who might have been a reincarnation of
the intolerant Tertullian, ostentatiously renounced communion with his archbishop. The pulpits thundered, the
pews shook, and the world wondered at the sudden outburst of excitement concerning a divine no longer obscure,
and a doctrine more obscure than ever. "I am old enough
to remember three baptismal controversies," said the
venerable Provost of Oriel, "but this is the first in which
one party has tried to eject the other from the Church."[1]

The remark illustrates the rising tempers and the rising
stakes for which the parties were now playing; after all,
intolerance is simply a struggle for control. But the
ambiguous questions of Christian doctrine, always difficult
and often dangerous to both sides, had now been submerged
in the graver problem of the supremacy of the Crown over
the Church, and the competence of the civil courts to
override an ecclesiastical tribunal.

The debate whether a judge whose authority is essentially secular can decide an issue which is essentially spiritual
goes near the foundations on which society and the State
are built, and men whose wisdom and piety are undoubted
have differed, and will long continue to differ, as to the
answer. Perhaps the most we can say on this intractable
subject is that in theory the spiritual must always be superior
to the temporal, but that in practice justice is much more
secure under State than under Church. There seems to
be some radical incapacity which prevents the clerical mind
from understanding the elementary equity that a man
should be heard in his own defence before he is condemned; and if justice is part of a divine plan, probably
the last place where one would look for it on earth
would be in a theocracy.

To Lord John Russell, however, the Gorham Judgment
raised no problem at all. To him, as perhaps to the
majority of laymen, baptism was merely a formal ceremony
of initiation, a species of ecclesiastical birth certificate,

[1] While the war of sermons and pamphlets raged, the insignificant author
of the ferment, who had become notorious in a night, was quietly instituted
in his benefice. Not, however, by the still pugnacious Phillpotts, but by the
ecclesiastical Court.

and the judgment of the Privy Council in his opinion was "to the satisfaction of all friends of liberty of conscience."

In reply to an episcopal outburst of perhaps unusual heat, he simply remarked that "nothing but the erection of a priestly supremacy over the Crown and people would satisfy the party in the Church who now take the lead in agitation." This may in fact have been true, but it was not quite the whole question at issue, and the reply reveals at once the strength and weakness of its author.

Russell's mind had the directness and simplicity of the ordinary straightforward Englishman, and his idea of strategy was the nearest possible approach to a straight line. He would certainly have confounded subtlety in action with subtlety in thought, but the two qualities are in fact very different.

Subtlety in action deceives, because it is intended to deceive. Subtlety in thought illuminates because it is inclusive of other than the obvious and immediate points of view; it may sometimes delay action, but it is more likely to lead to right action. The way of a bull with a gate is often effective with the rough cut and thrust of everyday affairs, but in matters of high policy subtlety of thought is essential to a solution.

Russell had none of this, and his mind was hardly equipped for these fine issues. He was slightly anticlerical; not indeed with the bitterness of the Gaul, but with the amused contempt of the average Englishman, who regarded the squabbles over robes and ritual as very much a matter of women's clothes—important to the feminine type of priest, but of no particular significance to the masculine world of politics. He knew, of course, that behind these vestments and the claim to apostolic succession was the old desire for authority and power, but he knew, or thought he knew, that those things belonged to the past, and liberalism to the future. He did not understand that tyranny, like tolerance, is of all time; and a rude shock was preparing, which threw him off his balance.

2

The Gorham Judgment was delivered in March, 1850. In the following September, long before its echoes had died away, the Pope issued a Bull restoring the Catholic hierarchy to England, and instituting twelve new episcopal sees.

Shortly afterwards Cardinal Wiseman, now designated first Archbishop of Westminster, published a pastoral claiming that "Catholic England had been restored to its orbit in the ecclesiastical firmament"; and adding that "we govern and shall continue to govern the counties of Middlesex, Hertford, and Essex, as Ordinary thereof, and those of Surrey, Sussex, Kent, Berkshire, and Hampshire, with the islands annexed, as Administrator with ordinary jurisdiction." The language was obscure—it was said that Wiseman knew too many languages to write his own well—and perhaps a little inflated; but the event was, after all, one on which good English Catholics were entitled to congratulate themselves.

At this distance of time it seems obvious that it was more convenient to give Cardinal Wiseman the title of Archbishop of Westminster than the absurd style of Bishop of Melipotamus *in partibus infidelium*[1]; and it is equally clear that if His Holiness had created twelve hundred bishops instead of twelve, not one single Protestant need have been converted—or as the phrase went, perverted—into a Papist against his wish. But such elementary considerations were forgotten. The storm broke.

In those days good Christians used stronger language about Christians whom they thought less good than good manners would now permit. It was not many years since Peel had been called Anti-Christ because of his share in Catholic Emancipation, and the now forgotten Dr. Croly was emphatic that George IV had come to a premature end and the Houses of Parliament had been burnt down in token of divine displeasure at that regrettable lapse from sound Protestantism. A later and more agnostic age may permit itself to doubt whether heaven was more concerned

[1] Melipotamus was actually an extinct diocese in China.

with George IV than George IV with heaven; but the credulous Croly found many to believe him, and these passions had increased rather than diminished since a few famous Puseyites had gone over to Rome.

England—or at least that large part of England which took its politics and prejudices seriously—was immediately in an uproar at what was at once dubbed the Papal Agression. The step could plausibly be represented as a challenge to the supremacy of the Crown; the Gorham Judgment was forgotten, and a panic which had no parallel since the days of Titus Oates swept the country from the Tweed to the Tamar.

The actual results of the manifesto were ludicrously small in comparison to the hubbub. The old Catholic families were annoyed, perhaps alarmed, and the Duchess of Norfolk wrote in some anxiety to the Queen, who reassured her. A few Tractarians who had hesitated irresolute on the brink took the plunge. A few more followed from time to time. But it soon became evident that conversions were to be in single spies, not in battalions; and after a time the Protestant heart of England, reassured as to its essential soundness, ceased these wild palpitations.

There was, it is true, one resounding splash. The proud and ambitious Manning, to whom power was the breath of life, had long been a pillar of the Anglican Church; and the memory of a notorious Guy Fawkes sermon, which had caused some scandal among the troubled consciences of Oxford, should have assured a vote of confidence in the Protestantism of the stout Archdeacon even at Exeter Hall. But the secession of Newman and the promotion of Hampden had shaken his faith; the Gorham Judgment and the acquiescence of the clergy in the supremacy of the Crown filled the cup of doubt to the brim.

A timely bishopric might possibly have restored his belief in the validity of Anglican orders, as it revived the fainting faith of Hamilton; but the Whigs were in and the Tories were out, and Lord John's bishops were broad and liberal prelates who would hardly even damn a dissenter. The Papal Bull decided the issue; and Manning, the friend of Gladstone, the brother-in-law of Wilberforce of Oxford,

THIS IS THE BOY WHO CHALKED UP "NO POPERY!"—AND THEN RAN AWAY!

and the chief ornament of the diocese of Chichester, was hailed by Wiseman as the firstfruits of the restoration of the hierarchy.

The political repercussions of the affair were peculiar. When the Bull was issued in September, Stanley, the Tory leader, was more likely to be interested in partridges than in the Papacy. But he kept a cool eye on the possibility of a general election, wondered whether the cry of "To hell with the Pope" would make the Radical dissenters forget their inconvenient interest in cheap bread, and on the whole rather favoured the slogan of "Protestantism, Protection, and down with the Income Tax" as a possible winner.

Its efficacy was never tried, for Lord John Russell, a little quicker at the uptake and more precipitate in action than Stanley, had intervened at once.

The Papal Bull had not in fact come altogether as a surprise to him. The Catholic hierarchy had recently been restored in other countries; and he must have known this. It had recently been introduced in British colonies, with the concurrence of the Imperial Government and without the slightest objection from the Colonial Office; and he must have known this. It is difficult to suppose that the subject had been entirely ignored at the Minto-Pio Nono affair three years previously, since it had been openly discussed in London at that time, and an article on the topic had appeared in the *Quarterly Review*. Moreover, Lord John Russell was personally acquainted with Wiseman, and had had an interview with him before the future Cardinal left London for Rome a few weeks previously. Whether the subject was actually mentioned then or not—Wiseman had not expected to return as Archbishop when he was summoned to the Vatican—is not clear, but the priest was given no indication by the Prime Minister that what had been permitted in the British colonies would not be tolerated at home. Wiseman was not a good judge of character, but he could take a hint as well as any man, and he was utterly astonished at what followed.[1]

[1] It is strange—or perhaps it is not strange—that none of these facts, nor the Pope's appeal to the British Government in 1847, are mentioned in the

Lord John can, therefore, not have been surprised at the action of the Pope. He was indeed offended at the rather grandiloquent language of the Bull and the Wiseman Pastoral; but he was not in the least alarmed, though he properly took the advice of the Law Officers as to the constitutional aspect of the hierarchy. But he confessed himself more disturbed at the action of the Tractarians, who had unsettled the minds of sound Anglicans of the old persuasion, led them to the brink of the precipice, and then left them to fall over.

Thus in a letter to the Queen, who fully agreed with him, but in an evil moment for himself, Lord John remembered the success of his Edinburgh Letter, and recollected the existence of an old friend, the Bishop of Durham. To this stalwart Dr. Maltby he wrote a letter destined to become notorious.

> There is an assumption of power [he said] in all the documents which have come from Rome; a pretension of supremacy over the realm of England, and a claim to sole and individual sway, which is inconsistent with the Queen's supremacy, and with the rights of our bishops and clergy, and with the spiritual independence of the nation, as asserted even in Roman Catholic times. I confess, however, that my alarm is not equal to my indignation.
>
> Even if it shall appear that the ministers and servants of the Pope in this country have not transgressed the law, I feel persuaded that we are strong enough to repel any outward attacks. The liberty of Protestantism has been enjoyed too long in England to allow of any successful attempt to impose a foreign yoke upon our minds and consciences. No foreign prince or potentate will be at liberty to fasten his fetters upon a nation which has so long and so nobly vindicated its right to freedom of opinion, civil, political and religious. . . .
>
> There is a danger, however, which alarms me much more than any aggression of a foreign sovereign. Clergymen of our own Church, who have subscribed the Thirty-nine Articles and acknowledged in explicit terms the Queen's supremacy,

---

official "Life of Lord John Russell." Some of these things may have been unknown to the official biographer, but it is incredible that they can all have been unknown. The truth about a man is usually found in the biographies of other men.

have been most forward in leading their flocks "step by step to the very verge of the precipice." The honour paid to saints, the claim of infallibility for the Church, the superstitious use of the sign of the Cross, the muttering of the liturgy so as to disguise the language in which it is written, the recommendation of auricular confession, and the administration of penance and absolution—all these things are pointed out by clergymen of the Church of England as worthy of adoption, and are now openly reprehended by the Bishop of London in his charge to the clergy of the diocese.

What then is the danger to be apprehended from a foreign prince of no great power compared to the danger within the gates from the unworthy sons of the Church of England herself?

I have little hope that the propounders and framers of these innovations will desist from their insidious course. But I rely with confidence on the people of England; and I will not abate a jot of heart or hope, so long as the glorious principles and the immortal martyrs of the Reformation shall be held in reverence by the great mass of a nation which looks with contempt on the mummeries of superstition, and with scorn on the laborious endeavours which are now making to confuse the intellect and ensnare the soul.

If you think it will be of any use, you have my full permission to publish this letter.

This was strong stuff, even for an age of full-blooded religious invective; probably few practised theologians could have beaten the politician on their own ground. It was also ridiculous stuff, for a careful reading betrays the fact that the Law Officers had advised the Prime Minister that there was nothing unconstitutional in the restoration of the hierarchy; if there had been, proceedings could have been taken against Wiseman on his return, and the Ecclesiastical Titles Bill would have been unnecessary. But the statesmen of that age were accustomed to employ a mass of resounding rhetoric to say what could be said in two sentences; and the fact is that Lord John Russell detested the Roman Catholic Church, and distrusted the Tractarians.

It is perhaps natural that a generation which is more sceptical, not only of religious belief but of the sincerity of political professions, should assume the Durham Letter to have been mere propaganda, an appeal to the mob written tongue in cheek. But the diagnosis will not do.

Undoubtedly Russell expected his Durham Letter to be popular; he would not otherwise have suggested its publication. Undoubtedly, too, his always incisive literary style was sharpened by resentment at the Pope's desertion of Liberalism three years before. But undoubtedly he believed every word he wrote; for he used precisely the same language in his private correspondence and throughout the whole of his public career. It is consistent with every word he wrote or spoke from the cradle to the grave. The world may possibly have seen many men whose Protestantism was as strong as Lord John Russell's. It can hardly, human limitations being what they are, have seen any stronger.[1]

But the very fact that he believed every word of the Durham Letter should have given him pause. Had his mind had any self-critical apparatus it would have shown him a weakness in his political philosophy. He was in favour of full civil and religious liberty. But if it was right to give Catholics liberty, why was it wrong of them to use that liberty for the purpose of forwarding their faith? Was emancipation conditional on cessation of propaganda? Does liberty only exist for the purpose of not being used?

In his simple and straightforward way Russell would probably have regarded the question as an abuse of reason. But in fact it cuts deep into the ancient controversy between authority and liberty.

Authority will tolerate no liberty that it does not specifically approve. Is liberty, then, bound to tolerate authority that it does not specifically approve, merely because it holds libertarian principles? If so, within what limits? Is it bound, in virtue of its own principles, to tolerate an authority that denies those principles, tacitly it may be, while it uses them to obtain control, and then openly? If not, at what point shall liberty deny its own first principles

---

[1] Even as late as 1873 he called a public meeting in London at the age of eighty to support Bismarck's Kulturkampf against the Pope. His " Recollections," written at the same time, show that although his memory had then begun to fail, his militant Protestantism still survived.

in order to retain its identity? And does liberty in fact retain its identity when it refuses to tolerate a particular system, simply because that system may beat it out of the field?

These are pertinent questions which go to the very root of social order. But Lord John Russell not only never answered them. There is no indication that he ever realized their existence.

He would have said, no doubt, that he was a man of action, not a philosopher. The reply is only partially convincing. A statesman is certainly a man of action. But a statesman may easily find himself in a situation in which the whole question of action or inaction is determined by the philosophy he holds; and if he has no particular philosophy, but only a mere bundle of admirable but not always applicable axioms, he may find that he has acted extremely foolishly. This was precisely an occasion of that sort.

At the moment, however, Russell was not concerned with principles, but with practice; and the Durham Letter seemed likely at first to repeat, perhaps even to surpass, the success of the famous Edinburgh Letter five years before. The Protestants were in a majority, and the Protestants were naturally enraptured.

Cobden certainly thought it "a disgusting display," and said so; Bright, as usual, agreed with him; and Palmerston, of all people in the world, was jealous of his chief launching a new policy without consulting his colleagues. But Russell had certainly taken the wind out of the Tory sails; he had trumped the Papacy, and they had only the discredited Protectionist suit to fall back upon.

Harcourt, soon to be a rising star of the Liberal party, was enthusiastic. "Lord John with his usual astuteness," he wrote, "is raising a little wind in favour of the effete Whig Government. It is not a bad notion. If the Whigs choose to take up the strong Protestant side, they will gain much support from all those who are justly alarmed by the hierarchical projects of the Puseyites."

The Whigs did choose, and for the moment they had wind and tide behind them. An Ecclesiastical Titles Bill

was introduced in Parliament amid immense enthusiasm,
and Lord John made an excellent speech. But Gladstone
made a better one, on a higher level; and now for the first
time perhaps was felt the full force of that magnificent
and fiery mind that was soon to dwarf all competitors
in Parliament and outshine Russell and Palmerston and
Gladstone's master, the great Peel himself.

The Bill was passed, but it remained a dead letter.
The Romans remained Catholics, the Puseyites remained
pernicious, and the Protestants were left protesting. But
burnt straw will not burn again, and the fire had been too
fierce to last. There were not enough Catholics to keep
it going.

John Morley, as an undergraduate, was presently to
notice that Oxford itself had begun to tire of the Oxford
Movement, and had turned again towards that very rationalism which Pusey thought so much more dangerous than
Romanism. The tide in fact was at the full when the
Durham Letter was published, and it had already turned
when the Ecclesiastical Titles Bill was introduced.

The Prime Minister had miscalculated. *Punch*, which
had been as strongly anti-Roman and anti-Tractarian as
the *Times*, published a cartoon of Johnny Russell as the
small boy who chalked "No Popery" on the door and ran
away. Russell never ran away, but in this case he was
simply left standing, with a broken stick in his hand.

The results were personally unfortunate. The Durham
Letter, like the Edinburgh Letter, had been written
on his own initiative, as an individual and not a party act.
It had nevertheless committed the party to follow the
individual.

Such methods are never convenient in great corporate
bodies of opinion; the very Popes took counsel with their
officers before they committed the Church, and the Liberal
Party could hardly be less liberal than the Vatican. Leadership of this kind can be tolerated only on one condition;
that it is uniformly triumphant. The first time had been
successful. The second had promised well, but turned
out ill. A third might be disastrous.

The Whigs now remembered their first doubts of

Russell's leadership over the Hampden appointment, and cogitated. That was a mere affair of outposts, and could be overlooked; but the Durham Letter was a main engagement. Nominally the victory was theirs, for the Act was on the statute book; but the victory was, after all, not worth having, for the Act was dead, and no action at all had in fact been necessary.

Moreover, it had cost something. The Whigs were sound Protestants, but Catholic votes were always useful and sometimes essential, and it was foolish to provoke unnecessary opposition. What was the use of emancipating Catholics if you intended to insult them? It would only make them vote Tory, and the last state of the party would be worse than the first.[1]

Lord John Russell remained Prime Minister for a space, but the Durham Letter ruined his chance of becoming Prime Minister again. A commander can be forgiven for losing a battle that is forced upon him; but when he challenges he must win the day or lose his commission.

It is dangerous to teach people that your bark is worse than your bite. Over in Germany the pious Döllinger puzzled and wondered why all the talk should end without decisive action; and the less pious Bismarck, from the other side of the hedge, also wondered, and then drew his own conclusions—which were not forgotten twelve years later, when he had to do with Russell himself.

It is possible that far away in the recesses of the Vatican the College of Cardinals smiled. If the Papal Bull had not converted England, it had at least shaken England's Prime Minister; there would be no more confidential missions from Lord John's father-in-law to encourage authority in the way of Liberalism.

Pio Nono had won the second round. But there was yet to be a third ten years hence.

[1] The shrewd Stockmar commented later: "The Roman Catholic Irish have been the chief supporters of the Whig Ministry. The Pope possesses now a compact phalanx in the House, and after long centuries the Pope has again caused the fall of an English Premier."

CHAPTER XV

FALL

I

THE world swung back steadily to normal secular interests when it found that the Bishop of Melipotamus was not after all to be prosecuted for calling himself Archbishop of Westminster; and Russell soon reverted from No Popery to the more familiar political sphere with the startling announcement that a new Reform Bill had become necessary.

The position was personally an awkward one, for Russell had always regarded the Act of 1832 as a final settlement, and had often said so with his usual frankness. He had explained that it might, of course, be necessary to amend it in some small details as time went on, and any obvious flaws that developed in working would naturally have to be eliminated. But subject to such minor and, in effect, trivial adjustments, Lord John had held for eighteen years that the work of parliamentary reform had been done once for all.

It is strange that he should have thought so, for there is no special sanctity about a particular schedule, and the Radicals of course knew it. Russell seems to have looked upon the high-water mark fixed by the Whigs as the flood level for all time, and the Radicals of course knew better.

The 1832 Act was not, in fact, founded on any particular principle except that it went as far as the Whigs wanted to go. It seems, indeed, to have been itself a compromise between the Left Whigs who would have been willing to go a little further, and the Right Whigs who would rather not have gone quite so far. Clearly there was no stuff of permanence or principle in such a settlement. But Russell had argued so long and so often in the face of recalcitrant Tories and rebellious Radicals that the Grey schedule was the only true system that he had ended by convincing himself.

He had never protested against the name of "Finality Jack," and although he had long associated with Radicals in the House of Commons, he had never given them Cabinet office,[1] and never shown the slightest sign of leaving the Whigs or adopting such dangerous heresies as universal suffrage. He had, it is true, always favoured the ballot, long since advocated by Grote, the Radical banker, and others in that camp; but it was not this that converted him to a second Reform Bill.

What potent influences, then, changed the views he had long held on the subject in which he was the acknowledged master and leader of contemporary opinion?

To some extent, no doubt, the sad failure of No Popery as a political cry affected his judgment of the tactical position. A new party programme was clearly needed. Everyone said the Whigs were worn out. Some of the Whigs themselves admitted it. Clarendon proclaimed it, if not from the house-top, at least from the dining-room table. If the expectant Tories and Radicals were waiting for the spoils, a new Reform Bill would show them there was life in the old dog yet.

These things counted, and Russell, as a good party man, would have been the last to deny that they counted. But they were not enough to convert him. Russell was an ambitious man, who liked office and wanted to stay there. But he was also an honest man, who would not have held office at the price of honour, and who certainly would never have proclaimed a changed opinion as a political conviction unless it had been sincere. He knew well enough that a new Reform Bill might restore the personal prestige that No Popery had lost, but he would sooner have retired from public life altogether than advance his personal interests at the expense of the State. And there were, in

[1] He had thought of offering Cobden office in 1846. Lansdowne had no objection, but thought he would be rather a liability than an asset, and as Cobden's private affairs were in confusion, the idea lapsed.

fact, two genuine reasons which accounted for his conversion, quite apart from the tactical advantages that would probably accrue.

It is clear that, as time went on, the technical arguments advanced by the Radicals on the ground of inequality of representation between town and country increased in force. Ten years after the first Reform Bill the continued growth of the great cities could be dismissed as insufficient for another constitutional change. Twenty years afterwards the argument had gained greatly in substance. It was manifestly only a question of time before it was recognized as overwhelming all other considerations.

But in the main it seems to have been the orderly nature of the Chartist demonstrations, when compared with the Continental revolutions of 1848, which convinced Lord John of the pleasant truth that his own countrymen were worthy of every constitutional blessing that could be bestowed upon them, and that a wider franchise would be an asset rather than a liability to the State. There was in fact some substance in this view, as Gladstone and Salisbury both discovered subsequently.[1]

These two considerations, added to the prospective party advantage, seem to have been decisive. The more Lord John thought about Reform, the more he liked it. Unfortunately the more he explained it to his colleagues, the less they liked it. When the time came, it might be necessary to make another bid for power, but why this particular bid? Why give the Radicals everything and the Tories nothing? The Radicals would only ask for more, and the Tories, when all was said and done, asked for nothing. Why not give it them?

Russell pressed the idea steadily on his colleagues; he wanted to bring it forward definitely in the session of 1851 as a Cabinet project for the future, if not as an actual Cabinet measure. He was now on familiar ground, and his arguments can hardly have been without weight. But the Durham Letter and its sequel had lessened his

[1] Salisbury strongly opposed the franchise extensions of 1867 and 1885. He said afterwards, "We made a great mistake; they (the new voters) are very conservative."

VISCOUNT PALMERSTON IN 1846

(From the Painting by John Partridge. Copyright National Portrait Gallery.)

influence in the Cabinet, and he found he could do nothing against the deadweight of resistance he encountered.

Lansdowne, his oldest political friend and the Nestor of the party, would not touch it. Palmerston had never changed the anti-reform attitude he had learned from Canning in his political youth; moreover he always had been frankly bored by franchise problems, and would have nothing to do with it. The rest of the Cabinet were unwilling to move.

Lord John relieved his mind by declaring publicly that a new measure of reform was necessary; but the studied indifference of his colleagues showed that nothing was to be expected in the Parliament then sitting, and it must be added that the general apathy of the country on the subject made it unlikely that anything in the nature of reform was to be expected in the next.

Lord John must have reflected bitterly that a prophet is without honour in his own country. But this prophet's last excursion into the wilderness had failed. If it had not been for No Popery, the Whigs might have been less distrustful of their leader, the Government might have been reconstructed, and the second Reform Bill have been carried after the usual rousing campaign in which the Liberals did the work and the Whig Olympians signified an aloof approval. In that case there would have been no Aberdeen Ministry, and the Crimean War would probably have been avoided.

It was not to be, and the fact that it was not was in one respect fortunate, for it removes any suspicion of Lord John's sincerity. As things fell out, he devoted a great part of the rest of his life to propagating the idea, very often to his personal disadvantage. It is largely due to his untiring efforts that the second Reform Bill of 1867 was passed. But though he sowed and tended, he did not reap; he was to see the harvest gathered, but it came too late. As with the abolition of the Corn Laws in 1846, Fate cheated him of his reward, and the measure was ultimately carried by his opponents, with the old pioneer merely a spectator at the finish. These are the bitternesses of party politics, and Lord John Russell had perhaps rather more than his fair share of them.

2

The problem of reform, both in its technical and its political aspect, influenced the rest of his working career. But meantime Russell was still Prime Minister, and the current daily task involved troubles enough of its own. An awkward question now arose between Windsor and Downing Street that steadily undermined his own position, and in the end brought him down.

The Court was constantly complaining that Palmerston, as Foreign Secretary, took action in the Queen's name without taking the Queen's advice. Decisions were made, policies drafted, and despatches sent off to British agents abroad before they had been seen by the Queen; or if seen, they were submitted so late that the document had already left the country before the copy was approved.

These complaints were in fact justified. But Palmerston had a ready answer. The business of the Foreign Office was increasing month by month; twenty-eight thousand despatches were received and sent by his department in a year, and with many, perhaps most, of these it was necessary to deal promptly, often at considerable length. A Secretary of State is, after all, not a clerk, but the responsible servant of the Crown; and unless intolerable delays were to be permitted, with consequent damage to the interests of the country, the speedier method must often be used.

There was substance in the defence, and it was rendered the more telling by the fact that the Court was frequently out of London. For at least half the year Buckingham Palace was left to the caretakers. Windsor, it is true, was practically a suburban residence now that the railway brought it within less than an hour of Downing Street. But the Queen had bought Osborne for the sake of the children, and was often there herself; and the new residence at Balmoral was being more and more used by the royal family. However good the new communications, Balmoral was a thousand miles out and home. To send despatches there for approval involved a delay of at least three days.

To summon a busy Secretary of State there for a conference meant that the most important work of the department was at a standstill.

On this matter Palmerston knew he was on strong ground. But one feels that neither party put forward the real burden of its complaint; perhaps neither felt itself quite strong enough to be sure of winning. The difficult question of prerogative lay in the background.

The Queen was no longer an inexperienced girl taking the good Melbourne's good advice and in effect doing what she was told; Victoria was now within sight of what that period would have regarded as almost middle-age, and she was what that period would also have detested had it known her better—a strong-minded woman with strong common sense on many unexpected subjects.

There was, indeed, a strong strain of rationalism in her character. She would have no nonsense about Days of Humiliation when the country was at war, and told her archbishops so with disconcerting frankness; and when they wanted to ordain special prayers against cholera, she rated them like silly schoolboys. "In 1837 the influenza was notoriously more fatal than the cholera had ever been, and yet no one would have thought of having a prayer for that. It would be difficult to define the number of deaths which are to make a (special) form of prayer necessary."

It was no use attempting to answer downright and straightforward plain dealing of this kind; and it gradually became clear to those in close touch with the throne that this was no meek Griselda or pious Priscilla, but a formidable personality who meant to do her duty by her Ministers, and meant them to do their duty by her.

Undoubtedly she was in a difficult position, from the mere fact that the business of the State was both more complex and more considerable than a hundred or even fifty years before. To oversee the whole of it was not possible, even if it had been desirable; and it was not always easy to draw the line between mere matters of routine that it would obviously be absurd to bother her with, and matters of principle on which she must not only be formally consulted, but allowed in the last resort to express a decisive opinion.

She did not want to become a slave of the office like Philip II, but she felt that if she gave way to Palmerston she would be as much of a cipher in the State as the first two Georges; and it was her business to maintain, if not increase the prerogative, which in any event was tending to decline from the mere pressure of routine business.

Palmerston, on the other hand, was a masterful man, with the peculiar objection to supervision and correction that attaches to the type.[1] He felt that he could do his best work when playing a lone hand. The idea was not quite well founded, for while Palmerston's tongue never ran away with him, it was notorious that his pen often did, and a little pruning would have saved many a protest.

But behind all this lay Palmerston's suspicion of Prince Albert, which now amounted almost to a mania. The Foreign Secretary maintained in private that the Queen's husband was becoming the power behind the throne, that he aimed at being the benevolent despot who would substitute tame courtiers for constitutional Ministers responsible to Parliament, and that he was in effect using the British Empire to support German political and Coburg dynastic schemes all over the Continent.[2]

What Foreign Secretaries say in private over the mahogany is soon public property, and the Press speedily began to insinuate suspicion, and then openly to express resentment of the unseen influence behind the Queen's petticoats. The scapegoat is an ancient and familiar

---

[1] Years afterwards, when Palmerston was Prime Minister, the Queen asked for a choice of names in regard to Church appointments. It was not an unreasonable point, as Gladstone tacitly recognized subsequently by often submitting more than one candidate; at any rate it was a check on ministerial favouritism, and on a repetition of the Hampden affair. But Palmerston replied that this "in some degree implies a reference of a recommendation from your Majesty's responsible advisers to your Majesty's irresponsible advisers." A very high and stiff answer.

[2] His suspicions were naturally increased by the fact that the German Baron Stockmar was often called in to advise. Actually his advice was perfectly honest, and sometimes better informed, from residence abroad, than that of Palmerston.

symbol, and the foreign husband of an English sovereign fitted the part to perfection.

Prince Albert suddenly found he had become one of the most unpopular men in the country. If he made one of those innocuous royal speeches that sound well and say nothing, it was suggested that there was more in this than met the eye, and that some sinister design would presently be revealed beneath the honeyed sentences. If he supported some academic project for a scientific museum in Kensington, it was hinted that this was merely a cloak for a speculation in real estate in a rising suburb. If the wretched man did nothing at all, it was said that at last his sins had found him out; he was only silent because a reluctant but exasperated Ministry had seen the danger to British liberty, and had had him conveyed secretly to the Tower, where he was to be tried and shot as a traitor. So circumstantial was this report that several thousand Londoners assembled on Tower Hill to see if they could catch a glimpse of the prince in prison; and the crowd only dispersed when somebody announced that he was not to be sent there after all, as the Queen had declared she would go with him.[1]

By some strange oversight the detractors of the Prince Consort seem to have forgotten to put it about that he was a Roman Catholic. It is almost a pity that this artistic finish was lacking, for the British public was in one of those absurd moods when the most impossible story is instantly believed. The excitement over the Papal Agression still inflamed the popular mind, and the mob would quickly have jumped to the conclusion that this member of an ancient Protestant house was a Jesuit in disguise.

Prince Albert's real crimes were two: he was a foreigner, and he was not a fool. That excellent Consort, who bulked so large in the gossip and scandal of the day, and has since become one of the obliterated personalities of history, was of a type which is rather more common in

---

[1] It is odd how deeply the Tudor-Stuart tradition of confinement to the Tower had bitten into the public mind. A precisely similar canard ran through the country in 1914 about Prince Louis of Battenberg, an excellent British naval officer of German descent.

Germany than England. A serious and sensible if rather heavy-minded man, who was neither the genius his wife imagined nor the dangerous conspirator the country supposed, he was utterly without wit or humour; but he had the genuine integrity of those Princes who believe in constitutions rather than despotisms, in culture rather than pomp, and in solid work rather than tinsel show.

Such Princes are seldom popular. They may become a power. But Prince Albert could never be more than an influence, for he was more interested in principles than persons, in things than men; and in England at least we regard the man who thinks in principles as the mere expert, and rank him lower than the man who deals effectively with men. In the rough world of politics, at any rate, this national prejudice succeeds; for the one political idea of Prince Albert's miscarried. The formation of the Aberdeen Government was right in theory. But in practice it was a hopeless failure.

It was complained that the Prince had no charm, and that his manners were constrained. But this was largely due to the fact that he was in a false position from the start, and that so far from being a free agent he had to maintain an inexorable watchfulness lest he should say or do the wrong thing. He was well aware of the faults and foibles of his adopted countrymen, which are perhaps not altogether invisible to the naked eye; and a chance sentence shows that he was equally well aware that a foreigner who alluded to these defects would never be forgiven. A man whose main object is never to make a mistake will never make much of a public success.

Had the Prince Consort been a lesser man he might have sunk to a popular nonentity; had he been a greater, he might in fact have become a public danger by attempting to dominate his wife and, through her, the difficult country of which she was the sovereign. He influenced the Queen, but on the whole she had much the stronger personality as well as the stronger position of the two; and it is clear that he knew his place, even if he sometimes resented it. He had the good sense to refuse the Commandership-in-Chief which the Duke of Wellington had the bad sense to urge upon him; and the supreme tact to die at the very moment when he had rendered a real service to the country.

3

As things were, Palmerston had to put up with him; and Palmerston's belief that the Queen should attend to her nursery and the Prince should attend to the Queen came into collision with the steadfast sense of public duty which both possessed. Again and again the Queen complained that she was not informed of the policy of the Foreign Office until too late; no remonstrance had any effect, and the repeated warning that it must never happen again made not the slightest difference. Palmerston apologized for the unfortunate oversight, and blandly went on as before.

Lord John was in a difficult position. He had no particular love for Palmerston, but Palmerston was the main prop of the Government; he was quite ready to transfer him to Dublin or to the House of Lords, or the Colonial Office, but Palmerston was perfectly happy at the Foreign Office, and would not go. Moreover, Lord John's only idea for filling the Foreign Office was Lord Minto— a proposal which not unnaturally astonished the Queen, who knew that his Vatican mission had been a failure, and thought that the chief merit of this kindly peer lay in the fact that he was the father-in-law of the Prime Minister. The Whigs were already a family party, but there are limits to all things.

The question was postponed owing to debates in both Houses on foreign policy, and a decision was perforce delayed by an extraordinary parliamentary triumph of the recalcitrant Minister. One Don Pacifico had had his house in Athens pillaged by a Greek mob[1]; the historian Finlay also had a claim against the Greek Government. They sought the assistance of the British authorities, and Palmerston could not resist the opportunity. The British

---

[1] Dean Church, who was in Athens at the time, says that the affair originated in the police forbidding the customary Easter amusement of burning a Jew in effigy. As the mob were deprived of the imitation Israelite, they attacked

fleet was ordered to the Piræus to make a hostile demonstration, and a peremptory demand for settlement was sent to the unhappy authorities at Athens.

Palmerston had a cheap success, but this bullying of the weak was too much for Parliament, and the House of Lords condemned him. But in the Commons, Palmerston faced his critics in person. He spoke one day from dusk to dawn, and claimed that as the Roman of antiquity could hold himself free from indignity when he could say *Civis Romanus sum*, so a British subject, in whatever land he might be, should feel confident that "the watchful and the strong arm of England will protect him against injustice and wrong." The British subject was, in fact, a Mediterranean Jew, and his claim for compensation was swollen out of all proportion to the injury; but the false analogy and the false rhetoric deceived a willing House, and on the morrow Palmerston was the idol of the party he had saved and the nation he had flattered.

For the moment it was out of the question to remove the audacious Foreign Secretary, but the Queen was not deceived. She told Russell that there was no hope of Palmerston reforming himself at sixty-seven, and another few months showed she was right.

An Austrian General, whose cruelty had been a byword in the late revolution, came to England and was roughly handled by some workmen at a London brewery. Palmerston sent an official letter of apology to the Austrian Government, but could not resist expressing his regret that the General had chosen to come at all. The affair was trivial, and Palmerston withdrew the expression; but a few months later the trouble began again.

Kossuth, the Hungarian nationalist, came to England, and it was with some difficulty that Palmerston was restrained from receiving him at the Foreign Office. Russell requested his colleague not to receive the famous foreign leader even at his private house, as this would be

the house of a real one—"pillaged, gutted, and all but demolished it, and were with difficulty prevented from demolishing the unhappy Jew himself."
Did Russell happen to remember Playfair's adage about the activity and perseverance of mankind defeating the folly of their governors?

a quasi-official recognition that must be offensive to Austria and Russia. Palmerston replied tartly: "There are limits to all things. I do not choose to be dictated to as to who I may or may not receive in my private house. I shall use my own discretion. You will, of course, use yours as to the composition of your Government."

The incident blew over. But soon afterward the Liberal friends of Kossuth addressed the Foreign Secretary in those tones in which democrats love to denounce Emperors at a safe distance, and Palmerston was too fond of doing this sort of thing himself to rebuke them. Again the incident was smoothed over, Russell tactfully assuring the indignant Queen that it was important to maintain "the popular confidence which your Majesty's name always inspires," and that although "somewhat of the good opinion of the Emperor of Russia and other foreign sovereigns may be lost, the goodwill and affection of the people of England are retained."

The Queen was sometimes deceived by flattery, but she was seldom duped by fustian, and nonsense of this kind can hardly have impressed her. But she had not to wait long for Palmerston to slip.

On December 2, 1851, the *Coup d'État* took place in Paris which transformed the Second Republic into the Second Empire. The Foreign Secretary, in conversation with the French Ambassador, expressed his entire approval of the change—in complete contradiction to the line of strict neutrality which British Court and Cabinet had alike desired.

The news soon reached the Queen, who thought (or at least affected to think) it incredible; she directed Russell to inquire, and he reported that as he received an explanation which was "quite unsatisfactory, he thought himself compelled to write to Lord Palmerston in the most decisive terms." The pretext—it was little more—was sufficient. Palmerston was summarily dismissed, and the Court spent a happy Christmas.[1]

[1] The Court had no objection to the *Coup d'État*, only to Palmerston's precipitance. Thirty years later (August 8, 1880) the Queen wrote that she remembered the Prince Consort saying, when the Empire was first

Lord John's mood was less joyous. It is true that he was tired of being umpire between the Court at Windsor and the Palmerstons at Broadlands; "my patience," he said to Clarendon, "was drained to the last drop." But if Palmerston was a good friend, he might be a dangerous enemy; and Russell can hardly have been ignorant that Lady Palmerston was circulating her private version of the affair in expectant drawing-rooms. "John has behaved shamefully ill," wrote that loyal spouse; "no doubt the Queen and Prince wanted to get Palmerston out and Granville in, because they thought he would be pliable and subservient, and would let Albert manage the F.O., which is what he always wanted. John has behaved like a little blackguard."[1]

Such things are meant to get back to those of whom they are spoken, and get back no doubt they did. The Government was already weak. The substitution of the amiable but unforceful Granville for Palmerston could not fail to weaken it still further. The Cabinet had never had a compact majority in the House, and the Irish Catholics on whom it depended were only biding their time to avenge the Durham Letter. Negotiations were opened with the Peelites, but they were far too prudent to book their passages in a sinking ship.

There was a moment of hope when Palmerston made the inevitable explanation at the opening of Parliament in 1852, and it was coldly received. But he was only holding his hand for a favourable opportunity. On February 20, 1852, he defeated the Government on the Militia Bill, and the Cabinet resigned next day.

established, "though he was not predisposed in its favour, that he considered a great danger to this country to be averted when any monarchy was restored to that country."

[1] Clarendon appears to have agreed with this estimate of the Court. "The Queen and Prince," he wrote, "are wrong in wishing that courtiers, rather than ministers, should conduct the affairs of the country. They labour under the curious mistake that the F.O. is their peculiar department, and that they have a right to control, if not to direct, the foreign policy of England. They now fear an independent-minded man as a scalded dog does cold water." It is an ironic comment on this letter that four years previously the Prince Consort would have liked Clarendon to be Premier in the event of Russell resigning.

"I have had my tit-for-tat with John Russell," laughed Palmerston, "and I turned him out on Friday."

"It's all fair," was Russell's comment; "I dealt him a blow, and he has given me one in return."

But the last Whig Government had fallen.

CHAPTER XVI

LOAVES AND FISHES

THE confused three years that followed the fall of Lord
John Russell is one of the oddest periods in our
political history.

It has become the fashion to say that the country was
never better governed than between the first and second
Reform Bills. The truth is that for several years the
country was not governed at all. There was a captain on
the bridge and a crew on deck who sometimes received
orders and occasionally obeyed them. But the ship of
State simply followed the prevailing current, while other
captains piled their craft on the rocks or ran them aground.

The fall of the Whigs naturally brought in the Tories.
But they were in no position to rule England. Peel was
dead, and the Conservative host would certainly not have
followed him had he been alive. Bentinck, the last hope
of the Tory Protectionists, was also in his grave. The
flamboyant Disraeli, the loquacious Jew who was slowly
conquering the dumb Christians, was fully aware that his
hour was coming, but had not yet come. There remained
Stanley, the Rupert of Debate, to carry on.

The fifteenth Earl Derby, the new Prime Minister, was
the most versatile and vacillating of all the Stanleys since
the famous ancestor who waited on Bosworth field to see
which claimant won before he risked his troops in action.
Everything by turns and few things long, he had been a
sportsman and a poet as well as a politician; and in politics
he had been a Canningite, a Whig, a Conservative, and a
Protectionist. He had yet to become a Free Trader and
Reformer. At the moment he was a Protectionist who
was willing to give it up if the country would not have it;
which meant in practice that he was a Conservative trying
to rebuild the ruin left by Peel.

The time, however, was not yet. The smash of 1846 had been so complete that Derby, unable to obtain the support of the Peelites, had the novel difficulty of finding the men to fill the offices—he called them his babies—and it was said he was not personally acquainted with some of his colleagues till they were introduced to him at the Cabinet table.

Obviously, a Government like a kindergarten was not likely to last very long. The Whigs might have bitten the dust, but they were still in better trim than the Tories, whose only sphere of influence was now the counties and shires. The Whigs, too, were impatient to get back—they were never so ready to play the waiting game as the Tories—and already in August, 1852, Clarendon noted that "Russell is dying for a fight and for office. In a letter to the Duke of Bedford this morning, he says he shall not hesitate on every occasion to vote against the Government, as no worse one could possibly be found." In another year Lord John was himself to be a member of a worse one.

Twenty years before, when Derby and Russell had both been members of the same Whig Government, it was Derby who whispered to Graham, "Johnny has upset the coach." It looked as though history would repeat itself with the usual difference, but this time other hands were to deal the blow.

There was not long to wait. The Free Traders were alarmed and intolerant, for Derby had favoured the admirable idea of Free Trade within the Empire, with tariffs against foreign goods, and this was anathema to the antinational and anti-imperial Bright and Cobden, whose prophecy that the whole world would soon adopt Free Trade had not yet been falsified by events. When Parliament resumed, in the late autumn of 1852, no quarter was given by the Manchester Liberals, and on December 17 the Government was beaten.

In later years Disraeli said that had the Derby Government remained in office, there would have been no Crimean War. What Disraeli said is not necessarily evidence, but the statement is not in itself entirely improbable,[1] and it may well be that the Free Traders' insistence was unfortunate for the country. However that may be, the Free Traders themselves were among those who paid the penalty, for Bright and Cobden both lost their seats later as a result of their peace policy.

Undoubtedly Russell had at first anticipated that the Derby Government would form no more than a brief interlude in his own career. He expected soon to be back in Downing Street as Prime Minister, with a Reform Bill and without Palmerston, or at least with Palmerston in some position where he could do no harm. The Tories might be momentarily in office, but they were certainly not in power, and they were far too broken and inexperienced for the country to give them a real majority at the polls. What then remained but for the Whigs to come back with Russell at their head, when all things would be as before?

He was soon undeceived. The first half of the calculation, indeed, worked out correctly: the Tories were out. But the Whigs were not in; at least they were not in as masters, with himself as chief of the tribe. He had forgotten the Peelites.

But there was worse to come. At sixty Lord John Russell had the bitter experience of discovering that office had alienated most of his friends and exasperated most of his enemies. The Court, once so friendly, remembered only that for four years he had failed to dismiss Palmerston. The country only remembered that after four years of close association he had dismissed Palmerston. That cold colleague Lord Grey, whose colonial policy was as sympathetic as an icicle, told the Prince Consort that Lord John had mismanaged matters in Cabinet and Commons. Clarendon, who was at least a human being, agreed that the Whig party was as decrepit as it was exclusive. Harcourt,

---

[1] On this point at least the Queen would hardly have agreed with Disraeli. She wrote to Granville years later (August 30, 1880): "To threaten and not to act upon it was too often tried formerly, and was also a maxim of Lord Derby, who was the most difficult and unsatisfactory minister she or indeed anyone had to deal with." (But this last sentence was written before her most difficult moments with Gladstone.)

despite the Protestant alliance, sneered at the fallen minister in the new *Saturday Review* as the last doge of Whiggism.

However that might be, the Whig family party, remembering the Hampden affair and No Popery, had come to distrust Russell's judgment, and the territorial magnates were not enthusiastic over the prospect of seeing him as Prime Minister again. They would accept him at a pinch, if nothing better offered; but they did not want a raging reform campaign, and they did want some ballast in the Cabinet boat. The Dukes mattered less in the country than before, but within the party their judgment was likely to be decisive; and the Dukes now remembered that Lord John's own father, the late Duke of Bedford, had said years before that his boy would ruin his chances in life by his recklessness and lack of judgment. The prophecy had come home to roost.

The verdict was not seriously disputed by the ordinary Liberal member of the Commons, who resented Russell's cool aloofness to the rank and file, and remembered that even in the midst of a foreign crisis Palmerston had always had time for a friendly word or a cheery nod as he passed through the division lobbies.

Outside the purely political circle, too, Lord John found himself unpopular. The English Universities had never loved a man who had only been to Edinburgh; but since he had appointed a Royal Commission in 1850 to inquire into their discipline, state, and revenues—in a word, to modernize them—the very name of Russell had been anathema in every common-room. The physic was overdue, but the physician was detested.

Among the ecclesiastics, the High Churchmen naturally hated his Broad Church Bishops and latitudinarian Deans; and that ambitious intriguer, Wilberforce of Oxford, who had hoped for York and dreamed of Canterbury, and been disappointed of both, said sourly that Lord John Russell was the cause of brother-in-law Manning's conversion. The Tractarians naturally hated the Durham Letter and the Ecclesiastical Titles Bill, and the Low Churchmen and Dissenters hated him for raising their hopes of a No Popery cry and frittering away the chance.

Most successful statesmen have to suffer a period of eclipse and temporary unpopularity at some time of their lives; like clergyman's throat and publican's liver, it is a disease of the trade, and the only cure is rest and change of occupation. Unhappily Russell did not see this. He complained of intrigues, which no doubt existed (though Clarendon denied them), but the real trouble was not the pulling of strings by Tapers and Tadpoles, but the fact that people preferred Palmerston. He at least rebuked Emperors for the error of their ways, whereas Lord John only lectured the Pope.

But Palmerston's time had not quite come; it would probably have been better in the end for Russell's peace of mind if it had. The Peelites had to try their hand.

Two days before the fall of the Derby Government, Lord John had gone to Woburn, whither the Duke of Bedford had already invited Lords Lansdowne and Aberdeen. At this meeting the Duke asked his brother what course he thought the Queen ought to take in the event of the Conservative Cabinet being beaten, and Lord John replied that she should send for Lansdowne and Aberdeen, both disinterested men, one the doyen of the Whigs, the other of the Peelites.

The advice was sound, but Lord John did not know that the Queen had herself asked the Duke of Bedford to put the question to him, nor was he informed of the circumstance till three days later. He naturally felt that his brother had not treated him quite fairly. But Bedford had himself been placed in an awkward position; and in view of the house-party and previous negotiations for parliamentary co-operation between Russell and Aberdeen, which had been resumed as recently as the last summer, it is difficult to see how Russell could have given different advice even if he had known that his brother was an agent and not merely an interested host.

However that may be, the Queen acted on the advice. Lansdowne was unable to obey the royal summons on account of illness, but he wrote a letter in which he stated his own desire not to take office—he was now seventy-two years of age—and recommending the Queen to "desire

Lord J. Russell and Lord Aberdeen to meet and to determine what arrangement of persons and situations would be best with the double view of official aptitude and of selecting those whose appointments would be most gratifying to the feeling of the friends and supporters of both parties."

The order in which the names were mentioned, the politics of the writer, and the known friendship of Lansdowne for Lord John, suggest that he envisaged a Whig administration under Russell with a Peelite wing; and such a Cabinet might possibly have been formed but for the fact that Palmerston was practically indispensable for public confidence in any Whig Government, and Palmerston had sworn he would not again serve under the man who had dismissed him. But before the Queen received Lansdowne's letter, Lord John met Aberdeen again, and told him that he would probably accept office in an Aberdeen Government. This, of course, altered the position completely; the question was no longer of a Russell Government with a Peelite wing, but of a Peelite Government with a Whig, or at least a Russell, annexe.

Lord John had, therefore, not merely contemplated but himself actually offered, to step down from first to second place. The fact is important, in view of subsequent jealousies and disagreements.

He had certainly expected to see himself Prime Minister again; the succession was his as of right. But it seems equally certain that he found in the interval that he would have no enthusiastic following, and that without Palmerston his Government would soon collapse, and his credit as a statesman suffer further and perhaps final damage. Only on this assumption can we understand his decision to abase himself from acknowledged head to second in command. He might hope in time to recover the position he had surrendered, but none knew better that ground so lost is not easily reconquered.

It was an evil moment for the little man, but he took his medicine without grimacing. Unfortunately the acrid taste remained in his mouth, and caused much further trouble.

But now confusion became worse confounded, and largely through Lord John's own indecision, true index of his inner grief of mind at the sacrifice that was being forced upon him. In the hypothetical Aberdeen Government he had designated himself Foreign Secretary—which would bar the way for Palmerston's return—and leader of the House of Commons. The one post entailed heavy office work, the other prolonged attendance and unhealthy hours.

It was clear that he would have his hands full, perhaps too full. He remembered Peel's remark, that no man had ever led the Commons after sixty; and on reflection he began to doubt whether he had not promised more than his never too robust physique would let him perform.

He carried his doubts to Lansdowne; and while the two friends were in conference, Macaulay chanced to come in. The eloquence of that great talker, combined with the recent death of Russell's old friend the Duke of Wellington, proved decisive. "I reminded him," wrote the historian in his diary, "that the Duke of Wellington had taken the Foreign Office after having been at the Treasury, and I quoted his own pretty speech on the Duke. 'You said, Lord John, that we could not all win battles of Waterloo, but that we might all imitate the old man's patriotism, sense of duty, and indifference to selfish interest and vanities when the public welfare was concerned; and now is the time for you to make a sacrifice. Your past services, and your name, give us a right to expect it.'"

It is hard to have one's moral precepts recommended for personal practice; and in the end Lord John offered to lead the Commons and to accept a seat in the Cabinet, but without office. There was some doubt whether the arrangement, which was certainly novel, was entirely constitutional, and a compromise was effected; Lord John agreed to take the Foreign Office for a few weeks, and to resign it at his own option to Clarendon; while Aberdeen in turn proposed to hand over the Premiership to Lord John "whenever circumstances should permit, and as soon as I could do so without breaking up the Government."

The whole arrangement was extraordinarily muddled, and almost bound to lead to trouble; indeed, it is difficult to think that any worse solution could have been arrived at. As events proved, so far from being a solution, it merely aggravated the situation. But this was only a small part of the difficulties that had to be overcome.

Party interests have to be considered by good party men, and the division of the spoils must at least appear to be fair. But the cake was not large enough to go round, and the clubs were loud in protest. The statesmen followed suit: "Of 330 members of the House of Commons," wrote Lord John to Aberdeen, "270 are Whig and Radical, 30 are Irish brigade, 30 are Peelites. To this party of 30 you propose to give 7 seats in Cabinet, to the Whigs and Radicals 5, to Lord Palmerston one."

Such frightful injustice shrieks to heaven, and is not to be borne by mortal man; in the end the six Peelites were balanced by six Whigs in Cabinet, with one Radical thrown in. Even then there was trouble over minor appointments; "I am afraid," lamented Lord John, "that the Liberal Party will never stand this, and that the storm will overwhelm me." It was all very well for Macaulay to talk about the Duke's indifference to selfish interest and vanities. Macaulay had his history to write, and wanted nothing more, but Russell had to feed the hungry, and loaves and fishes must be provided lest the faithful should desert.

The Peelites were admittedly a party that contained more leaders than followers, and nobody ever accused them of asking less than their due. Those prudent statesmen had refused to join Russell's sinking ship a year before, but now the position was reversed; this was a new craft with their own captain, and the Whigs must take what places were left over by the Aberdeen crew. The real trouble in this, as in every other coalition, was that there were at least two aspirants to every post; and "it is melancholy," wrote the ever-melancholy Graham at this time, "to see how little fitness for office is regarded on all sides, and how much the public employments are treated as booty to be divided among successful combatants."

We need not pursue the dismal theme; to be fed one must sometimes put one's feet in the trough.

CHAPTER XVII

COALITION

A T length the agony of forming the Coalition was over;
and if there were sore hearts among those who were
left out at the last moment, the Court at any rate was
delighted at the brilliance of the result. The Derby
Cabinet had contained one known man and a dozen medio-
crities; but here, it was said at Windsor, was a Ministry
of All the Talents.

Even more; Aberdeen himself, the new Prime Minister,
according to the Prince Consort had all the virtues. It is
true that others, who preferred something more robust,
said he looked like a Methodist minister, and Palmerston
laughed at him as a piece of antiquated imbecility. But
Palmerston may have been jealous; after all, a man must
have enemies, and it was easy to poke fun at the gaunt
frame and sad face and formal manners of the pious Scot.
The gossips whispered that he was other-worldly, had
second-sight, and saw visions of his dead wife. But others
remembered that Wellington had said that Aberdeen did
everything he undertook to do better than anybody else,
and were content. When the great Duke approved a man
the commendation was final.

On his record, too, Aberdeen could stand comparison
with anybody in politics. Admittedly he was a bad
speaker, but that mattered less in the Lords than the
Commons. The Upper House attended to matter rather
than manner, and were less easily swayed by emotion. As
Foreign Secretary in Conservative Governments he had
been conspicuously successful in his quiet way, and if there
were none of the alarums and excursions and resounding
triumphs of Palmerston, there were also none of the scrapes
and shifts of England's pocket Canning.

He stood frankly for peace and conciliation, and he had

succeeded; and when men complained that Peel had no foreign policy, they forgot that Aberdeen, as Peel's Foreign Secretary, had found England and France biting thumbs at each other over the Mehemet Ali affair, and had made an *entente cordiale* that was only ruptured when Palmerston returned to Downing Street. They forgot, too, that our relations with the United States had been strained when the Peel Government came in, and that it was through Aberdeen that the troublesome Oregon affair had been patched up. Metternich had certainly once said that Aberdeen might have taken a firmer line over some negotiation, and hinted at possible weakness; but a Minister who stood openly for conciliation might legitimately answer that the way to make friends is not to stamp on other folks' toes.

In one matter, it is true, even the excellent Aberdeen had failed to keep the peace. The Scotch Kirk had been beset with doubts; not indeed, like its erring Anglican sister, of the iniquity of the Scarlet Woman, but of its internal organization and relations with the State. True to his love of unity and concord, Aberdeen had done his best to keep the peace, and failed; and the furious belligerents, who feared to be frustrated, had loudly assailed him with charges of bad faith.

But sensible men know that these things are the small change of ecclesiastical commerce. Aberdeen was foolish to imagine that any one layman can stop any two clergymen from fighting when they have a mind to, and the attacks upon his honour merely raised a smile in the profane world of politics, where the wise mariner—as Russell had discovered to his cost—steers clear of theological typhoons.

It was natural for contemporaries to compare Aberdeen, the peace minister of England, with his friend and admirer Guizot, the peace minister of France. But the comparison was unfair to Aberdeen. Guizot was merely an intellectual pedant, who fell into the pocket of Louis Philippe, and fell out again through a hole in the bottom. Aberdeen had no particular intellect, but he was certainly not a pedant; he was simply ineffective in a real difficulty.

Palmerston dealt with foreigners booted and spurred,

and cracked the whip as he pleased. Aberdeen's diplomacy wore carpet slippers, hoped for the best, and never prepared for the worst. His real misfortune was that Peel had died two years before, and the Peelites chose him as their leader; otherwise he would never have been the alternative to Palmerston, and his modest reputation would never have been dogged by the memory of a peace coalition that drifted into war.

This ideal second-in-command was now tried in a situation that would have taxed the powers of a far stronger man.

The coalition arose almost inevitably out of the difficulties of the parliamentary position, in which no leader and no party had a majority or any prospect of getting one. For some years the House of Commons had been supreme over the Cabinet, and it was at this period that Gladstone found it necessary to warn the Queen that if the tendency was not soon changed, the House might begin to encroach upon the remaining prerogatives of the Crown.[1]

Liberty was certainly safe when any Government could be thrown out any afternoon between prayers and dinner; but Englishmen are accustomed to take liberty for granted, and there are, after all, other important things in the world. A weak executive may sometimes be as much a public danger as a strong one; and half the troubles of the Russell Government, and all the troubles of the Derby Government, had sprung from the fact that they were at the mercy of any chance combination in the House of Commons.

It was the business of the Crown to see this, and the Crown had seen it for years. Now at last it seemed certain, or almost certain, that a coalition would surmount the difficulty of party government by parties that were not strong enough to govern. Safety, like truth, proverbially lies in the middle, and the formation of a great centre group would give stability to the Government, which would

---

[1] This appears to have been common form among the Tories of the day. At this time Croker wrote: "The harder we die the easier will be the resurrection, but die this constitution will and must. The Queen is already a puppet. The House of Commons is King." The "Letters of Queen Victoria" certainly do not support the puppet theory. The prerogative was declining, largely owing to the multiplication of business, but the influence of the Crown was increasing as the Queen gained experience.

draw support from that great majority of moderate men of all parties, leaving opposition to the small knot of intractable Tories on the extreme right, and the equally small group of ardent Radicals on the extreme left. The fanatics at either end of the scale could be ignored when once the mass of opinion solidly supported the middle.

It seemed probable that such a Government, faced only by such an opposition, might look forward to something like permanent power. Other nations would no longer have reason to complain of the lack of continuity in British foreign policy. The country would be safe under a ministry that was at once Liberal and Conservative, and the Court would be spared those distressing crises in which the Queen had had to compose schoolboy quarrels among elderly statesmen, to appease the vanity of one, to soothe the wounded dignity of another, and to plead for a little more restraint from a third.[1]

The theory promised excellently, but almost from the first it failed to work in practice. Experience revealed the odd fact that in party politics, unlike physics, gravitation is away from the centre. Men are mentally either static or dynamic, either authoritarian or libertarian, either conservative or liberal, and they divide and work together naturally along those lines. Individual minds, it is true, are not all of a piece. Manning was an authoritarian in religion and a radical in politics, Pusey a political Whig and a religious Tory, Selborne a Liberal in politics, a Conservative in religion, but a radical law reformer. But taken politically and in the mass, men divide by right and left, and the cross-bench mind is rare.

Had it not been so, the sensible Tories who believed that some reform was necessary in 1832 would not have been

[1] The Queen reverted to the idea of a Coalition more than thirty years later. "I do wish there was some patriotism instead of Party, Party, in all this painful question. I long for the moderates of both sides to form a third party which would be a check to both the others and prevent this mischief the violents are making." (Oct. 7, 1884.)

And again, Dec. 3, 1885: "We want a strong coalition and to that end every nerve must be strained."

The Queen forgot few things, but apparently she forgot that the Aberdeen Coalition was weaker, not stronger, even than other Governments of the time.

overborne by the stupid Tories who believed that all reform was revolution; and the Liberals who believed that Ireland could be reformed without Home Rule need not have left their party fifty years later. The extremists, it is true, always get the loudest cheers, but they seldom get to the top; it is the moderate but decided men who become Prime Ministers. But in their equipment decision on principle is as necessary as moderation in expression, because the business of a Government is to act as well as judge, and the cross-bench mind makes for weakness in action.

Now, a coalition is nothing but the cross-bench mind imposed on men who are naturally partisans. It may indeed diminish opposition without; that is in truth the main virtue of a coalition. But it is likely to do so by increasing opposition within, and for a simple reason.

In every form of Government men have to compromise their opinions and accommodate their prejudices to fit the views of their colleagues. But in an ordinary party Cabinet those colleagues are at least agreed on essentials, and if it is not always easy to compromise on detail, it is at any rate not impossible, and should leave no sense of grievance behind. But in a coalition the colleagues are unlikely to be agreed on essentials; they may even disagree as to what constitutes an essential. Now, men seldom give up a principle without a struggle, and the better the man the more he struggles for his principles. And in a coalition Government men will therefore spend far too much time in trying to convince each other, and far too little on the proper business of administration; and the better the men, the worse the Government may be.

Every sensible man recognizes that there are great evils and as great absurdities in party government. A system which deliberately applies half the political ability of the country to frustrating the other half is evidently not an ideal method of carrying on any social undertaking. But party government is at least a natural growth. The evils which it produces have seldom proved insupportable, and they are on the whole to be preferred to a Coalition Government, which is likely to be indecisive in policy even if

strongly led, and certain to drift when weakly led. A
Ministry of All the Talents is a glittering sham, a pretended
panacea that first cancels out and then fizzles out through
lack of agreement on first principles.

So it was to be with the Aberdeen Government of which
Lord John Russell was now a member. It is, indeed,
natural to blame the mild Aberdeen for the troubles that
followed, to say that weak men cannot lead strong men,
and that there are times when a little rough handling will
do more to straighten things out than a gentle pat, a quiet
whisper, and an appeal for delay and further consideration.

These things are true, and they account for many of
the difficulties that dogged the Coalition; of all possible
captains of such a team, Aberdeen was probably the worst.
Like the absurd Goderich—his only rival to the title of
the worst Prime Minister of the century—he would hardly
have succeeded in leading an ordinary party Cabinet. But
it is only fair to recognize that, as leader of a Coalition,
his difficulties were greater, and not less, than those of his
predecessors. The fact that he failed so badly may be
properly ascribed to his benevolent impotence, which
produced a result the exact opposite of what he desired.
But an angel from heaven would hardly have succeeded
in his place.

CHAPTER XVIII

CRIMEAN RESIGNATION

OUR narrative has now come to the most difficult and unsatisfactory period of Lord John Russell's life. Hitherto, with only an occasional brief spasm of that unpopularity which no leading man can ever quite escape, he had been almost uniformly successful. His name was identified with great causes fought, with great causes won; his reputation was firmly established, not indeed in that small band of supreme statesmen like Cromwell and the Pitts, but among that more numerous but still splendid company which includes the great Canning, the sober Walpole, the exquisite Harley, the formidable Strafford, and the cunning Burleigh—men who had set their mark on England for good or ill and would never be forgotten while our history survived.

But the sunshine of power had now suddenly vanished, and at sixty Russell found himself in the gloomy wood of politics astray. Ten years previously Gladstone, whose verdicts on his contemporaries were nearly always scrupulously fair, remarked that Lord John had risen with adversity. He now as conspicuously fell, and many years later Gladstone again delivered judgment: "A great reputation built itself up on the basis of splendid services for thirty years; for almost twenty it has, I fear, been on the decline. The movement of the clock continues, the balance weights are gone."

But this in turn was excessive. The Durham Letter, which Gladstone rightly marked as beginning the period of decline, had miscarried; and this failure of a sincere stroke that was also intended to be shrewd was the first of several shocks that led two years later to the fall of the Whig Government. For the next three years a veteran statesman committed almost every blunder that a raw

novice would have avoided. He then did ungraciously
what he should have done in the first instance—retired and
left the stage awhile. But then came a marvellous recovery;
and four years later, mistakes forgotten and only successes
remembered, he returned and enjoyed a long Indian
summer of public esteem and power.

The first blunder, as Russell afterwards recognized, and
the mistake which led to all the rest, lay in consenting to
serve under Aberdeen. It is not easy for a man who has
been Prime Minister to serve under another Prime Minister.
The thing can be done, and has been done with success,
as Russell himself proved seven years later, and Balfour
has shown in our own day. But it is difficult to do it
without an interval for readjustment from command to
subordination; and it is still more difficult when the new
leader is of another party, a different temperament, and
accustomed to other ways of thought and action.

Russell was quick at the uptake and often hasty in
action; Aberdeen was the reverse—slow, calm, patient, and
invincibly procrastinating. Russell was always ready to
start, Aberdeen always ready to stop. Russell was generally
in too much of a hurry to act, Aberdeen always believed
that things would come right in the end if only haste were
avoided. Russell was never a deep but always a clear
thinker. Gladstone has borne tribute to Aberdeen's un-
swerving honesty of mind; but many honest men never
think, and Aberdeen was one of them. There is no doubt
that Russell had the irritating consciousness of being the
better man, and there is no doubt he was right. But he
was handicapped by past mistakes, whereas Aberdeen was
not.

Almost from the first there was misunderstanding, if not
actual friction. Aberdeen hoped that having once taken
the Foreign Office, Russell would have held it at least
during a great part of the session of 1853. The idea was
certainly not unreasonable. But twelve days after Parliament opened he resigned the post, and from that time led
the House without portfolio. No Government can work
effectively if Ministers throw up their departments before
they know the office stairs.

Russell was now offered the Home Office, and seemed struck with the idea, but on Lady John's advice, refused to take it. There can be little doubt that she showed a careful wife's proper solicitude for the health of a husband whose physique was notoriously frail, and also a good Whig's jealousy at the supersession of her man by a flabby Tory. But the gossips at Westminster at once accused him of being under petticoat government.

The arrangement, however, by which he led the House without departmental responsibility was awkward[1]; and presently it came out that, with his usual loyalty to an old friend's memory, he was editing the poet Moore's literary remains on behalf of the widow. The occupation probably solaced his leisure with thoughts of sweeter hours in the past, but it gave an opening for Croker to sneer that Russell was doing "his public work without an office, and accepted the office of Moore's executor without doing the work." Russell was not, in fact, that rarest of all God's creatures, a perfect editor; but had he been Raphael from Paradise he would not have escaped abuse. It was a bad hour.

But for the time, at least, the Government seemed to prosper. Publicly, at any rate, the session of 1853 passed off well. Gladstone introduced and carried a great Budget, the Indian Civil Service was thrown open to public competition, and Russell made some modest contributions towards extending the system of public education, which prepared the way for the great Forster measure many years later.

It was admitted that Lord John led the House with tact and dignity. But in effect office without portfolio is much the same as office without power, or dinner without the *pièce de résistance* which satisfies the appetite; and neither Russell nor the importunate Whigs were indifferent to the loss of patronage.

The position irked and irritated him, and the following year tart notes were exchanged. "The Whigs write to

[1] To regularize the position he subsequently accepted the Lord Presidency of the Council; generally a mere sinecure for the senile who are politically dead but object to being buried. It was then complained that no Commoner had held the office since the reign of Henry VIII.

me imagining that I have some influence on politics and ecclesiastical appointments. It is a mistake." Thus Russell to Aberdeen; to which Aberdeen responded, "To say the truth, I thought I had done little else than comply with your wishes either at the formation of the Government or ever since."

Incredible though it sounds, both complaints were partly true. There were no more Broad Bishops; Gladstone saw to that. A Presbyterian might lead the Lords and a mere Edinburgh student might lead the Commons, but the member for Oxford University was not forgetful of his duty to the Church. But Whig appetites are as healthy as Tory, and they seem to have thought that if they had only half a Government it was no reason why they should not have all the patronage. Lord John wanted nothing for himself except the Premiership, but Aberdeen discovered that he wanted a great deal for his friends.

When things have come to such a pass between colleagues, it is better to resign. But Russell thought it was Aberdeen who should resign in his favour, and Aberdeen had in fact suggested at the start that he would probably do so after a short time, and sometimes in Cabinet and in private conversation with Russell himself played with the idea as a cat plays with a mouse.

Once, in 1853, when Lord John told Aberdeen he should still support the Government, the Prime Minister replied: "I know what that means: you would not turn us out till you had an opportunity." He was always talking about resignation, but when it came to the point he never resigned.

The Queen, a personal friend and, by residence at Balmoral, a neighbour of Aberdeen's, told him frankly that he was imprudent; and Lord John must have found his procrastinating indecision exasperating. Russell came of a stock that knew exactly what they wanted, and went after and got it if they could; and this maidenly coyness in a man near seventy, this affectation of would-and-would-not in the first office in the country, was hardly to be borne. In the business of government a man should get on with the job or get out, and Aberdeen would do neither.

It is impossible to acquit Aberdeen of much that is

ascribed to Lord John's perverseness. Aberdeen had neither policy nor push; Lord John had both. He was certainly deficient in subtlety and scope, but in common with all sensible men he regarded government as an instrument and not an end; whereas Aberdeen seems to have regarded it as an end in itself, and almost invariably replied to any suggestion of action with the objection that it would break up the Cabinet.

As things turned out it would have been far better to have done so. If anything could have been worse than Palmerston's bluster, which threatened war and remained at peace, it was this mild and benevolent drifter who talked of peace and slid gently into war. In the end, indeed, the nation turned to Palmerston to clear up the mess, and the main result of the antiquated imbecility of Aberdeen—the phrase is Palmerston's—was to give Palmerston himself ten years of power.

The mental calm of Aberdeen, in fact, was not the calm of the strong man conscious of his strength, but of the weak man who is merely conscious of the best intentions. The point is illustrated by two events, one in home, the other in foreign policy, and both operated to bring Russell down.

There was first the awkward problem of parliamentary reform. Two years before his own Government had fallen, Russell had brought before the Cabinet a plan for the extension of the franchise. But Lansdowne looked grave and Grey looked glum; and where the high priests of the temple were dubious it would have been easy to drop the whole matter. But Lord John was not so easily beaten. He acquiesced reluctantly at the moment, but in the session of 1852 he gave evidence of the seriousness of his purpose by actually introducing a second Reform Bill in the House of Commons. The Government fell almost immediately afterwards, but Russell carried his idea forward to the Coalition, and pressed it insistently on the Aberdeen Cabinet.

There was, of course, a good case for parliamentary reform; there always must be when population is growing rapidly and at the same time shifting from the country to the towns. There was equally no question that the case for reform would become stronger in a few years; the only question was whether it could be made effective at the moment.

Russell thought it could. Lansdowne and Grey thought it could not. Palmerston, in a famous letter, refused to be "dragged through the dirt" by Lord John. The party was split; most Whigs gave it some support on the platform, many damned it in private, and some—who afterwards formed the Cave of Adullam—were ready either to kill it by kindness in the approved parliamentary manner of amendment, or if necessary in the last resort to vote against it. In the end, the Adullamites and their allies delayed reform fifteen years, and deprived Russell of the personal triumph which his noble persistence in face of obstruction had richly earned. But we can see now that Russell was right; the second Reform Act was inevitable.

He was, however, in a difficult tactical position. As one of the old official Whigs, he could hardly as yet adopt the position which Gladstone took up twelve years later, in a famous declaration that startled the Queen: "I venture to say that every man who is not presumably incapacitated by some consideration of personal unfitness or of political danger is morally entitled to come within the fiat of the constitution." This was radicalism, not Whiggery, for the Whigs had always held to a property qualification. But even on Whig principles, Cobden had pointed out as long ago as 1846 that Manchester had only two members to Buckinghamshire's eleven, but double the property; and the illustration could easily have been multiplied from other counties.

Statements of this kind naturally moved Russell, and it was right that they should; his mind worked easily and rapidly in terms of borough schedules and county franchises. Something must be done, somebody must do it; why should it not be he, who had a kind of pre-emption over Reform Bills?

Unluckily there was his own famous declaration of 1837 against further reform, which had earned him the nickname of "Finality Jack." He denied firmly that he had ever applied the word "final" to the Reform Act of 1832, and the denial was true. But it was also true that he had definitely pledged himself against extending the franchise, and reform could take no other shape; and the delicate question arose: How long is a pledge valid?

It depends, of course, on the nature of the pledge. Unfortunately there was no limiting factor in it. The thing therefore required nice handling. But if on the narrow grounds of verbal consistency he was wrong, on the broader ground of consistent policy he was right; for the situation had in fact changed in the fifteen years of the new reign, and if the anomalies left by 1832 were not redressed, something much more drastic than Russell contemplated in 1852 would be demanded and conceded —as in fact happened.

It says much for the courage of the little man that he was able to convince the Coalition Cabinet that he was right, to carry the tepid Aberdeen and even the melancholy Graham, to survive Palmerston's resignation of the Home Office and his incontinent return, and even to threaten his own resignation and to be asked to remain.

But there were painful scenes with his colleagues, and at one Cabinet dinner where the whole matter was discussed, Clarendon noted that "J.R. was wrong in his facts, insolent in his assertions, and most ill-tempered in his replies. No spoilt child could be more perverse or inaccessible either to kind words or firm words, and his look was as if he had plied himself with wine in order to get courage for doing what he felt was wrong. Everybody was dead against him, though some said nothing. Aberdeen's conduct was a most remarkable contrast."

Aberdeen, in fact, cared nothing for the Bill, but only to keep an appearance of amity where no unity was; whereas Russell's whole heart was now set upon reform.

The Cabinet at length gave way to his persistence, and the Bill was eventually introduced in the Commons on February 13, 1854. The proposals were received, wrote Graham to Clarendon, with "much astonishment and no enthusiasm. But on the whole I should say that the country gentlemen expected something worse and the Radicals something more."

But the measure was doomed from the start. The House and the country were thinking of nothing but war, and within a few weeks it was necessary to postpone the Bill. In making the announcement Lord John admitted that this course would expose him to the taunts and sarcasms of his opponents and to the suspicions of his supporters; and here his feelings overcame him, his utterance was choked in the delivery, and he could hardly conceal his tears.

Through this difficult, and for Russell almost tragical, episode, Aberdeen had been kind. But the formal sympathy of this tepid chief was more irritating than the frank opposition of Palmerston—a man who, like Russell, knew exactly what he wanted and equally well what he did not want. This long fight followed by a public fiasco over reform clearly sapped some of Lord John's self-control; and parallel as it was to the long agony of Aberdeen's indecision in the dispute that became the Crimean War, explains certain actions which puzzled and distressed his contemporaries, and brought his reputation for the time being to the ground.

The history of the Crimean War has been written once for all by Kinglake in a book which Gladstone described as too bad to live and too good to die. Here we are only concerned with the struggle so far as it affects Lord John Russell, who found himself in the exasperating position of having to take full public responsibility for a policy of which he could not fully approve, and who suffered more than anybody from the flabby mentality of his chief.

The origin of the Crimean War was a dispute between the Greek and Latin Churches as to the Holy Places at Jerusalem, which caused conflicting demands from Russia and France to the Sultan of Turkey. Such a situation was potentially, and might easily become actually, dangerous; and Lord John, temporarily Foreign Secretary, wrote a despatch: "We should deeply regret any dispute that might lead to conflict between two of the great powers of Europe; but when we reflect that the quarrel is for exclusive privileges in a spot near which the heavenly host proclaimed peace on earth and goodwill towards men—when we see rival Churches contending for mastery in the very place where Christ died for mankind—the thought of such a spectacle is melancholy indeed."

The language was a little florid, the moral a little obvious, but Lord John did not content himself with words. The British Ambassador to Turkey happened to be on leave in England. He had offered to resign on the change of Government; the temporary Foreign Secretary, who knew a man when he saw one, obtained a withdrawal of the resignation, and sent him back to Constantinople.

He had acted more strongly than he quite realized, for the Ambassador was Lord Stratford de Redcliffe, one of those formidable personalities who control rather than obey instructions, and who act as masterful plenipotentiaries as soon as they are across the Straits of Dover. Aberdeen, who also knew a man when he saw one, and had all the weak man's instinctive distrust of strength, was instantly alarmed, and talked darkly about the necessity of preparing his instructions very carefully, of giving no more than moral support to the Turks, and keeping ourselves free to act as circumstances might require. The short English of this is that Aberdeen proposed to do nothing.

It is possible that the strong line which Stratford de Redcliffe intended to take up on behalf of Turkey against Russia would have convinced the Tsar that the time was inopportune for dismembering the Turkish Empire as he desired. It is possible that the weak line which Aberdeen wished to take up would have kept England out of the troubles that were bound to ensue while such a policy was accomplishing. But it is evident that the combination of a strong man on the spot and a weak man at home is bound to produce a situation in which war was not merely probable, but practically certain.

So it fell out. Through 1853 the negotiations continued, but by October Prince Albert noted that Aberdeen "was, against his better judgment, consenting to a course of policy which he inwardly condemned, that his desire to maintain unanimity at the Cabinet led to concessions which by degrees altered the whole character of his policy. . . . The Queen might now be involved in war, of which the consequences could not be calculated, chiefly by the desire of Lord Aberdeen to keep his Cabinet together; this might then break down, and the Queen would be left without an efficient Government, and a war on her hands."

The Prince Consort was a true prophet. The Tsar, who knew Aberdeen personally, could not believe that he would ever put his foot down; and had Aberdeen stood alone, the Tsar would have been right. But he failed to reckon with Lord Stratford de Redcliffe at Constantinople, with the bellicose attitude of Palmerston at home, and with the firmness of Russell; and between the three Aberdeen was a mere straw in the wind.

Russell's attitude was simple and consistent. Writing to Clarendon on March 20, 1853, he said, "The Emperor of Russia is clearly bent on accomplishing the destruction of Turkey, and he must be resisted. The vast preparations at Sebastopol show a foregone purpose, and that purpose is, I fear, to extinguish the Turkish Empire. In case I am right the crisis is very serious. My own opinion is that, in case of the invasion of Turkey by Russia on any pretence, we ought to send a messenger to Petersburg, and demand the evacuation of the Turkish territory, and, in case of refusal, to enforce this demand both in the Baltic as well as in the Dardanelles. We should of course enter into concert with France."

This opinion he modified in details as the negotiations continued during the remainder of 1853, but in essentials his view remained unchanged. He felt that the policy he advised was clear and straightforward, and he could not understand the hesitations of Aberdeen, nor was he fully in sympathy with the more cautious methods adopted by his old colleague Clarendon at the Foreign Office.

Since Russell was neither Prime Minister nor Foreign Secretary he was not directly responsible for the conduct of the negotiations. But as one of the most important members of the Cabinet he was generally responsible, and as leader of the Commons he had, of course, to defend Government foreign policy in the House. He discharged the duty adequately, but without zest, and a correspondence with Clarendon in the autumn shows that the strain was telling heavily.

The position "I have held this year has been, and is, and must be, a degrading one," he wrote. "I have deserved it, and I have borne it as best I could. Lord Aberdeen by his kindness and good feeling has done all in his power to make it tolerable. Still, on more than one occasion, I have had to summon all my patience to my aid. But you have made me feel my degradation more than I ever felt it before. You assumed that I was to be the chief organ for defending in the House of Commons that which I had no share in deciding, and of which I had previously recorded my disapproval. It was impossible that I could so lower myself, or that I should not feel the blow you had inflicted on me more than all the other humiliations I have endured."

This unhappy letter is a cry from the heart of an entirely honest but perhaps excessively sensitive man. The cynic will explain it easily enough by saying that Russell was jealous of being superseded by Aberdeen, and that the man who has held supreme command is thereby unfitted to take second place. There is more force in the latter than the former contention. But the simple assertion is inadequate to the facts.

Russell was certainly jealous of Aberdeen, but his feelings were not, I think, merely personal; he had the natural impatience of the first-class man who finds himself in a subordinate position while a second-class man is muddling grave issues. It is well to be patient and calm under difficulties, but it is not well to pretend that the right course is being steered when in fact the ship is simply drifting.[1]

Undoubtedly Russell should have resigned. He had blundered in joining the Government at all, and he should now have rectified that blunder by leaving it; the European crisis was not yet acute, national interests would scarcely have been seriously prejudiced, and some plausible excuse of health or private affairs could easily have been put forward. He did in fact resign soon afterwards, but withdrew his resignation; and here he blundered again. But the reason was simple.

---

[1] Aberdeen himself admitted this. "As we are drifting fast towards war, I should think the Cabinet ought to see where they are going."—Aberdeen to Clarendon, June 7, 1853.

Little as he liked the European policy of the Government, he believed he could influence it in the right direction; and above all, his interest was bound up in the Reform Bill. By that he hoped to restore himself to a commanding position in the State; and meanwhile he put up with the futile Aberdeen with what scant patience he possessed.

The Reform Bill failed; the Crimean War began. And now the incompetence of Aberdeen became more and more evident to his colleagues.

It is well to keep the peace and ensue it. But if you go to war, it is well to fight hard and not waste time in vain regrets. The Prime Minister could not see this, and we find Russell writing impatiently to Clarendon: "The great want is a head of the English Cabinet. If a head could be found, all might be well; but I cannot imagine how we can go on any longer without any head at all."

History has endorsed this verdict. Aberdeen continued to reproach himself with having gone to war, and to congratulate himself on having at least kept his Government together. The campaign was waged in dilatory fashion, at enormous cost, and as it seemed without the least prospect of any effective result. The troops were badly led, badly fed, the Army contractors were dishonest, and there were rumours of favouritism in high quarters. To infuse a little more life into the campaign, Russell advised that Palmerston should displace the Duke of Newcastle at the War Office. But the Duke was an amiable nonentity of the Aberdeen type, and like naturally preferred like. Again and again Russell tried to stir Aberdeen to action; but the pacific machinery of that gentle mind interposed an amiable resistance to anything that looked like excessive energy.

At last the end came. The British public is proverbially patient. But there are limits to its toleration of the limits of its governors. The country first became restive, then angry, and finally alarmed, as one story after another reached England of the mismanagement in the Crimea and the complacency in Downing Street; and when Parliament reassembled in January, 1855, Mr. Roebuck gave notice of a motion on the conduct of the war.

As Leader of the House of Commons it would fall to Lord John Russell to resist that motion. His heart would not have been in it, but many a leader has to make many a speech without his heart being in it, and a world which is run on the basis of team-work not only does not condemn but approves the simulated indignation, the forensic rebuttal, the solemn asseveration of sincerity, in these performances. We all do these things, and we all put up with these things, for reasons that have always seemed sufficient to all sensible men.

The doctrine of Cabinet responsibility, as Lord Salisbury remarked in another connexion many years later, implies a constant agreement of opinion that never in fact exists. But there is a point of conscience where the individual rebels; and that point had now been reached with Russell.

All the accumulated impatience and disgust and disappointment, personal and public in who shall say what confused admixture, welled up in that fiery little soul against the task with which fate had faced him; and he came to a momentous decision. Whatever the consequences to himself and his future, he would no longer publicly defend a Government in which he could no longer believe.

On January 23, 1855, the first night of the session, Mr. Roebuck gave notice of his motion. Russell attended to the formal business as Leader of the Commons, and when the House was up went home accompanied by Sir Charles Wood. No conversation of importance passed between the colleagues, and nothing was said to Wood to indicate a personal crisis, much less a personal resignation. But that same evening, as Aberdeen was sitting in his drawing-room, a red box was brought in by his son and private secretary, and it contained John Russell's resignation.

The thing might have been better done. But it was better done as it was than not done at all. Russell's real fault lay, not in resigning now, but in not having insisted on his resignation before. A year earlier he would merely have been mildly criticized; now he had to face a violent storm of obloquy.

Instantly the floodgates of wrath and denunciation were

opened. Resignation in such circumstances was unprecedented; therefore it was unforgiveable. Palmerston, who had at least waited to be dismissed, wrote a bitter letter. Greville, who was a loyal friend but who would certainly never have given up a job except on compulsion, went about calling Russell a cowardly skulker. Dasent, who with Delane had done more to expose the incompetence of the Government in *The Times* than any man in the country, remarked that Russell had not so much resigned as absconded. Even the Queen so far forgot the reticent traditions of Windsor as to accuse the minister of deserting her; and this was the more galling since Russell had but recently defended the Court in Parliament against the gossips who accused the Prince Consort of interfering in public affairs while he hid behind the Queen's petticoats.

Aberdeen, it is true, still maintained the monumental calm which nothing short of the Day of Judgment would have shaken. Like a flatfish at the bottom of the sea, he was hardly even aware of the fierce elements raging above; he quietly put down the whole thing to a piece of party spite, and still maintained that the Coalition had succeeded admirably.

The statesmen of England often deceive themselves. But by the mercy of Providence the House of Commons usually undeceives them. Within a week the Roebuck motion was carried by 325 to 148, and the worst Government of the century was out.

CHAPTER XIX

RETIREMENT

THE French Ambassador in London remarked, with the masculine logic of his nation, that England was waging war without an Army and without a Government.

Lord Derby, immensely shocked that a foreigner should tell the truth, was sent for by the Queen, failed to provide a Tory Government in the hour of crisis, and returned, a little shaken in public esteem, to his poetry and pheasants. Lord Lansdowne, more helpful in spite of age and gout, recommended first Clarendon, then Russell, then Palmerston. The Queen declined Clarendon as having no courage for Prime Minister—an odd objection after Aberdeen—and sent for Russell to "hear what he could do."

The next day began a melancholy pilgrimage in search of colleagues, and a British Government in embryo was touted round Mayfair. Russell called on Gladstone "at half-past two and sat till three, his hat shaking in his hand. Upon the whole," noted the cautious host, "his tone was low and doubtful."

Gladstone refused; he could hardly help the man who had brought the Peelites down. The ever-timid Graham told Russell he had been rash. The debonair Herbert admitted that the Peelites preferred him to the hateful Palmerston, but could not help the man who had torpedoed the ship.

The disgruntled Whigs were equally explicit. Clarendon, whom Gladstone regarded as the best of all the colleagues he had known in Cabinet, "would not step over the dead bodies of his friends" to the man who had killed them. Lansdowne, probably not sorry to be past work, politely regretted that he could not assist his young friend. The intractable Grey, who had wrecked Russell's chance in 1845, was omitted as impossible; one does not go to an icicle for warmth in winter.

Palmerston, who never bore malice, was cordial in tone but guarded in substance. His hour had come, and too much was at stake for complete frankness, but neither pope nor anti-pope would yet admit the supremacy nor advise the excommunication of the other.

The attempt therefore failed, and a few days later Palmerston kissed hands as Prime Minister, three years and two months after he had been dismissed from the Foreign Secretaryship. The Queen's objection to Clarendon, which was perhaps ill-founded, had in effect compelled her to accept as Premier the man she distrusted more than anybody in the kingdom.

At least she took her medicine with good grace; and the difficult Peelites, who had professed to prefer Russell as a man to his rival, presently changed their minds when it was now or nothing. Having refused to serve under Russell, they consented to serve under Palmerston. Perhaps we need not wonder that politicians suspect each other.

The long duel of Palmerston with Russell was over, and with one brief interruption the older man was to retain the keys of Downing Street till his death ten years later. But Russell in turn bore no malice against his successful rival. Palmerston at once offered him a post in the new Government—a fact which shows how little the denunciations of the cowardly skulker and deserter were worth. Russell did not accept at the moment—perhaps it was asking a little too much to expect him to do so—but he willingly engaged on an important temporary commission.

In the preceding summer the two Western powers had formulated a protocol defining the objects of the war—which I had forgotten to state was still being carried on—under four heads; and some time later the Tsar had been persuaded to accept these four points as a possible basis of peace. Negotiations were now taking place preliminary to a conference to be held at Vienna, and Russell was asked by the new Government to represent Britain as a special envoy. He was not very sanguine of success. "It would be awkward," he remarked, "to go to Vienna with a return ticket," but he consented to the mission.

While staying in Paris on the way there, Palmerston

again pressed his old chief to join the Government The difficult Peelites had after all found the new Prime Minister impossible, and resigned; and the man who had been denounced as an absconding traitor found himself much in request. He quietly accepted the Colonial Secretary-ship, on the ground that he was already familiar with the work, and proceeded to the Conference.

But worse difficulties arose even than he had anticipated. In the give-and-take of negotiations each party insensibly modified its ground, and the position became hopelessly tangled over a proposal to neutralize the Black Sea. The truth is that the war had not yet reached a stage at which the combatants were sufficiently anxious to make peace; and after prolonged but abortive discussions Russell returned home.

The French envoy resigned; and Russell, finding his advice rejected by the British Government, also tendered his resignation. He was persuaded, however, to withdraw it, and the result was disastrous.

He was unable to defend himself effectively in Parliament, for as envoy at Vienna he had approved proposals that the Government of which he was a member in London now found itself unable to accept. The position had developed quite naturally as the negotiations continued, but he was caught in the chain of circumstance. If he defended himself he would have to criticize the Government, and if he criticized the Government he would have to explain why he was still a member of it.

The situation was obviously an impossible one. Personal spite seized the occasion, party rancour magnified a tangle into a scandal; and there burst upon his head all the accumulated malice that had been waiting an opportunity to revenge itself for his torpedoing of the Aberdeen Government. The storm of denunciation became too severe to stand against, and this time Russell definitely resigned. He had accepted the Colonial Office on February 23; on July 13 he was once more a private member.

It would be excessively tedious to recapitulate the diplomatic and parliamentary details of this unhappy business; it was simply that the sequences were against him, and the real blunder that Russell made was the same as under Aberdeen. He was not wrong in resigning, but in withdrawing his resignation. It was the mistake of an optimist who hopes things will come right if he holds on.

At this point Lord John Russell reached the lowest stage of his fortunes. He was now sixty-three, and most men thought, or affected to think, that his day was done. He was still a member of Parliament, but for the next four years his attendances were rare and his speeches few. Like a sensible man he retired into private life until the storm had blown itself out, and occupied his leisure, after the manner of Whig statesmen out of work, with writing a life of Charles James Fox, the patron saint of Whiggery—who, unlike Russell, was greater out of office than in.

CHAPTER XX

RETURN

WALKING home with Palmerston from the House of Commons one evening early in 1858, a personal and political friend told the Prime Minister that he ought, like the Roman consuls at a triumph, to have someone to remind him he was not immortal. The cheers of an immense majority on the India Bill were still ringing in his ears; the next day the same members turned against him, and the Government was out.

The Queen, who was more loyal than many monarchs to her friends and servants, still had an affection for the amiable incompetence of Aberdeen. But the extraordinary rectitude of mind which Gladstone remarked in his sovereign never allowed private inclination to interfere with public duty, and no more coalitions were attempted.

Her range of choice was limited, and the inevitable Lord Derby constructed the inevitable minority Government, while Whigs and Liberals licked their parliamentary sores. But the wounds, being self-inflicted, were not deep; while the knowledge that office could practically be had for the asking whenever it was convenient to turn the Tory caretakers out made convalescence pleasant and reconciliation easy.

A decent interval of a few months elapsed; and then one afternoon old Whig, new Liberal, and surviving Peelites met by arrangement in Willis's rooms, rubbed noses, and made friends. Political differences between the groups were few; personal jealousies were many, and needed adjustment.

But where there's a will there's a way; and Gladstone, who in private detested the shifts and tricks of Palmerston, agreed in public to serve under him again.[1] Palmerston,

[1] "I have never ceased to rejoice that I am not in office with Palmerston when I have seen the tricks, the shufflings, the frauds he daily has recourse to"—Gladstone in 1857 ("Life of Wilberforce"). Two years later he apparently ceased to rejoice, and took office under Palmerston.

172

who in private regarded Gladstone as a bad colleague and a dangerous politician, agreed in public to accept his support. The charming but timid Herbert, who had sneered at Russell as a man who dropped his Reform resolutions as if they were his colleagues, agreed to be a colleague once more. And finally Russell, after four years in the literary shades, agreed that life and office were better than the dead and the company of Charles James Fox.

The time was getting short—he was now sixty-six—and though he willingly ceded the primacy to Palmerston, he insisted on being the second and not the third man in the next Administration. After all, Palmerston at seventy-five could not live for ever; and when Palmerston was removed to a world in which even a *civis Romanus* is perhaps no longer Prime Minister, the succession would be Russell's. So in time it proved to be, but death as usual had its sting; the victory came too late.

The usual pretext was found to defeat the usual Derby Government; and the Queen, puzzled by the rival and equal claims of Palmerston and Russell, sent for Lord Granville to enquire if the two elder statesmen whom she had reason to dislike would serve under a courtierly *tertium quid*, whom she had reason to like. The proposal relieved her embarrassment, but the suggestion proved impracticable.

Palmerston returned to the Premiership from which only death was to dismiss him; Gladstone resumed finance; Clarendon, whom the Queen would have preferred as Foreign Secretary, was shelved; and Lord John Russell returned to the post in which the Court disliked and distrusted him only less than Palmerston.

He was not to leave the Foreign Office for six years, and controversies whose reverberations and results still affect the world were to come directly to his notice.

CHAPTER XXI

ITALIAN UNITY

LORD JOHN and his Liberal friends had timed their return well. It was a critical hour for Europe, when the cause of Italian national unity must be lost or won.

A month before the Derby Government fell the battle of Magenta had been fought, and the Austrians defeated; a month after the Palmerston Cabinet was installed in Downing Street the Treaty of Villafranca was signed, and Cavour said in the bitterness of his heart "England has done nothing yet for Italy—it is her turn now."

The reproach was just. England had given asylum to the impracticable idealist Mazzini, still talking and dreaming of the Roman Republic that never came; and Garibaldi had received an enthusiastic welcome when the freighter he owned put in at a British port for a cargo. Popular feeling was all in favour of Italian, as of Hungarian freedom; but even under Palmerston, England could hardly go to war with Austria to liberate those subject provinces. Paris had indeed picked a quarrel with Vienna which had added a province to the rising kingdom of Piedmont, but Napoleon III had been well paid for his pains by the cession of Nice and Savoy, and there was no Italian territory that England desired.

But no Russell could be indifferent to a plea for civil or religious liberty, and both were at stake in Italy. The new Foreign Secretary was a man of action. He decided at once to reverse the foreign policy of his Conservative predecessors, which had been simple non-intervention and official acceptance of the existing order. A more adventurous note was henceforth to be struck, and the tocsin of freedom was soon to sound.

It was some months, indeed, before Russell understood the true position in Italy. For that, however, he was hardly

to be blamed.   He had had a long private interview with
the Prime Minister of Piedmont at Nice, on his way home
from a trip to Tuscany the year before.   But the astute
Cavour was always ready to economize the truth in the
service of his country, and it is manifest from Russell's
early hesitation when in office that as a retired politician in
opposition he had not been told more than Cavour thought
it good for him to know.

It is clear that Lord John, like most Liberal Englishmen
of the day, thought of the Italian struggle primarily in terms
of constitutional liberty, and only secondarily in terms of
national unity.   Actually the position was the reverse,
though it remained true that unity could not be secured
until liberty was attained.   But it seems evident that Cavour
realized that the sympathies of Englishmen would be more
readily given to a struggle for liberty than unity, and he
stressed the former rather than the latter consideration.

The reticence was wise—at least for Italy.   But the
misapprehension marked a critical weakness in the philosophy of Liberalism, and that weakness, as it happened,
became evident in Russell's subsequent conduct of other
affairs at the Foreign Office.

In any event, the situation in the peninsula was extraordinarily complex, and perhaps only two men in Europe
—the great Cavour and his antagonist Pio Nono at the
Vatican—were adequately informed both of the programme
of the forwards and the plans of the reactionaries.   Apart
from Piedmont, where Cavour was Prime Minister of a new
constitutional State and an ambitious King, there were
three major and several minor allegiances in Italy—the
Austrian provinces in the north, the Papal States in the
middle, and the Kingdom of Naples in the south; and these
three Governments might have been ranked in an ascending
scale of evil.

The Austrians were firm and unsympathetic, but they
understood the business of administration, and they were
seldom wantonly tyrannical unless openly defied.   The
Habsburg Empire governed a large number of communities
with different tongues, creeds, and customs, and in various
stages of culture.   The task was not an easy one, and it

was steadily becoming more difficult as provincial dialects rose into national consciousness. But so far Vienna had not altogether failed.

The Papal States, on the other hand, suffered many of the evils common to all secular autocracies combined with all the evils customary under any ecclesiastical authority. There is no class of men with more excellent qualities than the clergy. But their excellences are best seen in the individual, their defects most conspicuously exhibited in the mass; and since no class of men set authority so high or equity so low, it follows that clerical virtues flourish best in a lay society that is slightly anti-clerical, in the same way that some people feel most energetic in an east wind. A theocracy is in effect simply a double tyranny, that controls soul and body alike.

There was, indeed, some excuse for the political evils that had long afflicted the Papal States. The Popes were concerned with the maintenance of Catholicism all over the world, and their primary business was not their patrimony at home but propaganda abroad. The best men at the Vatican were occupied with the spiritual affairs of the time, and Cardinals who are engaged on high problems of the Immaculate Conception and the mystical Procession of the Holy Ghost can perhaps be forgiven for neglecting the agriculture of the Campagna and paying scant attention to the petty concerns of peasants and fishermen at Ravenna. Be that as it may—and the argument in extenuation is in fact destructive of the whole case for an ecclesiastical temporality—the Vatican had neglected the joint advice of the Powers to carry out political reforms in 1831, and the evil condition of the States of the Church was one of the recognized scandals of Europe.

It might seem incredible that Italy could produce a worse Government than the Temporal Power; but as the sombre imagination of Milton found in the lowest depths of hell a deeper still, the traveller in the peninsula found the abominations of Naples worse than the abuses of Austrian Venice and Papal Rome, and the rule of the native a fouler thing than the rule of foreigners and priests.

There was something almost comic in the Neapolitan

POPE PIUS IX

Army. "Dress them as you like, they will always run away," said the candid King to a son experimenting with a new uniform for the royal troops. But there was nothing comic about the wholesale spying, the leakages from confessional to police, the corrupt courts, the perjured witnesses, the outrageous sentences, the stinking prisons in which men whose worst crime was some liberal opinion were chained in irons to some ruffian whose best defence was that he did not always murder the victims he robbed.

Such was Naples under the infamous Ferdinand, a European with the cruelty of an African, a Christian whose methods might have excited respectful attention in Dahomey or Benin. It may be that the worst indictment of liberty is that few men make good use of the freedom they possess. But it is also true that fewer men still can be trusted with absolute power; and in any challenge to autocracy the names of Ferdinand Bomba and his incompetent son Francis are assured a conspicuous place.

But it was one thing to condemn the governments of Italy; it was quite another to replace them. Palmerston, Russell, and Gladstone, the three leading men in the new British Cabinet, had denounced these evils in despatches, pamphlets, and speeches, and had probably only intensified the abuses they exposed. In Italy itself the Austrians could fight well, as Novara and Solferino proved; the Pope was safe behind a garrison of French bayonets; and if Bomba's army always ran away, he knew that his subjects usually ran quicker.

Against these powers in possession it seemed absurd to set the gentle Mazzini, who wandered across Europe, loved by all but followed by none; the mystical seaman Garibaldi, whose tramp carried cargoes of coal and wine from port to port; and even the rough bluff Victor Emanuel, King of the rising province of Piedmont and the lonely island of Sardinia. Alone these three would have left the memory of an ineffectual rebellion, a gallant guerrilla warfare, and a high ambition; but the hour for once produced the man of genius, and the enthusiasm generated by dreamer and sailor and monarch was supported and controlled and finally directed towards effective action by the coolest brain in Italy.

Cavour was Machiavelli's ideal come to life; the subtle statesman who was alternately supple and stubborn, at once a man of principle and an opportunist who could admit he sometimes played the scoundrel for his country's good. Cavour had none of those doubts about ends justifying means which have distressed smaller and perhaps greater men; so long as the end was the union of Italy the means by which it was attained were of no particular consequence. Political roads are often dirty, and progress sometimes means muddy feet.

It might be England's turn, as a great Liberal power, to help Italy, and Russell had certainly no particular objection to deposing the Pope who had in effect deposed him. But what, after all, was England to do? A large party held —and Russell was inclined to agree—that an independent Kingdom of Naples suited British Mediterranean interests. And although Russell himself would willingly have made war on Pio Nono, it is not for British Foreign Secretaries in this conventional world to invade the Vatican at the head of a Protestant legion. Faced with the intractable problem of the Temporal Power, he did indeed suggest that the Pope should have a life-interest in his dominions, which should then be administered by the State of Piedmont; but this odd proposal, a little reminiscent of Disestablishment strategy at home, fell on inattentive ears, and ruder methods were to cut that knot ten years later.

In other matters he was more vigorous and successful. His objections to the cession of Nice and Savoy, which increased the power of Imperial France, were indeed of no avail; the bargain had been struck and the contract carried out for a consideration, and nothing could be done. But when the question arose whether Tuscany and Modena should be restored to their late rulers by foreign forces his whole soul was roused in protest.

He contended that the policy proposed would be a "return to that system of foreign interference which for upwards of forty years has been the misfortune of Italy and the danger of Europe"; and to the surprise of the

House of Commons and the scandal of Windsor, he quoted the leading Whig case of William III as the example to be followed in Florence and elsewhere.

The Queen was frankly alarmed and angry. Her sympathies were on the whole with Austria and the exiled Grand Dukes; she naturally disliked a policy which she feared might lead from words to war; and the allusion to William III was openly resented.

Tart notes followed: on January 11, 1860, the Foreign Secretary wrote:

> Lord John Russell presents his humble duty to your Majesty; he has just had the honour to receive your Majesty's letter of this date.
>
> Lord John Russell has sent to Lord Palmerston the proposal he humbly submits to your Majesty.
>
> He will therefore only venture to say that the doctrines of the Revolution of 1688, doctrines which were supported by Mr. Fox, Mr. Pitt, the Duke of Wellington, Lord Castlereagh, Mr. Canning, and Lord Grey, can hardly be abandoned in these days by your Majesty's present advisers. According to those doctrines, all power held by Sovereigns may be forfeited by misconduct, and each nation is the judge of its own internal government.
>
> Lord John Russell can hardly be expected to abjure these opinions, or to act in opposition to them.

The sovereign replied as sharply to her masterful Secretary:

> The Queen has received Lord John Russell's note of this day, in which she is not able to find any answer to her letter, or even an allusion to what she had written, viz., that Austria and France being asked to abstain from interference, such an arrangement would be partial and incomplete unless Sardinia (Piedmont) was pledged also to non-interference. The Queen cannot make out what the doctrines of 1688 can have to do with this, or how it would necessitate Lord John to abjure them.

Further exchanges followed, and tempers rose; a month later "the Queen must demand that respect which is due from a Minister to his Sovereign. As the Queen must consider the enclosed letter deficient in it, she thinks Lord

John Russell might probably wish to reconsider it, and asks Lord Palmerston to return it to him with that view."[1]

Lord John would reconsider anything except the principles of 1688 and their application in 1860. The Queen, who must more than once have wished for the easier-going Clarendon,[2] naturally would not go to war with France or Austria for the sake of Italian unity, but short of that she could do little to restrain her impetuous Foreign Secretary. It was not merely that the cause of Italian liberty, happily combined as it was with No Popery, was immensely popular in England—although no doubt public applause was more sweet than ever to Russell after several years of neglect— but he was backed in Cabinet by the two strongest men in the Government. Palmerston and Gladstone could agree on nothing else, but at least they agreed in supporting Russell's encouragement of Italy.

All things come to those who wait, and the fair wind and tide of liberty and success were now with the little man again.

[1] There was perhaps a little family pride behind these exchanges. The Queen frankly admitted that her "family was brought over and placed on the throne of these realms solely to maintain" the Protestant religion. ("Letters of Queen Victoria," Nov. 23, 1866.) But she did not want to be reminded of it too often, and Lord John was well aware that the Russells were among those who were already here and who issued the invitation.

[2] She was grateful for any help in this emergency. Nearly thirty years later, on the death of Lord Halifax, she recalled that he was "always a true and loyal friend and servant, and in 1859 when Lord Russell and Lord Palmerston did, and wanted to do still more, mischief, he was a great and real help."

CHAPTER XXII

THE RIGHT TO REBEL

THE decisive moment for Italy came in the summer of 1860. Cavour had never under-estimated the difficulties in his way, and he knew that the chances even at the best were heavily against success; that was inevitable when the aggressor had such small resources, and three different opponents. But he knew that if he waited the situation might get worse instead of better, and an enterprise that was now admittedly hazardous might become merely foolhardy.

Looking back with a knowledge of subsequent events, we can only be amazed at the extraordinary prescience and precision of his judgment. Cavour was that rare type of man in whom great courage is tempered rather than checked by natural caution, and he was well aware of the grave risks he was running. He did what he could to reduce them to something like manageable proportions, and then acted promptly. He could not have carried out his plans before, because the preparations were not complete. But had he postponed the attack, the risks would have been still greater; more, he himself would have been dead, and without that cool but daring brain it is difficult to see how there could have been a united Italy, for Cavour had no successors.

But the great moment had now come, and Garibaldi was despatched, without official support but with full unofficial approval, on the conquest of Sicily. The campaign that followed is one of the romances of history. The island fell before his magnetic personality and splendid generalship; but Sicily was only an outpost of the Kingdom of Naples, and the Straits of Messina had yet to be crossed.

This was the opportunity for international action against a leader whom the people rightly regarded as a hero, but whom every Government correctly regarded as a mere

brigand. Austria and Naples naturally made diplomatic
representations to Britain and France, the two naval powers
who could prevent Garibaldi from crossing the Straits; and
Napoleon III was inclined to agree.

He had recently warned the Pope that it would be "more
conformable to the true interests of the Holy See to make
the sacrifice" of the Papal States. But the alarm which
this declaration caused among the French Ultramontanes
on whom the Second Empire so largely depended for
support made him fearful of further complications, and more
particularly of an attack by Piedmont or Garibaldi on Pio
Nono, which would involve the French Papal garrison. He
had gained his own throne by revolution, but he held it
—a little insecurely—by conservative and clerical influence;
and it was dangerous to go too far in forwarding an Italian
movement that was being denounced from every French
pulpit as the Revolution against Religion.[1]

He therefore proposed to the British Government that
joint orders should be given from London and Paris to
protect the coast of Calabria against the conquering legion.
Had these orders been issued, the Neapolitan kingdom
would have survived, and the whole plan of Cavour have
crumbled.

Russell was at first disposed to fall in with the French
Emperor's proposal, less apparently on the ground of international law than because he thought the forward movement in Italy premature. Fortunately he was persuaded to
change his opinion, at one of the oddest but most fruitful
diplomatic conferences in English history.

It happened that a gentleman named Lacaita had been
Gladstone's guide and mentor during the visit to Naples
that had resulted in a famous pamphlet against the iniquities
of Bomba's rule. For this heinous offence Lacaita had
been exiled, and England, kinder to him than his own
country, had received him, naturalized him, and knighted
him. The Piedmontese Minister in London now warned
him of the danger that Garibaldi might be stopped at the
Straits by the joint action of England and France, and

[1] Even Newman, in England, characterized the Piedmontese army from
the pulpit as "a band of sacrilegious robbers."

Lacaita, who was ill in bed, at once rose and called at Lord John's private house.

Lacaita was a personal friend of the Russells, and the servant informed him that Lord John was engaged at that very moment with the French Ambassador, and that strict orders had been given that nobody was to be admitted except the Neapolitan minister. Clearly there was not a moment to lose, and Lacaita asked to see Lady John.

She, too, was ill in bed. But Lacaita was a man of resource. Taking a card from his pocket, he wrote on it, "For the love you bear the memory of your father, see me this instant," and sent it up. Lord Minto, her father, had sympathized with Italy and had personally assisted Lacaita; and Lady John was not her father's daughter for nothing.

Disdaining convention, he was shown to her bedroom, hastily explained the position, and persuaded her to send down to her husband the message "Come up at once." Lord John, afraid his wife was suddenly taken worse, excused himself to the French Ambassador, and rushed upstairs. A situation that might have enlivened a farce met the astonished eyes of the Foreign Secretary, but Lacaita quickly explained, and made an impassioned appeal to the friend of liberty. If Russell's principles meant anything, he must not stand in the way of Italian liberation by closing the Straits; if he wanted to be forever loved in Italy, he would permit Garibaldi to pass; if he wished to be forever hated he would protect the rotten fragment of Naples with the British Fleet.

Luckily Russell was always quick at the uptake, and that very hastiness in action which more sober English politicians sometimes condemned was now an asset. "Go to bed," he said to the coughing Lacaita, "and don't be so sure that I am going to sign the treaty yet."

Lacaita's intervention proved decisive. A day or so previously Palmerston had practically promised the French Ambassador to stop Garibaldi. Two days later Russell informed the amazed French Government that "no case had been made out for a departure on their part from their general principle of non-intervention; that the force of Garibaldi was not in itself sufficient to overthrow the

Neapolitan Monarchy. If the Navy, Army, and people of Naples were attached to the King, Garibaldi would be defeated; if, on the contrary, they were disposed to welcome Garibaldi, our interference would be an intervention in the internal affairs of the Neapolitan kingdom. If France chose to interfere alone, we should merely disapprove her course and protest against it. In our opinion the Neapolitans ought to be masters either to reject or to receive Garibaldi." [1]

The lofty superiority of this despatch, which certainly showed no sign of sudden conversion in a sick-room, was sufficient. Napoleon refused to act alone; Garibaldi crossed the Straits, and Naples fell. [2]

Russell had, in effect, intervened decisively by simply refusing to intervene. It was not often that Liberal, Conservative, and Manchester School policy synchronized so happily. But this was not enough, for the crisis was not yet over.

Official Europe was officially shocked at the prospect of revolutionary Piedmont annexing conservative Naples and the greater part of the Papal States that lay between. There seemed a possibility that some untoward intervention might yet wreck Cavour's plan; and Russell, stirred to the depths of his soul by the prospect of tragedy overtaking the work of liberation, determined to take the bull by the horns and leave no doubt whatever as to the British attitude.

On October 27, 1860, he wrote the most famous despatch of his life.

> There appear [he said] to have been two motives which have induced the people of the Roman and Neapolitan States to have joined willingly in the subversion of their Governments.
>
> The first of these was that the Governments of the Pope and

---

[1] Once Russell was convinced, he became a whole-hogger. Sir J. Hudson, who was in a position to know, told Lord Malmesbury that Russell encouraged the King of Piedmont to invade Naples, by asking his aide-de-camp at Richmond whether the King was not afraid to do so. This, said Hudson, was quite enough to send the King anywhere.

[2] The wretched King of Naples was so terrified at Garibaldi's advance that he telegraphed five times in one day for the Pope's blessing. Cardinal Antonelli, perhaps with some suspicion of the value of his wares, sent the last three without troubling to refer to His Holiness.

the King of the Two Sicilies provided so ill for the administration of justice, the protection of personal liberty, and the general welfare of the people, that their subjects looked forward to the overthrow of their rulers as a necessary preliminary to all improvement in their condition.

The second motive was that a conviction had spread, since the year 1848, that the only manner in which the Italians could secure their independence of foreign control was by forming one strong Government for the whole of Italy.

Looking at the question in this view, her Majesty's Government must admit that the Italians themselves are the best judges of their own interests.

That eminent jurist Vattel, when discussing the lawfulness of the assistance given by the United Provinces to the Prince of Orange when he invaded England and overturned the throne of James II, says, "The authority of the Prince of Orange had doubtless an influence on the deliberations of the States-General, but it did not lead them to the commission of an act of injustice; for, when a people from good reasons take up arms against an oppressor, it is but an act of justice and generosity to assist brave men in the defence of their liberties."

Therefore, according to Vattel, the question resolves itself into this: Did the people of Naples and of the Roman States take up arms against their Government for good reasons?

Upon this grave matter, her Majesty's Government hold that the people in question are the best judges of their own affairs. Her Majesty's Government do not feel justified in declaring that the people of Southern Italy had not good reasons for throwing off their allegiance to their former Governments. Her Majesty's Government therefore cannot pretend to blame the King of Sardinia (Piedmont) for assisting them.

It must be admitted, undoubtedly, that the severance of the ties which bind together a sovereign and his subjects is in itself a misfortune. Notions of allegiance become confused; the succession of the throne is disputed; adverse parties threaten the peace of society; rights and pretensions are opposed to each other, and mar the harmony of the State. Yet it must be acknowledged, on the other hand, that the Italian revolution has been conducted with singular temper and forbearance. Such having been the causes and concomitant consequences of the revolution of Italy, her Majesty's Government can see no sufficient grounds for the severe censure with which Austria, Prussia, and Russia have visited the acts of the King of Sardinia. Her Majesty's Government will turn their eyes rather to the gratifying prospect of a people building up the edifice of their liberties, and consolidating the work of their independence amid the sympathies and good wishes of Europe.

The effect of this historic statement was immediate and profound. It could not be other than unpopular at Windsor, and it was read with some trepidation even by Russell's own political associates—the timid Granville and the perhaps jealous Clarendon in fact stigmatized it as "the revolutionary doctrine of Ivan Ivandvitch," and for some little time the rather crude sense of humour of the inner political circle made it the correct thing to allude to the Foreign Secretary as Ivan Ivanovitch.

But the country at large, with its generous love of freedom (and a watchful eye on the Pope) cheered this forcible and direct language to the echo, and it rang through Europe like a challenge. It was as though an electric shock had been sent out from Downing Street to every throne on the Continent.

Cavour had recently been somewhat annoyed by a warning from Russell—stimulated probably by the Queen—that Italy must not go to war with Austria to liberate Venice. But when he read this despatch early in November, 1860, reported the British agent at Turin, "he shouted, rubbed his hands, jumped up, sat down again, then began to think, and when he looked up tears were standing in his eyes. Behind your despatch he saw the Italy of his dreams, the Italy of his hopes, the Italy of his policy."

His agent Villamarina said the despatch was worth a hundred thousand men, and this was more than the usual meaningless hyperbole. For Italy now stood practically alone in Europe. Napoleon III had seriously strained the clerical supports of his throne by telling the Pope he should have set his house in order, and refusing to defend the States of the Church against Piedmont. Austria was only waiting a favourable opportunity to overthrow the whole policy of Cavour by direct attack. Russia lamented that only geography forbade her to defend Naples. The King of Prussia, still hesitating between complete autocracy and a microscopic dose of popular government, would have supported his imperial brethren had they moved. He said openly that the Russell Note was a tough morsel, but at least it destroyed all appetite for revenge on Turin by suggesting that Britain would be found on the side of Italy if any attack were made on Piedmont.[1]

Its effect was therefore precisely what the author intended, and Italy had good reason to be grateful. Whether Cavour's policy was to be regarded as robbery under arms or the natural rights of man, it had succeeded in uniting all Italy except Venice and the city of Rome, which were to be added as opportunity arose during the next ten years; and in that success Lord John Russell had had a real share.

But this famous despatch was entirely characteristic of its author; indeed it was one of the most revealing acts of his life as a confession of political faith.

Lord John Russell, as was said in an earlier chapter, had a simple and direct mind. Incapable of strategy or subtlety, he never beat about the bush, and he said exactly what he meant. It is certainly not the highest type of mind—it cannot compare in range with Gladstone, in richness with Burke, in depth with Morley or Balfour, and it is not in the same class as the discoverers of new truth. It is imitative in artistic appreciation and deficient in scientific understanding, and it leaves large tracts of life and human interest unexplored. It cannot brood over the unknown, because it instinctively goes straight for its limited objective, as in the Edinburgh and Durham Letters and this famous Note; but if its weakness is that it cannot handle a situation like that which Cavour managed with the reserve of truth that Newman commended and Lord John always detested, its strength is that it tells the full truth as it sees it, and is incapable of being misunderstood.

Such a mind, which we like to think of as being peculiarly English—though it is as frequently met in France and Germany—is incomparable for certain types of action. It sets out straight for its particular objective, and gets there because it means to arrive there and nowhere else; in a word, it is stronger in character than intellectual equipment.

[1] A few weeks later the Emperor of Austria tried to arrange a personal interview with Queen Victoria. The British Government nipped this dangerous scheme in the bud.

If it is seen at its worst in a Redvers Buller, who cannot even deceive the enemy in war, it is seen at its best in Russell, when confronted by a tangle of European complications which can be better cut than unravelled.

The doctrine to which Russell appealed in 1860 sprang directly from the Whig Revolution of 1688, and it might also have been fortified with the Declaration of Independence of 1776, which had derived the just powers of governments from the consent of the governed.

"Is it true, Lord John," the Queen is reported to have asked, "that you hold a subject is justified in certain circumstances in disobeying his sovereign?" To which Lord John replied, "Well, speaking to a sovereign of the House of Hanover I can only say that I suppose he is." The retort was both courteous and conclusive, nor does the Queen seem to have been offended, for she never forgot her Whig upbringing or the advantage of a constitutional over an absolute monarchy. Now the whole theory of a constitutional monarchy is necessarily based on contract, written or implied, between Crown and subject, not on any divine right of Kings. And a contract that is broken by the one side may be rescinded by the other.

Few were likely to dispute that doctrine openly at a day when the divine right of kings was regarded as an even greater absurdity than the parallel superstition of apostolic succession. But Russell's confident generalizations had, as usual, exposed rather more surface than was actually necessary to the case, and raised larger issues than were required.

It so happened that three political crises of the first magnitude lay ahead, one in America and two in Europe. All three occurred while Russell was at the Foreign Office; and each was to test from a different angle the validity of a political philosophy that justifies rebellion against the State.

CHAPTER XXIII

THE RIGHT TO SECEDE

HISTORY is occasionally comic, often tragic, and—in spite of Hardy—rarely ironic. But by an odd chance it perpetrated one of its major ironies on Lord John Russell, the least ironic of men.

In October, 1860, the British Foreign Secretary had justified rebellion against constituted authority on the high ground of natural right. In November of that year he received preliminary warning from Lord Lyons, the British representative at Washington, that the Southern States intended to rebel against the constituted authority of the American Union; and since there could be no question of any divine right of kings in a republic, it was evident that the claim to secede must also be founded on natural right.

Here was an awkward practical comment on a recently affirmed theory; a theory, moreover, which Russell had set out without any of those qualifications or limitations of time and place which a more cautious statesman would have inserted.

It would not have been possible for Gladstone, with his different political ancestry, to have written the famous Italian despatch of October 27, 1860. But had he done so, we may be quite sure that some ingenious reservation which the ordinary man would not have noticed would have been introduced, which confined the general argument to the particular event, and could have been triumphantly quoted afterwards to show that it had no possible relevance to any other political event that could ever occur, and more particularly to the event that actually occurred almost immediately after. Russell's mind was too straightforward, too simple, and too direct to do these things; a principle to him was a principle, and that was the end of it. Unluckily, in this difficult world, that is sometimes only the beginning of it.

As between the contemporary cases of the United States and Italy the objective, it is true, was reversed. Naples and Sicily seceded from the Bourbon in order to make a larger Italian union. South Carolina and the rest seceded from Washington in order to make a smaller American Union. But the fundamental rights of the individual are independent of the size of the State. The principle, therefore, was the same in America as in Italy.

Further, if one person is entitled to rebel against constituted authority, any number of persons must be similarly so entitled; for although men are physically and mentally unequal, it is implicit in Russell's theory that they are politically equal, and the natural rights of equal individuals must everywhere be the same.

Moreover, on that doctrine, the right must reside in the individual to contract out of the State, and there can be no contrary coercive right in the State to compel the individual to stay in; for to admit this would manifestly reduce the whole theory to an absurdity.

It follows, then, from Russell's principle, that South Carolina was as much entitled to secede from the American Union as Sicily from the Kingdom of Naples; that Charleston would have been as much entitled to secede from South Carolina as South Carolina from the Union; and that the individual citizen of Charleston would have been as much entitled to secede from Charleston as Charleston was from South Carolina.

Human institutions are not, in fact, built that way, and would not last long if they were. But this problem of rebellion ultimately goes down to the roots of our social and political being, and it is therefore not very surprising that men who agreed on all other subjects disagreed as to the justice of the American Civil War, and men who had previously been content to disagree on all other subjects were vexed to find themselves agreed on this.

Palmerston was not a man who indulged in abstract political theories, and he regarded the American Civil War simply as an unnatural and fratricidal conflict; but as a practical statesman he seems to have thought from the first that the best solution would be a friendly separation of Northern and Southern States.[1]   Cobden, whom he detested as a mere commercial traveller in politics—Cobden had recently suggested to Metternich that Austria should sell Venice for cash to Piedmont—thought the same as Palmerston at the beginning of the American campaign, and rather favoured the Southern States as being Free Traders, whereas the North had mysterious leanings to high Protection.

John Bright, on the other hand, who had never yet differed from Cobden, saw that there was more at stake than a fiscal problem, and was hotly in favour of the North, emancipation of slaves, and reunion.   He was the stronger man of the two, and he succeeded in convincing Cobden.

John Morley, a young Lancashire pacifist and agnostic whose voice was not yet known in politics, held all war to be wrong, but reluctantly admitted that the one cause in history which was right was the cause of the free North against the slave South.   Selborne, a profound Liberal lawyer and ardent High Churchman, who would have hesitated to agree with Morley on any other subject, agreed with him in this, and remarked in the restrained language habitual to him, that "the North were within their rights in resisting dismemberment."

His colleague Gladstone, now almost a Liberal and always, like Selborne, a High Churchman, saw so many issues at stake in the American quarrel that his earlier pronouncements were merely unintelligible.   But when

---

[1] According to Gladstone, in 1862 Palmerston "desired the severance as a diminution of a dangerous power, but prudently held his tongue."   But Gladstone is not quite a safe witness against Palmerston, and Palmerston did not hold his tongue in private letters.

Had he really desired the diminution of America as a dangerous power, he would have urged the recognition of Southern independence on the grounds of high policy, and pressed co-operation with Napoleon III when the latter wished to recognize the Confederates in 1862.   Palmerston was not averse to recognition or Confederate independence, but he regarded it as a matter of current political convenience, not high policy.   There are no indications that he considered the United States a dangerous power.   He would have reserved that compliment to France.

these oracular confusions were resolved, he came down decidedly on the side of the South—to the grave embarrassment of the Government of which he was a member.[1]

The inscrutable Tory Disraeli, wiser in this instance than his rival, kept silence. He neither lectured the North nor hectored the South, and contented himself with the remark that the difficulties of the Washington Government were so great that it was only fair to put a generous interpretation on their actions. On the whole, he seems rather to have favoured the North, but he was well aware that many of his party took the other side, and since the fight was not his fight in any case, discretion was here the better part of Opposition.[2]

There were even family divisions in which father and son had to be content to differ. That robust old Whig the great Duke of Argyll was a hot Northerner; his son Lorne, a convinced Southerner. The old Campbell's wrath kindled at the thought of slavery, the young Campbell's at the thought of compulsory reunion.

It is impossible to understand the British attitude towards the American Civil War unless we realize this background of divergent political theory among statesmen accustomed to thinking out high constitutional problems; and to this must be added a further confusion of the popular mind on other issues of the conflict. The upper classes were inclined to support the South as more aristocratic, the lower to support the North as more democratic. But the middle classes were openly divided.

Slavery, of course, could no longer be tolerated, and this influenced them against the South. They would hardly, indeed, have taken the American statesman Sumner's view that "the rebellion is slavery in arms, revolting, indecent,

[1] The Gladstone family had been connected with the slave trade in the previous generation, but this does not appear to have influenced him at all. He was not alone in his confusion. Carlyle, for instance, remarked that "No war was to me more profoundly foolish looking; neutral am I to a degree." But this simply means that the sage of Chelsea had not troubled to understand the issues; he was too deeply engrossed in the "History of Frederick the Great" to bother about his own times.

[2] Similarly Hartington, among the Liberals, rather favoured the South, but kept quiet because his constituents took the other view.

imperious"; to the middling Englishman the war from this point of view was rather freedom in arms, challenging, chastising, cleansing.

But on the other hand, Liberal individualism was then in the very heyday of its reputation. Men spoke openly of the possibility of the British colonies peacefully seceding from the mother country at no distant date, and of the State as a mere voluntary association of citizens who found it a convenient social form, but a form whose authority was better restricted to those minimum police duties which unhappily could not yet be dispensed with. To men used to thinking along these lines, it was very strong measure for the North to compel the South to return to a Union it had formally repudiated; and the case against coercion seemed even stronger in America than Europe in view of the relatively recent and voluntary nature of the Union, and the notorious fact that a large party within the republic had always emphasized State rights rather than Federal authority.

On the whole, then, at that day the preponderant weight of Liberal popular opinion supported the North on the definite ground of emancipation, but was inclined to agree that the South was as much within its rights in seceding from Washington as the people of Sicily and Naples had been a few months before in withdrawing allegiance from their King.

From this conflict of mind no enthusiastic support could be forthcoming, such as that which had cheered the spectacular crusade of Garibaldi a few months before. Then love of liberty and hatred of the Pope had accidentally united in one stream; now love of liberty was accidentally divided into two streams, the one insisting on the freedom of the States to rebel, the other on the right to freedom of the individuals within the State.

And Liberal popular opinion, it must be remembered, was practically decisive in the country at that time. Actually the Tories were less ardent emancipists than the Liberals, and on that ground inclined to favour the South; on the other hand, they could give no countenance to rebellion, and on that ground were compelled to support the North.

But the Tories were still a divided minority caste, and what they thought did not much matter.[1]

But the conflict divided men within their own parties on still other grounds. While the upper classes admitted that slavery was indefensible, even for aristocrats, the lower classes lamented that the lack of raw cotton from the South meant distress and unemployment; and this was a serious consideration to thousands of good Lancashire men whose sympathies were wholly with the North while their pecuniary interests were entirely with the South.

For once, Bright put sympathy first and trade second, and remained a staunch Northerner throughout; with Gladstone the position was exactly reversed, and it was the suffering of Lancashire from the cotton famine that finally led him to favour the South. But nobody, even among those whose business it was to watch the struggle closely, seems to have realized that the conflict was not merely political and social but economic—a struggle over the transfer of power from agriculture to manufactures, from country to town, from solid to fluid capital, similar to that which had so recently troubled England.

Fortunately Lord John Russell, as Foreign Secretary, had in some ways a simpler task in America than Europe. If there were angry belligerents to deal with, there were fewer covetous and suspicious neutrals. If France tried to fish in troubled waters, as she had done recently in Italy, at any rate Russia, Prussia, and Austria could give the best of all proofs of disinterested honesty—they had nothing to gain or lose whichever side won.

There were likely to be, and in fact there were, many difficult and even critical days ahead. But at least it was not necessary to write despatches to Washington on the rights of man in order to harry Emperors and Pope. The business in hand was simply to keep the British peace and, if and when opportunity offered, to hint willingness to mediate between the contending parties.

---

[1] Lord Derby, the Tory leader, was more concerned with relieving the distress of his native Lancashire than with the rights and wrongs of the contest. Malmesbury, late Tory Foreign Secretary (who had been pro-Austrian and anti-Italian) expressed no opinion, even in his diary.

It must not be overlooked, however, that this attitude of benevolent neutrality implied a positive decision of fundamental importance. In politics the difficulties of friends are the opportunities of rivals, and it would have been easy for England to pay off old scores against the United States in their hour of trouble. Had Britain recognized the independence of the Southern States on the basis of Russell's famous Italian despatch, and supported them with her Fleet,[1] the action could have been defended by a simple reference to the policy of Washington itself in 1812, when the United States had gone to war with England over the rights of neutral trade.

The Northern States could not have obtained a countervailing ally in Europe. Napoleon III was already casting covetous eyes on Mexico and stood to gain by the weakening of both North and South; in any case he could not afford to risk the chance of war with Britain. The new-comer Bismarck had other fish to fry in Central Europe for the next ten years, and Russia was unable to help America for the same geographical reason that had prevented her intervention in Italy.

It was frankly recognized in Britain that alliance with the Confederates meant the end of the United States as a political unit, and much else besides. With British naval and financial backing, the Confederate States could hardly be subdued by Washington. But when peace was made they would be too weak to stand alone. They would therefore probably emerge as a weak Republic economically dependent on Britain as a market for their produce, and politically more or less dependent on the support of the British Government against the rival power at Washington.

The latter, it is true, would probably attempt to make good the loss of the South by expansion in the North, and Canada might be invaded by Yankee armies. The outcome of that adventure no man could foresee, but one thing was certain, if such a policy were seriously undertaken

---

[1] British diplomacy counted for little in Continental Europe during these years, as we shall see in subsequent chapters, because of the smallness of the army. It would have counted for much in America, because sea-power came into play.

in London. It meant not merely a long and exhausting war between Britain and America, but an uneasy peace after the war, that would be worse than war itself. It meant the end for all time of trust and goodwill between two peoples that sprang from the same common stock, acknowledged the same common law, and spoke the same common tongue. The political gain would need to be great indeed to compensate for a disaster of that magnitude.

It is to the honour of the British Government that the Cabinet did not for a moment consider such a policy. England had, on the whole, been more friendly to the United States than the United States to England—forty years before, Castlereagh had remarked that we could have had war by raising a finger over the Oregon affair, but the cry of "Fifty-four forty or fight" was American, not British, and since Aberdeen had settled that matter on the very day the Peel Government fell, there had been no open sore —and there was no disposition whatever to take advantage of what was commonly felt almost as a domestic calamity.

Palmerston as Prime Minister had indeed no particular prejudice against war on general principles, and he could not resist improving the present occasion by pointing out that "man is a fighting and quarrelling animal, and republics where the masses govern are far more quarrelsome and far more addicted to fighting than monarchies which are governed by comparatively few persons." But the position of England, as he saw it, was to play the judicious bottle-holder to the American combatants, and his only objection to Russell's desire to mediate between them was the common-sense feeling that until both sides had been well-blooded the peace-maker would have his trouble for nothing.

Russell held graver but more generous language than his chief. Before the war broke out, he rebuked some foolish person who had rejoiced in the House of Commons at the "bursting of the American bubble," and remarked, in words that obviously came from the heart, that the joy he had recently felt at the overthrow of Italian despotism was counterbalanced by pain at the fratricidal conflict of free institutions across the Atlantic. The trouble, he observed, "had arisen from that accursed institution of slavery; I cannot but recollect that, with our great and glorious institutions, we gave them that curse, and that ours were the hands from which they received that fatal gift of the poisoned garment which was flung around them from the first hour of their establishment. Therefore I do not think it just or seemly that there should be among us anything like exultation at their discord, and still less that we should reproach them with an evil for the origin of which we are ourselves to blame."

This was nobly and consistently spoken, and of itself more than sufficient to show on which side Russell's instinctive sympathies lay. But the Civil War was not one which he could follow with the enthusiastic assurance that the right would conquer. In Italy he had seen the light of liberty triumphant, and it had been as grateful to his eyes as the vision of Jerusalem Delivered to Torquato Tasso. But that light was now split and sundered as though it had passed through a prism; for if the North stood for the freedom of man, the South stood for the freedom of the State.

What is to be done when these tragic contradictions thrust themselves forward to be answered? The Englishman in Russell could not conceal the feelings of a lifetime when slavery was mentioned, the Whig recognized frankly that in another aspect the struggle was for independence on one side and for empire on the other. Between those conflicting ideals the old Whig was more likely to be attracted by the call of independence than empire, and the old Englishman who had sat in a Cabinet that had freed the West Indian slaves was more likely to be attracted by the call of emancipation than secession.

The conflict of ideals is clearly exhibited in Russell's American policy. Before the war started the old Englishman was to the fore, with his generous reference to slavery. Then the old Whig came to the front, with his belief in independence. Finally the old Englishman prevailed, and Gladstone noted that "Russell rather turned tail"; the recognition of independence was postponed, and emancipation won.

Actually, then, Russell was well equipped to hold to

the strict and strait path of neutrality which was required of him as Foreign Secretary, since his conscience could give neither side his full and free support. But in the circumstances of the day, it seemed likely that neutrality would soon become almost impossible.

The Washington Government naturally urged the British authorities not to recognize the Confederate States, or to deal with their agents. The inference was plain that the Federals regarded the Confederates as rebels without rights rather than seceders. They were to be treated like the Hungarian rebels against Austria twelve years before, who had no official position in foreign countries save as private citizens, or political refugees.

A Conservative Government would very likely have agreed almost at once, since Conservatives normally hold rather high doctrine as to the unity and authority of the State. Another Liberal Government might possibly have conceded the point, albeit reluctantly; for it had been admitted by sound Liberals that international comity forbade the official recognition of the Hungarian rebel Kossuth in England. The ordinary Liberal would no doubt have pointed out that the case of a federal State seceding from a federal Unit was not on all fours with a subject province rising in arms against an autocratic Empire which has subdued it by force; and it is in fact difficult to argue that an association of States which has been voluntarily agreed should not be as voluntarily determined. But with a little grumbling about the natural rights of man, the ordinary Liberal follower of the ordinary Liberal Government would probably have acquiesced in the technically correct official attitude.

Lord John Russell was, however, of all men in the world the most awkwardly placed to reply to such a request. It was notorious that the British Government of which he had been Prime Minister ten years before had refused to receive Kossuth, and that Russell had had high words with Palmerston at the bare possibility of the Hungarian refugee crossing Palmerston's private doorstep. But it was equally notorious that the British Government of which he was now Foreign Secretary had encouraged rebellion less than a year before in Naples and Sicily, and that it would not have been seriously perturbed had the immediate subjects of the Pope thrown off both their spiritual and temporal allegiance.

Lord John had not, indeed, either received or refused to receive Mazzini or Garibaldi, and had not technically recognized them. But he had written a famous despatch which had sent shudders down the spine of every court in Europe; and that despatch in effect supported not only Garibaldi but rebellion as rebellion, for it made the people and not the Government over them the judge of the rightness of their cause. What was sauce for the Neapolitan goose was equally sauce for the Confederate gander.

The embarrassments which afflict generous minds are no doubt to be preferred in retrospect to the cold detachment of the pure egoist and the merely selfish statesman. But there are moments when the best of us would give a good deal to be as unprincipled as the ungodly; and although Russell gave no outward sign of annoyance, he would not have been human had he not cursed the ill-luck which made South Carolina follow Sicily within a year.

Faced by this difficulty, he naturally played for time, and became oracular and obscure. At the start he merely told the American Minister in London that it was neither the wish nor the intention of the British Government "to pronounce any judgment on the causes which had induced some of the United States to secede from the rest. Whether, as to the past, those States had reason to complain that the terms of the compact of union had not been observed, or whether they had reason to apprehend that, for the future, justice would not be done them, were questions upon which Her Majesty's Government did not pretend to decide. They had seen in the United States a free and prosperous community, with which they had been happy to maintain the most happy and amicable relations. Now that a secession had taken place, they were in no hurry to recognize the separation as complete and final. But, on the other hand, I could not bind Her Majesty's Government, nor tell how and when circumstances might arise which would make a decision necessary;

that I must therefore decline to enter into any further discussion at the present moment, and could only assure him of our regret at the events which had recently occurred."

Thus Russell on April 6, 1861; the author of the Italian despatch could hardly have said less, the Foreign Secretary could hardly have said more at the moment, and plus and minus in combination amounted to exactly nothing. But there are occasions when wise diplomacy intentionally says nothing, and this was emphatically one of them.

The truth is that even on the spot the position was extraordinarily obscure, and it was practically impossible for anyone in London to form an accurate judgment. Russell had never visited America, but James Buchanan, the outgoing President, was well known in England, and Buchanan had committed himself to the remarkable proposition that while no State had a right to secede from the Union, no State had a right to force another to stay in. Russell in his simple and straightforward way may well have thought that Buchanan was not a metaphysical Scotsman and Presbyterian for nothing. But Buchanan's time was now up, and of the incoming President Lord John knew little save that his name was Abraham Lincoln, that this suggested a background of English ancestry—the Lincolns were said to be originally East Anglians from Norwich—and that he was actually a small-town lawyer who had been born in Kentucky.

The almost mystical halo that has gathered round the martyred name of Lincoln wherever English is spoken makes it difficult for us to put ourselves back to the time when this gaunt genius of the common people was less famous than Polk or Zachary Taylor. The American Presidents since Andrew Jackson had been ordinary politicians of no particular weight or consequence, and that splendid office, which had itself been dignified by the great men who had founded the Republic, seemed in process of becoming as superior to its occupants as the Papacy to the immediate successors of St. Peter.

All that was soon to change, but at the start there was nothing to distinguish the new occupant of the White House from his immediate predecessors. His unassuming

ways made no impression on visitors; and Lord Hartington, then on a visit to America, wrote to his father the
Duke of Devonshire after a talk with Lincoln that he seemed
"a very well-meaning sort of a man, but almost everyone
says about as fit for his position as a fire-shovel. I should
suppose that Seward did very much as he liked with him."

This was clearly the current impression in Washington,
and for some little time there was nothing to modify it.
The new President's inaugural message merely exhorted
the seceding States to return to their allegiance, and his
early speeches showed that he, like Seward, his Secretary
of State, still thought there was a chance that the ruptured
Union could be restored without war. Actually the crisis
had not yet come to a head, and Lincoln had to feel his
way towards a policy in a situation he did not yet understand.

But the Lincoln legend grew very slowly, and the slightly
theatrical swagger of Jefferson Davis in the Confederate
camp quite eclipsed the homely caution and often foolish
language of the greater man. In any case, after the recent
examples of Kossuth, Mazzini, and Garibaldi, the age saw
its hero naturally as rebel, and was more inclined to worship
the man who hurled defiance at the State than the man
who was merely trying to keep it together. To many
Europeans of the time Lincoln must have looked very much
like an ineffectual American Metternich who had arrived
at Washington a little too late.

But unknown to all, the tide was now beginning to turn
against secessionist and revolutionary movements all the
world over, and to favour the cohesionist and unionist
impulse that binds men into States and Empires. The
hour of the picturesque rebel, leading a volunteer army and
proclaiming his independence solemnly before heaven, was
nearly at an end, and Jefferson Davis was to fail where
Garibaldi had succeeded. The day of the constructive or
at least conservative statesman was again at hand, and
Lincoln was soon to be followed by Bismarck and the
federalists of Canada, Australia, and South Africa in
emphasizing the unity and order of society rather than the
liberty of man to rebel.

The American Civil War in effect rescinded the Declaration of Independence, and turned back the tide of revolution which had flowed with such momentous results for Europe and the world since Philadelphia first unloosed it eighty years before.   On the day that the White House at Washington decided to fight secession till it was suppressed, the full Liberal doctrine of the freedom of the individual was challenged by the authority of the State, and for more than half a century ahead the State was to win.

CHAPTER XXIV

THE *TRENT* CRISIS

WITH Lincoln's advent to the White House the constitutional riddle of Buchanan was presently answered by war; and within a month of Russell's non-committal words to the retiring American Minister in London, the position had so far developed that the British Government formally recognized the Confederate States as belligerents. The announcement was made on May 13, 1861, and it was obviously timed to coincide with the arrival of the new Federal Minister, a member of the famous Adams family, who arrived in London the same day.

The recognition of the enemy, contrary to the expressed request of the North, at once provoked the most bitter feelings at Washington. It was assumed, of course, that the Confederate agents who were known to be in London had been successful in winning over the British Government to their side. And it was supposed that recognition of the Southern States as belligerents was merely a pre-liminary to formal recognition of their independence—a step which it was suspected would shortly be followed by assistance or even alliance, open or concealed.

For that belief there was not in fact the slightest justifi-cation, but we can hardly be surprised that Washington anticipated the worst consequences from the British Government's action. The gulf that separates the mere rebel from the recognized belligerent is a broad one. But the line between the recognition of a belligerent and the recog-nition of his independence is a very thin one indeed. It exists; but its existence in international politics may be compared to that of the ether in physical science, in that it is more evident in theory than in practical fact.[1]

[1] The commonsense King of the Belgians held that recognition of belliger-ent right automatically implied recognition of independence, "as no fraction

The reasons for Lord John Russell's actions are not, however, far to seek.

It is, in the first place, more convenient for a neutral Government to deal with two recognized belligerents than with a State divided against itself. And this is particularly the case where the line of division between the combatants is sharply geographical, and where the neutral's own subjects have long had large commercial dealings with both parties.

It is, in the second place, obvious that there comes a point at which rebellion against constituted authority is so extensive, and so homogeneous, as to be something more than the revolt of a discontented minority; it must then be regarded as a catastrophic scission of the whole unit. It may be difficult, and indeed impossible, to fix the precise point at which a local rising becomes a general civil war —a Liberal like Russell would be inclined to fix the point rather lower than a High Tory—but of the fact there can be no doubt whatever. Eighty years before the Americans had been justly offended because the British regarded General Washington as a rebel. But the revolt of the colonies against Britain was certainly not more impressively united than the revolt of the Southern States against the North.

But it is clear, in the third place, that almost from the first the British Government and probably most of the British people—including many of those who actually favoured the North—assumed that the Confederates would eventually establish their independence. It happened that

of States could make war on the remainder in this regular way without being independent." ("Letters Queen Victoria," Nov. 20, 1862.)

But the lawyers argued differently. Selborne (then Roundell Palmer, British Solicitor-General) notes that the United States "were offended at our recognition of the Confederates as belligerents, and complained much and often of it as an unfriendly act; though on what other footing they could have maintained a blockade of the Southern ports, visited and searched British merchant ships at sea, and seized British vessels for contraband as breach of blockade, was not explained."

The reasoning is legally conclusive. But recognition of a belligerent in fact gives him a status of independence before the world which the mere rebel cannot possess. The thing is unavoidable, but so also is the annoyance of the State whose rebels are recognized.

they were wrong, but they could only judge from the
evidence before them, and from that evidence the idea that
the Confederates would make good their secession at least
appeared to be fully justified during the first two years of
war.

Russell seems to have assumed from the start until nearly
the end that the Confederates would succeed. In March,
1862, he thought the war would be settled in three months;
which meant, in the then condition of affairs, that he
expected the Washington Government to recognize the
independence of the South. Even as late as 1864 he
remarked that if the result of the war were the restoration
of the Union, it would be to him most unexpected.

Judging the position as he did from a distance, and
without previous personal knowledge, we can hardly be
surprised at his conclusion. The new American Minister,
who was soon a welcome if somewhat silent guest at most
of the great houses, sensed the feeling as general through
English society[1]; and he knew that, in spite of Russell's
sincere sympathy with the North in its struggle against
slavery, the Foreign Secretary's own Whig principles as
proclaimed in the famous Italian note must incline him
more than a little to the independent and secessionist
standpoint proclaimed by the South.

The new Minister seems to have trusted Russell as a
man and to have distrusted Palmerston. He complained,
indeed, that Lord John ignored him, a little forgetful, perhaps, that the British Foreign Secretary was also concerned
with France, Italy, Denmark, and Poland in these years.
Mr. Charles Francis Adams, who had all the force of character which seemed hereditary in that famous family, was
rather a difficult person to ignore successfully. But Russell
was torn between the two rival freedoms and the two rival
compulsions of North and South, and for the first time in
his life he must have been conscious of the inadequacy of
orthodox Whig doctrine to solve this dilemma. It is unpleasant to discover a weakness in the political creed that

[1] It shows clearly enough in a letter from the Queen to Palmerston (May
30, 1861), in which she speaks naturally of "the remnant of the United
States."

was accepted without question almost with one's mother's milk, and particularly unpleasant when these things happen at nearer seventy than sixty. It is probable, therefore, that Russell did not encourage Mr. Adams to call on him more than was actually necessary.

However that may be, troubles now came thick and fast. There followed almost at once a whole crop of difficulties with Washington.

On May 1, before the recognition of the Confederates, the British Minister at the Federal capital had been warned by Seward, United States Secretary of State, that *Peerless*, an iron steamer, had been sold to the *de facto* Southern Government, and was on her way out to Lake Ontario as a privateer. It was believed she flew the British flag and that her papers were in order, but Seward had instructed the American naval officers to seize her "under any flag, and with any papers." Lord Lyons, the British Minister, persuaded him to give way on pledging himself solemnly that, if the facts were as stated, full satisfaction should be given by London. But although this trouble was smoothed over, the American Secretary continued to use threatening language, apparently in the hope of overawing such powerful neutrals as Britain and France.

This was hardly a hopeful beginning. Cobden, whose judgment of persons was often better than his judgment of principles, remarked that Seward was simply an American Palmerston, who talked a similar kind of bunkum. It happened that Cobden was better acquainted with America and important Americans than most Englishmen of the time, and allowing for the fact that Seward was in a desperately difficult position, there seems to have been some truth in his explanation. (It would have been truer still to say that all statesmen used more provocative language for less reason then than now. International manners have improved, if international morals have not.)

But this was by no means a full explanation. Lord Lyons, on the spot, was profoundly disturbed, not merely by the language of Seward but by the temper of Congress, and he warned Russell that a sudden declaration of war against England was by no means impossible. To the cool heads of neutrals this must have seemed a crowning folly, for it would obviously have made the reunion of the United States not merely difficult but practically impossible; but when a nation is fighting for its life it sometimes throws caution to the winds, and precipitates the very catastrophe it most wishes to prevent.

Fortunately it was not so in this case. But the escape was a narrow one. It happened that the Confederates appointed two gentlemen, Mason and Slidell, to represent their case with the British and French Governments, and these agents were arrested by a Federal warship, while proceeding to Europe on the British vessel *Trent.*

The contingency had already been considered by the British law officers, who held that a foreign warship falling in with a neutral steamer, had the right to board her, open her mail bags, examine their contents,[1] and if the steamer were carrying despatches, carry her to one of the warship's home ports for adjudication. They maintained, however, that there was no right to arrest passengers, who might and in fact ought to be disembarked at some convenient port before the captured vessel was interned for adjudication.

The Americans, then, in the language of the General Confession, had done those things they ought not to have done, and left undone the things they ought to have done. It is true that they may reasonably have thought that the British interpretation of international sea law damned the things they were inclined to, and passed the sins they had no mind to. But the British authorities, who were historically more accustomed to the rôle of belligerents than neutrals, were not likely to strain the custom of the seas against belligerents in order to make out a special case which might subsequently be quoted against themselves, and it was never seriously contended that the opinion was unfair.

---

[1] Selborne was doubtful of the right to examine mails, on the ground that the ship's officers could not know the contents of the mail-bags. The two other British law officers thought there could be no limit set to the captor's right to examine. The question did not arise over the *Trent* affair, but it came up over the seizure of the *Peterhoff* two years later.

The American Minister in London realized the seriousness of the position better than his superiors at Washington, and at once assured Palmerston that the Federal ship had orders not to meddle with any vessel under a foreign flag.

He understood that the offending Captain Wilkes had come to intercept *Nashville*, a Confederate ship in which it was thought the envoys might have booked their passage, and had taken the law into his own hands. This seemed intrinsically probable, since Wilkes had told Mrs. and Miss Slidell, who were already in London, that he was acting on his own responsibility, without instructions from Washington; and this evidence was on the face of it more likely to be true than the report, which also reached Downing Street, that the seizure of the Confederate envoys had been discussed in Cabinet, and determined on with the full knowledge that it might lead to war with England.

In that event France was to be invited to join the Northern States as an ally, Quebec being used as bait. The scheme was a little crude, for Napoleon was now thinking more about Mexico than Canada, and more about Prussia than either; but an American attack on Canada was by no means impossible—some raiding parties in fact crossed the frontier from time to time—and as a precautionary measure a contingent of the Guards was sent up the St. Lawrence.

Meanwhile Russell drafted a despatch which demanded the release of the Confederate envoys, and an apology or expression of regret, failing which Lyons was to leave Washington within seven days. Gladstone, who had been generally in agreement with Palmerston and Russell on their Italian policy, thought this too severe, and wisely urged that we should hear what the Washington Government had to say before withdrawing the British representative; but he was overruled in Cabinet.

It was a weakness of that day—and particularly of Palmerston and Russell—to use strong language first and think about it afterwards. A long price had yet to be paid for that most foolish of all habits, but luckily in this case there was time for second thoughts.

It happened that Gladstone dined at Windsor that night.

A LIKELY STORY

CAPTAIN JONATHAN, F.N.: "Jist look'd in to see if thar's any rebels he·arr."

The conversation naturally included the *Trent* crisis, and Gladstone was the last man in the world to conceal his opinion either at Court or anywhere else. The next day another Cabinet was held, and Gladstone so far succeeded that the draft despatch was softened and abridged; but when it was sent to Windsor it was still considered too sharp in tone, and the Prince Consort, already on the alert through Gladstone's warning, suggested still further alterations.

These were willingly accepted, for on reflection Palmerston had come round to Gladstone's point of view; and in the end Russell told Lyons to say nothing about leaving Washington, and professed himself "willing to believe that the United States officer who committed the aggression was not acting in compliance with any authority from his Government, or that if he felt himself so authorized, he greatly misunderstood the instructions which he had received."

The sword had now become the olive-branch. As the action of Captain Wilkes had been officially approved by the Naval Secretary at Washington, and he had been thanked by the House of Representatives, Russell's "willingness to believe" was stretched to a point which he would have been the first to condemn in a Puseyite; but as a soft answer turneth away wrath, a blind eye is occasionally the most useful organ of diplomacy.

Lyons received the despatch at Washington on December 18. It was formally read to Seward on the 23rd; and on Christmas Day the Federal Cabinet met to consider the matter. Sumner, who had many friends in England, had been invited to attend, and he read aloud long letters which he had received from Cobden and Bright. Neither could by any stretch of the imagination be considered jingoes, and neither had a high opinion of Palmerston, but in the present instance both were agreed.

Cobden admitted that the Americans might be right in law, but insisted they were wrong in policy; things were said and done on their side, he declared, that made it very difficult for the advocate of peace in England to keep the field, and on the whole he did not blame the British Government or think the nation had behaved badly in view of the terrible loss of trade.[1]

Bright was even more emphatic. "At all hazards," he wrote, "you must not let this matter grow to a war with England. Even if you are right, and we are wrong, war will be fatal to your idea of restoring the Union. I implore you not, on any feeling that nothing can be conceded, and that England is arrogant and seeking a quarrel, to play the game of every enemy of your country."

A French despatch to the same effect was also read; and it must now have appeared that the bait of Quebec was less likely to tempt the Second Empire than had been supposed. But the question of peace or war still hung in the balance. Seward and Sumner were in favour of giving up the Confederate agents; the dogged and slow-moving Lincoln hesitated.

At last he consented, and the issue was saved. But had Russell's original despatch been sent, it seems certain, or almost certain, that the result would have been different.

This was the last, and perhaps the greatest, of the many services which the much misunderstood Prince Consort rendered his adopted country. He was already suffering from the disease of which he died, and ten days before the despatch he had amended reached Washington, the Queen was a widow. It is curious to reflect that in the matter of Italian unity, where he was well informed, his policy would have been wrong, whereas Russell was right; but in the matter of American unity, where he cannot have been particularly well informed, his policy was right, whereas Russell was wrong.

The Prince Consort may have been right in this matter because he realized that peace at this juncture was more important than prestige; or he may have been right simply because Gladstone aroused his old distrust of Palmerston and provocation. Our business, however, is not with the

---

[1] The British public appears to have kept its head very well. When the Confederate agents were eventually released, and landed at Southampton, Malmesbury noted in his diary that they were received with complete indifference.

Prince Consort but with Russell; and here the question is: Why was Russell wrong?

It would be easy to dismiss the problem with the simple supposition that he did not like Americans, or did not understand them, or that the English aristocrat despised the Yankee democrat. Unfortunately for the first of these assumptions, there is no evidence whatever that he disliked Americans, although there is a letter from him, in 1846, in which he deplored the fact that the Americans seemed at that moment possessed of a "rage of hostility" against the British. Unfortunately for the second assumption, Americans were recognizably human beings, and Russell was a very human individual, who understood most people reasonably well except Catholics, Puseyites, and Lord Aberdeen. And unfortunately for the third assumption, it was Palmerston and not Russell who had remarked a few years before that some of the American representatives in London hardly came out of the top drawer of society; but Russell had to do with one of the famous Adams family as United States Minister, and the whole world knew that the cream of republican Boston was at least as aristocratic as the most exclusive Whig.

The truth, I think, lies deeper. It was not that Russell disliked or misunderstood Americans, but that his political philosophy failed to understand the deeper issues underlying the American Civil War. And this failure on his part is worth probing, because it is fundamental to his whole attitude towards life.

It is the fact that he regarded the Italian struggle as being a war of liberty. But liberty was in fact only incidental, the canvas on which the picture was painted; actually the Italian struggle was a war for unity. It was the same with America; he was sound, as every Englishman was, on the question of liberating the slaves, but he never quite understood that, underlying the slavery issue, was the demand for restoration of unity.

No man can rise above his first principles, and while Russell could find liberty written large in the Whig doctrine of 1688, there was nothing there of national unity. There was no need for it in the England which dismissed

James II; for political creeds are the opposite of religious creeds in this, that they are silent on agreed doctrines, and only recite points on which parties disagree.

This is, I submit, the key to the missing word in Russell's Whig philosophy. He emphasized the freedom of the individual, and it was necessary to do so. But he forgot that man, by the mere fact of sexual division, cannot exist as an individual simply because he cannot propagate the species as an individual; and therefore man is fundamentally not an individual, but part of a social organism. And this need for unity of action with his fellows is stronger and more constant and more permanent than that other imperative need of the individual to stand alone. The former is felt by the many, the latter only by the few.

And of the mystical feeling of corporate union which underlies a nation, a Church, and even a school or a trade union, and gives it cohesion and strength, the Whigs had therefore no conception; nor could they understand the passionate devotion with which men would follow such a cause, and die happily that it might live. A few rare spirits here and there have sacrificed themselves for liberty; but thousands of men in all ages have given themselves and their children for their country.

The Whigs, in fact, regarded liberty as an end, whereas it is only a means—the means whereby men select or modify the type of society and social organism in which they do their life-work. They knew it was the oxygen without which men cannot live. But they were apt to forget that oxygen makes men hungry for more solid food.

Now Russell was the typical Whig, and he could never understand this. He worshipped at the Whig altar of liberty; but even in the country where liberty was more highly prized than anywhere else in the world, the Whigs were generally split, and the Tories generally united. He worshipped at the Whig altar of toleration, which is the religious form of liberty, and perhaps even more necessary than civil liberty—because the Church punishes opinions, whereas the State only punishes actions—but even in the country where toleration was more prized than anywhere else in the world, the Church strove for unity at the price

of exclusion, and regarded him as an enemy because he
strove to give it comprehensiveness at the price of doctrine.

He worshipped at the Whig altar of popular right to
choose the Government one prefers, and he could have
justified this doctrine by the Declaration of Independence
and a reference to Jefferson and the States' Rights school.
But he did not understand that when it came to the point,
the majority of Americans were willing to forget the States
and remember the Union.

The perfect Whig could not have done so. But the
Americans, like other men, were only perfect Whigs when
they chose to rebel; and when it came to repressing rebellion, they made very passable Tories.

CHAPTER XXV

THE ALABAMA

IN the spring of 1862 Russell thought the American Civil War would be over in three months—sufficient proof that he expected the South to win. He was probably misled, not only by his feeling that independence was the natural result of secession, but also by the false analogy of recent European campaigns, which had mostly been short; but as the year wore on, and reports came in of the determined spirit at Washington, it became necessary to revise that opinion.

After a time it was evident that one side or the other would be fought to a standstill, and while Napoleon III took advantage of the opportunity to interfere in Mexico —an apparently promising but ultimately disastrous adventure which Russell refused to countenance—the British Cabinet began to consider the possibility of mediation between the belligerents.

It is proverbial that good offices of this kind are apt to be misconstrued and resented by both parties. But in the present case the position was particularly delicate, for the military advantage lay so far with the South, and the only possible terms at that time were that the North should recognize the independence of the seceding States. But this was practically the point at issue; and the North, though slow to act—and at first incompetent in action— was certainly not beaten.

The three leading members of the British Government, however, were agreed that, providing France and Russia would unite in joint representations, proposals should be made to both North and South for an armistice; and if these were accepted, negotiations for separation should be begun. If both declined, Palmerston assumed that Europe would acknowledge the independence of the South.

Some suspicious Americans seem afterwards to have regarded the whole project of mediation as a conspiracy to wreck the United States, and every scrap of evidence that could be discovered was strained to fit that hypothesis. But the facts will not support the theory.[1]

It was assumed in England that the United States was already wrecked, and nobody conspires to achieve a *fait accompli.* Had any such idea been in contemplation, the *Trent* crisis would have furnished the occasion, but Gladstone did his utmost to smooth that difficult passage; and the idea of intervention six months later originated with Gladstone, who was impressed not only with the victories of the South but by the suffering of Lancashire in the cotton famine.

Palmerston for once agreed with him, and Russell—whose first principles made him lukewarm on union, and who had long thought the South must win—did not dissent. "I agree with you," he wrote on September 17, "that the time is come for offering mediation to the United States Government, with a view to the recognition of the independence of the Confederates. I agree further, that in the case of failure, we ought ourselves to recognize the Southern States as an independent State."

This was the critical moment, for we know now that Washington would not have tolerated mediation, and war must almost certainly have followed. But the plan, as things fell out, was ruined by Gladstone's own eagerness, and his personal indiscretion killed the proposal before it was born.

It happened that Gladstone had to make a speech at Newcastle, and he appears to have thought it would be wise to prepare the ground for mediation by some public reference to the conflict in America. The business was in any event a delicate one, and to be occult without being obscure was a difficult art that Gladstone never mastered.

[1] In the "Education of Henry Adams," Russell is definitely charged with the "attempt to break up the Union." The truth is that Russell thought the Union already broken by its own act. His view was always clear and direct, and the evidence that the United States was not united was sufficient for him, quite apart from his Whig doctrine of the right to rebel.

He meditated his words carefully in advance, but in this case he was neither occult nor obscure.

The next morning the world read with astonishment that in the opinion of the Chancellor of the Exechequer "the Northern States have not yet drunk of the cup—they are still trying to hold it far from their lips—which all the rest of the world see they nevertheless must drink of. We may have our own opinions about slavery; we may be for or against the South; but there is no doubt that Jefferson Davis and the leaders of the South have made an army; they are making, it appears, a navy; and they have made what is more than either, they have made a nation."[1]

The matter was not improved by one of those oracular explanations which had long since made the straightforward if stupid Croker accuse Gladstone of a jesuitical mind, and which gave the plain man cause to blaspheme. It seemed certain that such language could not have been held without the concurrence of the Cabinet, and if so, it portended British recognition of the independence of the South, and war with the North. The American Minister naturally read the speech in that sense, and confided to his diary that his stay in England was likely to be short.

A country which worships oratory has to pay for occasional slips of the tongue. This was rather more than a slip of the tongue, for even had there been any chance of successful mediation, the publicity of the Newcastle speech would have ruined it; but Russell was always a generous colleague—he had cause to remember one or two indiscretions of his own—and in writing to Gladstone a day or two later he contented himself with the remark that "recognition would seem to follow, and for that step I think the Cabinet is not prepared."

The Cabinet in fact was divided. Russell had consented to try Gladstone's idea, but he had not been deeply con-

---

[1] It has been suggested that in the triumphant atmosphere of a great banquet he said more than he intended. Such things happen, but in this case the evidence is clear that he prepared his speech in advance. It is odd he should not have realized that offers of mediation are not merely made privately, but usually informally, in the first instance, to ascertain if they are welcome.

cerned in it. His common sense now assured him that its author had defeated his own chances, but he was not deeply depressed by it.

When the American Minister dropped a hint that he might have to think of packing his carpet-bag, the Foreign Secretary showed momentary embarrassment, and then said frankly that the British Government regretted the speech, and that the policy of the Cabinet was to adhere to a strict neutrality, and to leave the struggle to settle itself.

This would not have been true a week before, but it was now in fact true. Adams was mollified, but the damage—if there was any damage—was done. There could be no more talk of mediation, and from that time relations between London and Washington, which had been much improved since the *Trent* affair, were once more, in the technical language of diplomacy, correct rather than friendly. It is an irony of politics, however, that they would certainly have been worse still had Gladstone been more discreet; for in that event a doubting Cabinet would probably have advised Washington that in the opinion of Europe, the time had come to cease a useless struggle.

Four months later Napoleon III, who was definitely anti-North, again suggested a project of mediation. Russell and Palmerston both agreed with him that the war ought to cease, but both distrusted the Emperor, both realized that intervention was now useless, and to Gladstone's disappointment, neither would act.

It was clear that the British Government would do nothing to assist the South. But it was equally clear that its leading members had no belief in the success of the North.

And now another source of difficulties arose. The combatants needed munitions and supplies, and ordered equipment and transport in Europe. England was suffering far too heavily from loss of normal trade to refuse this abnormal business, but it was recognized from the first that it needed careful watching, and when the Confederate States began to contract for warships to be built on the Mersey and Clyde, the British Government promptly became alert. Jefferson Davis might, in Gladstone's phrase, be making a navy, but if it were established that Britain was building it for him, then Adams would begin to pack his carpet-bag in earnest.

The position of the British Government was not, it is true, an easy one. There were many great shipbuilding yards in the north of England, and thousands of tons of shipping were normally under construction for ordinary purposes of trade. If any warships were being built it was certain that great secrecy would be maintained by the contractors, and it was quite impossible for Government officials to inspect every vessel being built in every yard at every stage of her construction. As it was, the Federal agents in England were constantly reporting suspicious cases, but when these were examined, they were mostly found to be innocent freighters.

There was, however, another difficulty in the fact that the law only took cognizance of ships capable of offensive action when they left British waters; it could not deal with an unarmed vessel built in British yards that was proceeding to a foreign port for armaments and munitions. The world has seen many an army that cannot fight. But British law had some excuse for holding that a warship which could not fight was a contradiction in terms.[1]

Actually six vessels were built in British waters to Confederate order as warships. Three were duly seized by the British authorities before they got away. One was seized, tried, acquitted and released; it became a Confederate cruiser, but did little damage. The remaining two became famous.

The *Florida* was the first. But when inquiries were made, it was shown that the vessel was under orders to proceed to Palermo, and that she was unarmed, uncommissioned, and incapable of offence. In fact she sailed for Nassau, was there arrested, acquitted, and proceeded to Mobile.

A few months later Adams drew Russell's attention to the fact that a warship was being built at Birkenhead. Inquiries were made at once, and no attempt was made to

---

[1] It must be remembered, of course, that naval architecture was then very different from what it is now.

dispute the fact that she was constructed to foreign order, and was intended for offensive purposes.

Then, unfortunately, a legal delay occurred. The papers were delivered to the Queen's Advocate on July 22, 1862, but he was too ill to attend to business. When the legal opinion was eventually given it was decisive; the Birkenhead case was a flagrant violation of the law. Orders were therefore issued to seize the vessel on July 28. But that same morning she slipped out of dock, the next day she dropped down the Mersey, and sailed for the Azores.

The British Government had not, in fact, anticipated this quick departure. Laird's, the shipbuilders, were a firm of high standing at Birkenhead, and the senior partner was Conservative member for the place, and a man of influence in his party. The Government obviously thought he would never play a trick on them; and no case had till then occurred to put them on their guard, said Selborne afterwards, against stratagem or surprise. Apparently they supposed that what had never yet happened never would happen. But men who go down to the sea in ships do not always wait for legal permission. And the British Government, of all Governments in the world, should have known that sailors are often awake when lawyers are asleep.

Had the vessel been arrested on suspicion there would no doubt have been an outcry in Parliament, and the courts would probably have ordered her release, since she was in fact unarmed and incapable of offence until fitted out at the Azores. But the fact that an attempt had been made to detain her and had failed would have been a strong point to urge in subsequent controversy with Washington.

Actually Russell, who had rather more than the ordinary layman's contempt for the niceties of the law, had suggested detention of the *Alabama*. But Westbury—the formidable Lord Chancellor who had "dismissed hell with costs, and deprived members of the Church of England of their last hope of eternal damnation" in an ecclesiastical suit—was naturally averse to such legal irregularities, and unfortunately the Foreign Secretary consulted his masterful colleague before, instead of after, taking action. The *Alabama* then began her fateful career.[1]

Russell sometimes acted too quickly; this time he had not acted quickly enough. He admitted afterwards that he had blundered, but it would be more true to say that he was the victim of circumstances. Had the Queen's advocate not been ill the delay would not have occurred, and had Westbury been less positive (or Palmerston more positive), Russell would have acted decisively.

But Westbury was a dogmatic and overbearing person whose reputation as a lawyer stood high. It is a grave matter for a layman's common sense to override a Lord Chancellor's practical folly; but in this instance the states-man should have remembered that the responsibility was primarily his, and acted while there was time.

In the following year other cases followed. The war-ship *Alexandra* was built by Laird's, seized by the Government, and tried. The jury acquitted, and after long legal argument she was released, and served the Confederates. The Federal Government frankly admitted that no more could have been done; but the very fact that so much had been done in the case of the *Alexandra*, and that the Federal Government fully recognized it, served as an additional argument against the inaction over the *Alabama*.

Subsequently other warships were ordered and built to Confederate order. Mr. Minister Adams protested vigor-ously, and on one occasion permitted himself to talk of war—a threat which, in the then circumstances of the United States, can hardly have frightened Russell more than Russell's similar threats to Russia and Prussia over the Polish and Danish questions frightened the Tsar and Bismarck.[2] They talked of war very lightly in those days.

In the particular case to which Adams referred, Russell had been advised that the law did not apply. But since the Laird affair, he had less patience than ever with the legal mind, and he had already arranged that the ships

---

[1] It was suggested that Russell connived at her escape. The evidence is decisive against that assumption; and Cobden is emphatic that Russell was very angry at the trick that was played on him.

[2] See Chapters XXVII and XXVIII.

should be purchased from the builders over the heads of the Confederates by the British Government. There were no more orders, or if so, they were not executed.

But the *Alabama* had by now become the terror of the seas. She was swift and she was sudden, and she left destruction wherever she went. Day after day she eluded the Federal Navy, but no peaceful merchantman that carried the Stars and Stripes seemed able to elude her. New York packets from Europe, New England and Philadelphia tramps from Brazil and the Plate, Boston clippers homeward bound from Canton, fell one by one before her: in two years the American flag had become little more than a memory in the China Seas and the great Capes.

In 1860 the Yankee clippers were the fastest and loveliest freighters the world had ever seen; by 1865 these splendid birds of the ocean were almost extinct, and British steamers took the trade that Massachusetts skippers grown wise in sail had carried for a generation or more.

At the time it seemed merely a temporary interruption, but the blow was mortal. The clippers had carried such a press of sail that they were becoming too costly for the freights they brought; whereas coal on the other side of the Atlantic was cheap, and the steady chug-chug of British steamers was independent of calms and doldrums. After the Civil War the rising generation in New England looked landwards and westwards, the old sea-lore that had come down from Devon and Dorset sea-dogs to the young Puritan colonies died out as the old captains knocked their last pipes and turned in, and the taste for salt water was lost as the centre of national gravity moved towards the middle of the Continent.

Nobody could have anticipated these grave results on that summer morning when the *Alabama* slipped quietly out of Laird's yard at Birkenhead. But they serve to explain why the Federal Government, now at last beginning to wear down its Confederate opponents, talked menacingly of heavy compensation, and pressed its claim insistently in London.

A few months after the *Alabama* escaped, Adams had forwarded a digest of the evidence, and warned the British

Government that he was instructed to solicit redress for the "national and private injuries received." Russell replied with elaborate arguments in a long despatch, which quoted largely from recognized American authorities to the effect that it was "not the practice of nations to undertake to prohibit their own subjects, by previous laws, from trafficking in articles contraband of war. Such trade is carried on at the risk of those engaged in it."

The argument was not conclusive, in view of the British Government's previous action in restraining the export of warships built to American order in British yards. But the demand for compensation was rejected point-blank.

If there is any equity between nations, the refusal was wrong; a blunder had been made, as Russell afterwards recognized, in not detaining the *Alabama* at Birkenhead, and respectable people usually offer to pay for their mistakes. It would have been difficult to agree on the amount, but it should have been foreseen that it would be impossible to maintain the absolute refusal to compensate.

The next suggestion from Washington might have been anticipated; it was proposed that the dispute should be submitted to arbitration. This was negatived with the statement that "Her Majesty's Government are the sole guardians of their own honour." Apart from the fact that Her Majesty's Government had scarcely been efficient guardians of their own shipbuilding yards, the attitude was absurd, for a man certainly does not lose his honour by consenting to arbitrate.

High-falutin' language of this kind deceives nobody. It certainly made no impression on the shrewd Minister Adams, who probably realized that statesmen only begin to talk about honour when other arguments have run dry.

Russell had, of course, a better reason for his refusal. Having replied so stiffly to Adams, he could hardly admit it in public, but in a private letter to Gladstone he declared that any possible tribunal of arbitration would decide against England on the ground that she was rich and it would do her good to be bled, and that he would sooner see the country pay twenty millions down than submit to arbitration. The latter argument was absurd; the former was almost prophetic.

These successive refusals only exasperated Washington.[1] The American Government knew they had a case, and they decided to press it to the utmost.

Unfortunately Russell's own blundering in Denmark, which we have yet to discuss, had meanwhile convinced the world that England would never fight again. But nations that do not fight their way have to pay their way; and it is a weakness of the pacifist doctrine that a country which is too fat to fight is so much the easier to squeeze. The Americans, impoverished by the war and the *Alabama*, decided that slim Jonathan should squeeze fat John Bull to the limit of his capacity.

It must be confessed that Russell's original blunder and his subsequent arrogance in discussion had given them some reason to pitch their claim fairly high. But they nearly ruined their chances, and for a moment seemed almost to justify Russell's refusal, by putting forward the most preposterous demands. Not only direct but indirect damage was to be included; the total suggested would have amounted to more than the whole cost of the American Civil War, or the entire amount of the British National Debt; and when it became evident that any nation would rather submit to war than to such demands, Sumner calmly suggested that the United States would waive the *Alabama* claims if Canada were ceded.

He had miscalculated. The British Empire was not for sale, and Russell would have opposed a blank negative to such absurdities. But Russell was no longer in office, and Gladstone as Prime Minister was less rigid and more anxious to arbitrate. But Gladstone himself admitted that the original *Alabama* claim "contained a mass of matter at once irrelevant and exasperating, and advanced claims and pretensions such as it is wholly incompatible with national

[1] In 1868 Stanley remarked in the House of Commons that "the grievance seemed to have been gaining importance in the minds of American statesmen and the American public, just as in proportion on this side of the water had grown up a feeling of desire to remove all other causes of difference." He did not recognize that grievances flourish best when least attended to.

honour to admit or to plead before a tribunal of arbitration," and declared that "the conduct of the American Government in this affair was the most disreputable he had ever known."

The indictment was true. The Civil War had lowered the tone of public as well as private morality in the United States, and few Americans to-day look back to the period of Grant's Presidency with pride. After the victory came the vultures, and the birds of prey were too hungry to be particular where they fed.

Russell had now retired from public life, but he retained his interest in the affair, and his indignation rather increased as the unsavoury business proceeded. After a prolonged wrangle, the claims were cut down, but they reappeared again when the Arbitration opened at Geneva. Lord Westbury, whose tongue would have blistered a rhinoceros, said bluntly that the American aim seemed to be to frame a special indictment against Britain for its whole conduct during the war; and even Selborne, whose language was always decorous, complained that the tone of the American argument was acrimonious and totally wanting in international courtesy.

In fact the United States bluffed up to the last moment, and then withdrew the more inadmissible claims as a concession. The final amount awarded was so much in excess of the claims that could be substantiated, with interest on them all, that a large balance was left, which Congress applied to purposes never contemplated by the arbitrators; but according to Selborne the three arbitrators were not well chosen.

One was a Brazilian, who naturally thought more of the goodwill of the United States than of Britain. The second was a Swiss, a man without a seaboard, whose sympathies were naturally on the side of a Republic. The third was an Italian, who was influenced neither by geography nor political theory but by a much more elementary consideration; for when Selborne suggested to him that the amount awarded to America was excessive, he replied simply, "You are rich, very rich." As Palmerston had already boasted of British wealth some years before, and the country had certainly grown richer in the subsequent decade, there was nothing more to be said.   The loser pays.

The result of the arbitration seemed to justify Russell's whole attitude throughout the controversy.   But in fact it did not; for if he had been less arrogant, the position of America would have been less assured.   It is a reasonable assumption that if the United States had had more confidence in British readiness to repair an admitted fault, her politicians might have been less grasping; even had they not, the British would have been in a stronger position to argue and refuse.

In retrospect, most reasonable men will agree that neither side had anything to be proud of.   Britain blundered and blustered; America bullied and bluffed.   If the *Alabama* affair did not quite reach the low-water mark of international statecraft, it certainly smelt rather strongly of the mudflats.

CHAPTER XXVI

PEERAGE

TOWARDS the close of the session of 1861 Lord John Russell, after long consideration and hesitation, took the title of Earl Russell and a seat in the House of Lords. The apparently immortal Palmerston would sooner have seen Gladstone leave his side in the Commons for the Upper House than his old friend and rival John Russell; but then Palmerston disliked and distrusted Gladstone as much as Gladstone disliked Palmerston. For Russell, now that the victory was won and his own precedence as Prime Minister assured, he could afford to feel something like affection—the easy affection of those who have often gone hunting together, and are agreed at last not to quarrel over the bag.[1]

The transition from commoner to peer was easy and natural. "The new Earl," wrote Mr. War Secretary Lewis to Clarendon on July 24, 1861, "took leave of the House of Commons last night. Some foolish people wanted to get up a valedictory debate. Eulogies on moving the writs of a dead man are borne, but eulogies on the living are intolerable."

It was in fact hardly an occasion for eulogy. The House of Lords may not be, as some of its critics suggest, a living tomb. But for old members of the Commons who cross the lobby to take the oath as Peers it marks the beginning of the end. It is the gilded entrance to the valley of the shadow.

"Oh, Johnny, what fun we'll have," was the greeting from Russell's old friend Lord Derby, as he attended his

---

[1] "Speaking confidentially, Viscount Palmerston would think himself doing better service by recommending the House of Lords for Mr. Gladstone than for Lord John Russell."—Palmerston to Queen Victoria, Jan. 1, 1861.

Two years earlier Palmerston had remarked that he at any rate would not go up to the Lords, because he could not trust Russell in the Commons.

first debate.   But the new peer was now within a year of seventy, and nearly half a century had passed since a frail and undersized Whig cadet had entered the old unreformed House of Commons as member for the Bedford family borough of Tavistock.   A different England had grown up since then, which Russell had had some share in making: he had gallantly fought his way to the top, and fallen and risen again; no man had ever shown greater parliamentary courage, and only two, according to Gladstone—Peel and Disraeli—as great.   He had beaten everybody of his time except Palmerston, but Palmerston had beaten him, and Palmerston seemed likely to go on living for ever.

The ashes were out of that business—why kick against the pricks?—but while Palmerston lived there would be no second Reform Bill, and when Palmerston died it would be another, and not Russell, who introduced the Bill in the Commons.   So it fell out in four years' time.

To go to the Lords, then, was to fling away ambition. These things are bitter in the mouth, but old statesmen know that there are more disappointments than successes in politics.   And meanwhile there were affairs to attend to.

Home politics, it is true, were very quiet, as they are apt to be when trade is flourishing.   Lancashire was becoming involved in the cotton stoppage with unhappy results, but apart from that the growth of wealth, in Gladstone's phrase, was intoxicating; and the decline of charity, to Shaftesbury's less complacent eyes, was an alarming accompaniment of the new plutocracy.   Men were too busy making money to think about philanthropy; the sleek sixties had succeeded the hungry forties.   The progress of Free Trade, remarked Lord John, was "constant, victorious, and irresistible"; but with money to burn there were no grievances to redress, and reformers might as well put up the shutters while the mills of Mammon ground so fast.

There was actually more life in the Church than the State at the moment, with a latitudinarian *Essays and Reviews* disturbing the clerical conscience—"Of all books in any language it was incomparably the worst," insisted the passionate Archdeacon Denison—and an astonishing new work called *The Origin of Species* disturbing more than the clerical conscience. These things showed, or seemed to show, that the Tractarian movement had lost its lead and Rome its recent fascination; the tide of Anglican secessions had evidently died down, and in spite of Gladstone and his Oxford friends, Palmerston saw to it that the Evangelicals and Broad Churchmen were having their innings again. But there were to be no more Hampden affairs or No Popery letters for the new Earl Russell. The burnt child dreads the fire, and Foreign Secretaries are fortunately not required to write despatches on heresy or biology.

Abroad, however, there was no lack of interest. Mr. Minister Adams had much to say, in his quietly forcible fashion, about affairs in America, and really seemed to believe his own assurances that the Northern States would win. The Italian question, too, again needed careful watching, now that Cavour was dead; for Austria and the Pope survived, and both were ready to try their luck against Piedmont if opportunity offered.

Trouble, too, was blowing up in Poland and Denmark, and Russia and Prussia were as far from adopting the sacred principles of Whiggism as ever. It was clear that the Liberal millennium was not yet in sight.

The chief prize of office might have passed, but there was still work to be done, and the new Earl Russell was as ready for the daily round as little Lord John had ever been. "Our old men," remarked Gladstone wistfully to his diary, "are unhappily our youngest."

CHAPTER XXVII

THE POLISH FIASCO

UNLUCKILY the next two adventures in diplomacy were a failure almost from the start, and they left a train of evil behind which hampered Britain for fifty years.

The famous despatch which Lord John Russell wrote in 1860 had helped the Italian national cause at one of the many critical moments of its advance towards unity; and there is ample evidence that its author watched with interest, with affection, and occasionally with anxiety, the policy which led step by step to the annexation of Venice, the capture of Rome, and the humiliation of his old enemy the Pope a few years after Pio Nono had proclaimed that the pontiff "neither can nor ought to be reconciled with liberalism and modern civilization." But that same despatch had not merely announced the interest and approval with which the British Government regarded a particular course of action in what was, after all, a local conflict. It had affirmed, in the wide and general terms of universal principle, that an oppressed people is justified in rebellion against its rulers. And it was not only in Italy and the Confederate States that this revolutionary doctrine was read, digested, and approved or reprobated. Echoes, and something more than echoes, of the Whig theory of 1688 were now to come from Warsaw.

Few Englishmen of that day knew more of what had once been Poland than the bare names of Kosciusko and Mazeppa. A few historians had heard of Sobieski, a few musicians knew Chopin, and one or two men of letters may possibly have heard of the great Mickiewicz. But few Europeans had crossed those sun-baked and snow-driven plains in which the hapless national insurrection of 1831 had raised its head and been beaten to the ground, and fewer still had any knowledge of the sweet musical tongue that was spoken by a passionate and gifted people from the pinewoods of Silesia to the solitudes of High Tatra and remote Bukowina.

The country had no longer a Government or a capital, and since 1846, when Austrian troops had entered the ancient city of Cracow—the traditional tomb of Polish kings, the peaceful home of Polish learning, the Oxford of the occidental Slavs—the last square mile of free Polish soil had disappeared. A martial but helpless nation now acquiesced, or seemed to acquiesce, in the loss of its identity. Some of the ambitious emigrated to America. Some of the artists settled in Paris. Some of the great nobles, to save their estates, came to terms with the new masters. Some of the students in the schools of Warsaw or the college at Lemberg described, in fiery prose or surreptitious verse, the glorious past when Polish armies had ruled the land from the Black Sea to the Baltic, and the great days when wide Volhynia and black Ukraine had trembled beneath the Polish horsemen on the road to far Kief.

But these things were no more than dreams; and unhappy Poland turned, as nations will turn in time of secular disaster, to the Church which assures them that the oppressions of the present world are only transient, and that a reward is prepared for the people of God. Perhaps this, too, is a dream, but at least it is a dream that lightens the night of tribulation; and the faith that would have enslaved the intellect of the rebellious West served to liberate the emotions of the unhappy East. In all the world there was no more docile and devoted daughter of the Church than desolate Poland, and no more gentle mother to her afflicted child than Rome.[1]

But patriotism was not dead but sleeping on those silent plains. From time to time the bound limbs stirred, and a movement was felt like that which touched the tops of the Polish forests when fierce Siberian winds drove summer south of the Vistula. It began like a sigh out of heaven,

---

[1] Gregory XVI was regarded by the West as a rigid and reactionary Pope, a clerical Eldon who considered all reform as revolution. But he defended the Poles vigorously against Russian persecution, as did Pio Nono against Bismarck's Kulturkampf.

it spread like a shout of resurrection as the autumn gale swept over wood and village and solitary farm, and it died down with a sob and a shudder as the one free thing in Poland passed to happier lands, leaving only wreckage and destruction behind.

There had been insurrection before in Poland. Each had failed, but the old still hoped, and the young, who learned at their mothers' knees to love the country whose past was all that remained to them, looked forward secretly to a day of reckoning and the coming of a national hero for their deliverance.

Such a time seemed to have come in the year 1862, when Italy had regained her freedom, and the Confederate States of America were justifying their rebellion by beating the Yankee armies. It was known that preparations were afoot for a rising of the Poles; it was thought that Hungary under Kossuth might repeat the rising of 1848; it was hoped that the British and French Governments, both of which had assisted Italy against Austria, might aid the cause of national liberalism in the east as well as the south of Europe.

Poland stirred, but Poland had miscalculated. There was some desperate fighting, and burning villages lit the indifferent skies. But no national hero rose for her deliverance, and the Russian Government was ingenious as well as alert. It adopted the effective method of conscripting the suspected youth of the country, and drafting them to distant provinces of the Empire, where they were helpless for good or evil. The hour of revolution came and passed, and no help came from the West.

Had Poland risen in the Crimean War, neither Britain nor France could well have abandoned her. But neither Britain nor France was prepared for another Crimean War when neither British nor French interests were at stake.

There was indignation at the rigorous treatment of the unhappy rebels, and the noble Shaftesbury held a public meeting of protest in London, and made a magnificent speech. But he noticed that subscriptions for the relief of Poland came in very slowly, and there appears to have been far less enthusiasm for the Poles in 1863 than for Italy in 1860 or Hungary in 1848. This was not due to any diminution of interest in the cause of liberty, but to the fact that Poland produced neither a Garibaldi nor a Kossuth. Principles require personalities to enforce them on the popular mind.[1]

Russell had all the generous sympathy which Burke had shown ninety years before for the miserable Poles, but he was well aware that Britain could do little for them. He was perfectly frank and explicit as to the attitude of the Government. "No statesman who has held the office which I have the honour to occupy," he said on March 25, 1862, "no Prime Minister of this country has, at any time, held out the prospect of material assistance to the Poles."

A little more than this cold comfort was attempted. Russell, who was described by his colleague Granville as a compound of a giant and a little child, still held a belief in the effect of moral suasion which seventy years of a rude world had not shaken. Others thought, or pretended to think, that a word spoken in due season might change a whole system of Imperial polity; and in association with Austria and France, a remonstrance was now addressed to Russia. A programme of six points—including a national Polish administration and the use of the Polish language in public offices and the Courts of Justice—was submitted to the Tsar's Government.

The liberal advice was in fact sound, and the system suggested for Warsaw was adopted in the Austrian province of Galicia, where it worked reasonably well for many years. But few of us are grateful for good advice, and the reply from St. Petersburg was emphatic.

It was intimated that Russell was not well informed as to the facts—a statement of doubtful accuracy, for he knew at least enough of the facts to recognize the old familiar

[1] Carlyle, who was glorifying (and whitewashing) Frederick the Great in these years, was anti-Pole. But he was authoritarian at heart, and in any event he had little influence. He was pro-German, but the British public was violently anti-German over Schleswig. The poets—Tennyson, Browning, Swinburne, Arnold, Meredith, Hardy—were silent. Tennyson was ardently in favour of Polish national freedom, but his official position would have made the subject a delicate one for him; the others, however, were free. The subject would have suited Hardy's sombre muse.

round of repression, rebellion, and repression again—but Russia would not even consider the remonstrance until the rising was put down, and then, of course, would not consider it at all.

If Russell had now expressed polite regret at the failure of his proposals he could hardly have been criticized, for geography had made England as impotent in Russia as Russia had recently found herself in Italy. But it was his weakness that he did not know when to stop.

The old difficulty of intervention by a foreign Power in the internal affairs of an independent Empire, which had vexed good Liberals before, now became acute. Russia refused to admit that other States had any right to consider the future of Poland; and in Russell's own phrase, "the question came to be whether the three powers should together urge their demands by force or relinquish the attempt."

The Queen was naturally alarmed when her Foreign Secretary mentioned force as a possible alternative; a European war is not, after all, to be entered into light-heartedly even when the quarrel is just. But she had further reason for complaint. She objected, precisely as the Prince Consort had objected eighteen months before to the *Trent* despatch, that Russell's language was too abrupt and peremptory, and pointed out that he was making threats which Russia knew would not be carried into effect.

The criticism was well found. The ordinary Englishman has little patience with levity in action, but for levity in speech, he had, at that time, a greater tolerance, and Tennyson's recent poetic justification of "our ancient privilege, my lords, to fling whate'er we felt, not fearing, into words," had not yet been exposed as a sport that looks cheap and costs dear. But even bubble and squeak have to be paid for.

Russell replied to Windsor in a minor key. The Government had "no wish or intention to go to war for Poland. But a declaration that they would in no case make war might give a licence to the violence and murdering habits of the Russian soldiery, which would be very grievous, and might kindle a war spirit in this country."

The Queen refrained from the retort that ineffective threats were just as likely to give a licence to repression as a declaration against war, and since Russell admitted that "at the present moment the contest in Poland does not appear to be a very bloody one"—the rebellion in fact was dying down—the matter dropped. She had exposed— but not for the last time—a weak point in her Government's armoury. Unluckily they did not learn their lesson, and were soon to repeat their blunder more publicly against a more formidable antagonist.

In the meantime the Poles surrendered once more to their masters. If Poland did not pay the penalty of Italy's success, at any rate Poland failed where Italy had succeeded. The fiasco was an unpleasant reminder that freedom, like authority, depends on force.

CHAPTER XXVIII

BISMARCK CALLS THE BLUFF

THE ineffectual struggle of Poland had evoked a certain amount of ineffectual sympathy in England, but the distant troubles of Warsaw were soon forgotten in the excitement of a political crisis and a military campaign nearer home. Events were now in train which led to the German-Danish War on the Continent, and to the downfall of the Palmerston-Russell school of foreign policy in England.

The Schleswig-Holstein controversy, which was the nominal cause of this upheaval, was one of the oldest and most intricate of the unsolved political questions of Europe. The origin of the dispute could be traced back by the learned to the Middle Ages, but the more the matter was explained the more obscure it became, until it was said by the flippant that only two men had mastered its history, one of whom had died under the strain while the other had gone mad.

However that may be, the actual issue was the dynastic allegiance of two duchies between Germany and Denmark. It is sufficient for our purpose to say that, when it came to the point, both Berlin and Copenhagen were equally unaccommodating and—if equity can be pleaded in international affairs—both were to some extent in the wrong.

There had been trouble over the subject between the two countries before, and when the King of Denmark died, in 1863, it was clear there would be trouble again. But the difficulties had been smoothed over before, and there is little doubt they could have been smoothed over again, but for a fresh factor. The King of Prussia had a new adviser, who had the novel idea that Prussia should displace Austria as the dominant power in Germany, and that Prussia at the head of a reconstituted German Empire should become one of the great Powers of the world. That adviser was Bismarck.

The King himself was typical of the later Hohenzollern stock; that is to say, he looked more than a King, and was less. Bold in appearance, he was timid in action; a splendid figure in public, he was weak and irresolute in private. He admitted he had no right to Holstein, and he was frankly terrified of the path along which he was being led. "I can perfectly well see where all this will end," he warned Bismarck. "Over there, in front of the Opera House, they will cut off your head, and mine a little while afterwards."

Bismarck knew his English history. But he also knew his Prussian, and he decided that Strafford and Charles I were not relevant precedents for Germany. The diagnosis was correct. From the very beginning he kept the annexation of the duchies steadily before his eyes, and the situation, as it happened, played into his hands. Nobody either at home or abroad could believe that the King would act. And nobody believed that Bismarck, a mere reactionary junker from the provinces, who laughed at the Prussian constitution and legislation and talked nonsense about a policy of blood and iron, mattered very much one way or the other.

Bismarck was new to his post in Berlin, and strange stories of a reckless youth were whispered about the mature Minister of forty-seven. The stiff courtiers of Potsdam muttered that this was the wild Pomeranian squire who woke late guests of a morning by pistol-shots at their bedroom door, and scandalized matrons in Charlottenburg shuddered over the coffee and cakes as they heard of the mad countryman whose ordinary drink at dinner was said to be a mixture of champagne and stout. This attractive beverage, which sounds more innocent under its English name of Sabbath Calm, is, in fact, an excellent refresher for the tired outdoor man; but the mere mention of a thirst apparently so titanic supported the rumour that Bismarck drove the drink out of him by long night gallops through forests and sleeping villages till his horse was found, still frothed and sweaty, in the stable next morning.

This rough-spoken hulk of humanity, half fact and half legend, scarcely seemed a man of the time, but rather some strange survival of a ruder age. Good Prussian Liberals could hardly listen seriously to a man who had none of the fine sentiments and high-sounding abstractions that every polished German loved to mouth and to hear mouthed in Parliament; the new Minister used the straight blunt speech of the soil. Admittedly there was a crude force about him that would impress a farmers' ordinary in Brandenburg, but mid-nineteenth-century Berlin preferred something more cultured.

Bismarck, it was agreed, was not quite civilized; and the day had gone by, men said, when politicians could defy public opinion and govern without Parliament. Perhaps it had, but all days are much alike to those who know how to use them.

There was nothing to show the diplomatic world that here, now that Cavour was gone, was the coolest and shrewdest political brain in Europe, and the portent was the more unexpected since Germany hardly produced one first-class statesman in a century. Nobody could have foreseen Bismarck, and nobody fully understood what he was at until his work was nearly done.

He had learned much from watching Cavour; and like Cavour, he was ready to deceive others with words where necessary, and to let his actions speak for themselves. But he never deceived himself with fine phrases, and so long as he was dealing with a concrete secular situation he made no mistakes. It was only later, when he set himself to fight an imponderable spiritual atmosphere with the weapons of temporal controversy in the Kulturkampf, that he had to admit defeat; and it is an extraordinary fact that the man who studied Russell's record and gave Russell his worst fall in the diplomatic field, should have imitated his antagonist by taking a tilt at the Vatican and have come down in like manner.

All this was far in the future. For his immediate problem Bismarck had tougher wood to work in, but fundamentally his problem was the same as Cavour's: to make a third-class State into a first-class one by deposing a dozen or so petty Dukes and Princes, and creating a united Germany.

If the end was the same, the method had to be different. Cavour had used the machinery of constitution and liberty, because Italy was under foreign and ecclesiastical rule; but Germany was at least governed by Germans. The problem, as Bismarck saw it, was that they were the wrong Germans and that there were too many of them in the trade. Cavour had to encourage liberty in order to attain unity. Bismarck, on the contrary, had to restrict liberty in order to attain unity. But he was careful not to go too far. He knew that German Liberalism had been an ineffective and on the whole a disruptive force, but he knew that, properly canalized, it might be a useful ally. He knew that a Parliament which ruled him would never unite Germany, but he knew that a Parliament which he ruled might prove at once a useful rudder and emotional index, like a dog's tail to its master. And above all he knew that honest German Michael was a rare combination of duty and docility that could be led anywhere, would always do what he was told and, what is more, believe what he was told. Less independent than the English, less uncertain than the French, and better men than the Slav, Providence seemed to have created the German tribes expressly to follow a leader to the end—and then forgotten to give them a leader.

Now all that was changed. Loyalty was strong in German hearts: therefore let them worship the King. But stupidity was strong in royal heads: therefore let the King be advised by Bismarck, and victory would follow.

The programme was envisaged in three stages. First, a war with Denmark, to put Prussia on the map of Germany. Second, a war with Austria, to put Austria off the map of Germany. And thirdly a war with France, to put Germany first in Europe. Within ten years all three wars had been forced and fought, and the game was won.

Nothing of all this was known to the timid King of Prussia in 1862; his paper reputation as the iron maker of Imperial Germany—which history has not endorsed—was still undreamed of. Nothing of all this was suspected at Versailles, where Napoleon III had known Bismarck and apparently misjudged him; the French Emperor was now busy with thoughts of Italy and Mexico, and his Empress with the pleasant flattery of clericals at home. Nothing of all this was thought of at Windsor, where the

meanwhile ostentatiously invisible at Osborne or Balmoral, the young Alexandra was constantly visible at Marlborough House; and the rumour of a royal rivalry at home was vastly more attractive than the dull details of a tangled squabble abroad.

Soon the story crossed the great divide of Oxford Street, north of which a grand lady once assured Lord Salisbury she never left her cards. Rumour spread it through what was then the rising suburb of Bayswater, and thence it travelled quickly all over London. Family lawyers shook scandalized heads in Bedford Row, and promptly took the savoury tit-bit to respectable homes in Highbury and Clapham, where it was retailed over the mahogany and the port to worthy City merchants, who felt more important than ever when they read the newspapers next morning. For *The Times* had begun to roar, the young lions of Fleet Street took up the baying, and soon the stray hyenas of the gutter press began to lick their chops at the promise of a sensation and a scandal in high quarters.

There was, in fact, a difference of opinion between Windsor and Marlborough House. The Queen, ignorant as yet of Bismarck's project—even her daughter in Berlin knew nothing of what was planned—thought her heart was all German until bitter experience taught her it was not in the least Prussian; the Prince of Wales, as Gladstone observed after a talk with the young bridegroom, "showed a little Danism." It did not amount to much more than strained relations with his sister in Berlin, but so far as it went the Prince had the people with him. Portly fathers remembered they had once been schoolboys, and when they saw big Germany threatening to invade little Denmark they promptly lost their heads, and cried aloud for action.[1]

There are majestic moments of grave national peril when the soul of England rises serene and confident above trouble that might overwhelm a lesser nation. But there are other moments when Britannia is as ridiculous as a drunken

---

[1] *Cf.* Lord John Manners to Disraeli. A war with Prussia would be "the most popular, the easiest, and the cheapest (for it can be waged by the Navy alone) of the century." He forgot that navies cannot fight on land.
Malmesbury makes it clear that the Tories were entirely pro-Dane.

charwoman trying to fight the police, and this happened to be one of them. Something must be done to keep Prussia back. But that something must not be war, because war costs money and breaks heads, and though heads are cheap, money is dear. Why not give a little good advice, suggest a conference and a compromise, and if that fails, try a horrid scolding?

The drunken charwoman generally hiccups before she is sick, and these elementary physiological processes concluded, returns to work with a headache. Unluckily it fell to the Cabinet of which Palmerston was Prime Minister and Russell Foreign Secretary to doctor the excited patient, and two more unsuitable physicians can hardly be imagined.

From their point of view the case had, indeed, certain novel and difficult elements. The attentive student of thirty years of Russell-Palmerston despatches is constrained to admit that they devoted rather disproportionate attention to the matter of rebellion, that they generally assumed that the people are right and the rulers wrong,[1] and that they thought of foreign affairs naturally and easily in terms of conflict between authority and liberty. In the new Prussia there had been, it is true, some conflict between authority and liberty, and it followed as a matter of course that the Bismarckian policy of blood and iron was wrong. But so far from there being any rebellion, the people appeared to agree with their new Minister, and the more he was criticized abroad, the more enthusiastically he was followed at home in his aggression on Schleswig-Holstein. Cavour had created a Parliament, and it had naturally followed him in liberating Italy. But Bismarck had tamed a Parliament, and it followed him docilely in the conquest of Denmark.

This was something new in Russell's political experience, and it is evident that he failed to understand it. His mind responded with its whole strength to the cry of liberty in Italy or Poland. It would have responded as readily to the same cry in America had two rival freedoms not met and challenged each other between North and South. But

[1] The Queen had once criticized an amusing instance. It was declared that a rebellion in Portugal had been suppressed with unparalleled severity. She pointed out that not a single life had been lost.

the new national movement in Prussia ran counter to liberty and Russell's life-long theories of constitutional and popular government; and the old man, already troubled by the proved inadequacy of Whig doctrine in the American conflict, could not fathom the novelty. As in the early days of the Tractarian movement thirty years before, he failed to realize the deep emotional springs of German patriotism from which Bismarck drew his real strength; he simply sensed another Tory in a new disguise, and instinctively opposed the enemy.

Of course Bismarck was a Tory, in the sense that he believed in authority, and saw facts as they were, not as he wished them to be. But because men profess the same creed, it by no means follows they believe the same things; a Presbyterian and a Catholic are both Christians, but in practice their only point of agreement is a denial of Anglican orders. Bismarck's Toryism was not the kind that Russell had in mind when he denounced the iniquities of William Pitt; and in comparison with the gentle compromise that Lord Derby understood by Conservatism, it was a pile-driver to a door-knocker.

It was precisely this failure to understand the situation that made Russell's course so uncertain and erratic, his defeat so certain and complete. It should have been easy to adopt an attitude of detached disinterestedness over Schleswig-Holstein and, when war broke out, of polite regret. It should have been easy to assure the House of Commons that the affair was none of our business, that no British interest could possibly suffer, and that we were ready to proffer good offices the moment mediation was desired. It is true that such an attitude would have achieved nothing. But it would have cost nothing, and lost nothing; not even respect.

But Russell and Palmerston would neither stay out of the ring nor stop in.[1] They seem at one time to have thought that Russia and France would join them in a

---

[1] The Queen at first thought that Russell himself was very fair, but that he was alarmed and overruled by Palmerston. Later, however, she was deeply hurt by a cold dry letter from Russell. There seems to have been little difference of opinion between the two men.

demonstration, perhaps even in war, against Prussia. But Bismarck had supported Russia in the Polish trouble a few months before, and the support had now to be paid for. Napoleon III was always ready for an intrigue, but this particular intrigue did not attract him.

Britain was, therefore, isolated. But Palmerston and Russell could not understand that isolation spelt impotence; probably because neither of them understood that Bismarck meant business. It is true that they admitted at Windsor —what the Queen already knew through her correspondent Granville—that the Cabinet was divided, and that Gladstone at least was for peace. But they muttered oracular nothings at Copenhagen. They baited the bully of Berlin with menacing despatches. They dropped hints of war in Vienna if the Austrian Fleet passed through the English Channel. They told Versailles they did not really mean to carry the thing through alone. They planned in Whitehall and countermanded their plans in Westminster. But one thing they did not do. They did not increase the army by a single man, and Bismarck naturally counted the soldiers and ignored the despatches. The available British army consisted of twenty thousand men. (There were probably more words in the despatches.) But the German armies numbered a million.

"Those two dreadful old men," as the Queen in a moment of exasperation called her Prime Minister and Foreign Secretary, seem to have forgotten that numbers have a certain relevance in argument; and they seem also to have forgotten the wise counsel of the statesman under whom they had both served thirty years before. "I am against exciting people," remarked the cool Melbourne in 1836, "to commit themselves to a warfare in which you cannot give them effectual support."

It is strange that Palmerston could never understand what is, after all, an elementary and commonsense political proposition; and perhaps it is stranger still that Russell, who had at least seen something of the Peninsular War in which British troops had certainly given effectual support to Spain, shared his colleague's delusion. But the facts remain on record. They talked. Bismarck acted.

Denmark fought Germany and was beaten; and Palmerston announced that we had not thought it consistent with our duty to undertake the task of armed intervention. Characteristically he coupled the retreat with a threat that Britain might yet act if Germany went too far, but nobody believed it. Probably he did not believe it himself; it was merely a rhetorical flourish, a bit of soiled bunting out of the political ragbag that had come in useful before. It was never used again, for the Prime Minister's day was nearly over.

The folly of Russell and Palmerston in this matter cost the country dear. Selborne, in his usual measured language, remarked that there was "some loss, never afterwards repaired, of authority in Europe." But this was an understatement.

The impression went all over the world that Britain would never fight again. Men remembered that Russell's famous Italian despatch was after all merely a matter of words without action; they recalled that in dealing both with the Pope and with Poland, his bark had been worse than his bite, and it was now merely a toothless growl. Neither the old dog nor his corpulent master mattered any more.

Prussia was poor and England was rich, but Prussia had won the day because the poor man armed is stronger than a rich man unarmed. The ghost of Canning's continental policy vanished when Bismarck called Palmerston's bluff; and from 1864 to 1914 German statesmen wrote Britain off the map of Europe.

CHAPTER XXIX

PRIME MINISTER AGAIN

ON October 18, 1865, Lord Palmerston died, at the great age of eighty-one.

The nation was surprised and almost shocked to hear the news. Ten years earlier colleagues and rivals alike had thought him past work. But he had begun his career afresh at a time when most men are content to finish, and a long decade as Prime Minister had made him seem immortal.

Even now, it was said, he was loth to go, for there were no farewells, and there was a legend of an open despatch-box being found on the table in front of him when he died. This was heroic fiction in the making; actually Palmerston died quietly in his bed, and Shaftesbury was doubtful whether he understood much of a religious service that the local clergyman held in the room.

With Palmerston dead, the political world stirred in its sleep. Two years previously, the personal and party aspect of affairs, which had been static if not stagnant since the Crimean War, was summed up by Forster in a frank letter to his wife. "The old Whig leaders are worn out. There are no new Whigs. Cobden and Bright are impracticable and un-English, and there are hardly any hopeful Radicals. There is a great prize of power and influence to be aimed at."

Gladstone was well aware of the prize, as he surveyed the changing scene without excessive lamentation at the passing of a colleague whom he had always disliked and distrusted. But his time had not quite come, and the decencies must be preserved. When Palmerston died Gladstone at once wrote to Russell on the assumption that the second man in the late Government would now be the first, while he himself remained Chancellor of the Exchequer as before.

The assumption was correct, but Gladstone noted musingly that the new Prime Minister's "physical strength is low, but I suppose in the Lords he may get on." It was hardly likely to prove more than a stop-gap Administration, but the thing would do for a time. The prize was so near that there was no need to hurry.[1]

Thus the last Whig pope survived the last anti-pope after all, and Russell stepped almost automatically into the seat he had vacated thirteen years before. But at seventy-three the shadows are lengthening, and that puny frame could hardly hope to last as long as Palmerston—actually he lived five years longer than his old rival, but not in office—and the time for what he had to do was short.

Things were so quiet at home politically that the new Government might easily have lasted four or five years had it been content simply to carry on and let the men of business continue to make fortunes. But the new Premier's sincerity was put to the test by his new office, and as usual he answered it triumphantly.

A Russell Government, as all the world knew, was a Reform Government. There was every excuse for doing nothing, for opinion was admittedly apathetic, but almost at once it became known that the little Whig intended to have his last fling at the franchise. A pledge was a pledge to John Russell, and this one dated back to pre-Crimean days.

But it would evidently be a close thing, for it was still a Palmerston Parliament. Russell in the Lords could do little; the main fight must be in the Commons, and the main burden of the fight must fall on Gladstone, the new leader of the Commons. Gladstone was now, indeed, an ardent reformer, and ready to go further than Russell himself. But he was untried as a leader, some of his best friends lamented that he was more hated than loved, and it was doubtful whether his masterful temper would not provoke more enmity than it allayed.

[1] Dasent wrote to Delane (Oct. 27, 1865), "Everyone dislikes and distrusts Russell, and I had no notion how unpopular he was." This was probably excessive, but it seems clear that nobody expected the new Government to last long.

As it chanced the Bill failed, but the fault was not Gladstone's. Aware that the country was silent and Parliament would probably be hostile, he introduced it in the Commons on March 12, 1866, in a studiously moderate speech which frankly admitted that "the limbo of abortive creations was peopled with the skeletons of reform bills." Bright supported the Bill as an instalment, with the remark that beggars could not be choosers. Disraeli, the leader whom the Conservatives distrusted and followed, did little.

There was no need, for half the Liberals, who were nominally in favour of reform, were secretly antagonistic, and wished the Bill at the devil. The history of the first Reform Bill, where a third of the Whigs detested what two-thirds of the Whigs supported, seemed likely to repeat itself, but it repeated itself with a difference. The Liberals could not decently oppose their own principles in public, but there are more ways than one of killing a cat, and the hour brought forth the man.

Robert Lowe, whom his contemporaries were to forget under the title of Viscount Sherbrooke and whom a later age has forgotten almost as completely as the melancholy Graham, was one of those destructive spirits who can momentarily dominate a transitory situation and twist it to their purpose as genuine greatness cannot always do. He had resigned a secondary office in the Palmerston Government a year or so before on a scruple; and when the question arose of re-appointing him in the reconstructed Cabinet, Russell recalled that he had been violently and even virulently opposed to reform, and told Cardwell he would not have Lowe for a master in office. Cardwell answered "Then he will be your master out of office," and Granville said, "It is political suicide"; and both, as things turned out, were right.

Lowe had seen democracy at work in Australia and America, and from practical experience he disliked it intensely. He spoke well, he wrote well, he hated well; and he was soon the effective head of the *ad hoc* opposition to the Russell-Gladstone Reform Bill.

Popular Government has admittedly many grave defects, but hardly those that this most illiberal of Liberals attributed to it. Clever rather than wise, his principles were all prejudice, and when he spoke it was with the hiss of an angry cat at bay, for his lips were filled with gall. "If you want venality, ignorance, drunkenness," he cried, "if you want impulsive, unreflecting, violent people, where do you look for them? Do you go to the top or the bottom?"

It may seem to some of us, as to young Lord Salisbury —the future Premier was then a minor member of the Commons and an opponent of reform—that the virtues are distributed vertically rather than horizontally. But a threatened caste prefers denunciation to argument, and Gladstone's retort that after all the people at the bottom were our own flesh and blood had no effect in mitigating the verbal class-war.

Lowe's arguments were in fact constructed to justify his position, but he could claim that his position was the result of personal observation of democracy at close quarters, and nobody could contradict him. He was perfectly sincere in his stand, but the truth is, of course, that this hard-headed lawyer had no sympathy with the poor, and very little sympathy with anybody else.

There was neither sweetness nor compassion in him. Compared with Lowe, Wellington was a man of sentiment and Bismarck a man of pity. They only hurt when it was necessary to hurt; Lowe hurt because it was his nature to hurt, and the wounds he made were poisoned. He was the type of man who seldom gets to the top, but when he does a revolution follows.

However, it was his hour. His passionate prejudice carried everything before it, for a large number of the Liberals, having got the franchise themselves, had no belief in the franchise for others. Their talk was all of liberty, but in their hearts they believed in privilege. No doubt they loved God as good Christians should, but no doubt their God only loved the middle-classes. The vote was for those who could afford it.[1]

[1] Karl Marx was living in London in these years, and the attitude of the Liberal opponents of reform must have confirmed him in his opinion that the State is an executive committee for managing the affairs of the governing class.

The Liberal malcontents formed a dissident if not actually mutinous group, immortalized by Bright as the Cave of Adullam, and the Bill was doomed. On April 28 the Government majority sank to 5 in the Commons; on June 18 it was beaten by 11.

Across the corridor in the Lords the unhappy old Prime Minister watched his last great measure being slowly murdered; he was powerless to help by vote or voice, and he kept a dignified silence while Gladstone bore the brunt of the battle. He had, after all, known disappointments before, for politics is a rough school, and he had not forgotten that Grey's stiffness let him down in 1846, that Aberdeen's softness let him down in 1854, and that Palmerston's stubbornness let him down in 1859. But this was his last chance, and desertion and defeat by those who had called him their leader and pretended to advocate reform wounded him deeply. The truth is that he really believed in liberty, and he now discovered that half the Liberals only believed in talking about it.

These things are bitter in the mouth. For the time he said nothing, but years afterwards the resentment came out. The Adullamites, he wrote in his recollections, were "divided into three columns or gangs, the first consisting of the selfish, the second of the timid, and the third of those who were both selfish and timid. The timid inspire pity, the selfish indignation, the timid and selfish contempt. There were no doubt some honest men in the Cave of Adullam; but upon the whole I have never, in my long political life, known a party so utterly destitute of consistent principle or patriotic end. When these bandits, uniting themselves to the Tories, had put the Government in a minority, the Cabinet thought it right to offer their resignation."

The Queen, however, protested. She pointed out that the country appeared to be entirely apathetic to reform—Russell admitted this to be true—it was impossible to form another Government, and the state of Europe, with war pending between Prussia and Austria, made their continuance in office imperative.

The last consideration would have been more relevant

THE NEW FOREIGN SECRETARY

JOHNNY RUSSELL : "I can confidently recommend this young man, Clarendon, your
 Majesty, and I taught him writing myself!"

THE QUEEN : "Indeed, John; then I hope he'll mind his P's and Q's better than
 you did."

(By kind permission of the proprietors of "Punch.")

had anybody in Europe cared twopence what the British Government thought about continental affairs. But Bismarck knew that Russell's foreign policy, like the Adullamites' reform policy, was only words, and forgot him; and this time there was not even a growl from Downing Street.

The attempt to carry on the Government was made; it did not last a week. Russell maintained that Parliament had dishonoured itself by the way it had treated the reform question for fifteen years, and clung tenaciously to his ideas, and it became clear that he would sooner die with reform than live with Adullam.

It was just possible, Gladstone thought afterwards, that "an appeal to the country, unhesitatingly made, would have evoked a response similar, though not equal, to that of 1831." But at the moment it seemed unlikely. The defeat was accepted, and the opportunity passed.

It was not, of course, impossible to construct a new Government, for the inevitable Lord Derby was at hand, ready to form his third minority Ministry. The Tories were ardent and hungry after so many years in the wilderness; the promised land was in sight, and the spoils of office were allotted even before the offices were vacant.

A strange reversal of parts now followed. A month before the Russell Cabinet fell, Derby had written to the Queen that the Reform Bill was fatal to the Constitution; within a year the pledges of Disraeli and the principles of Derby had gone by the board, and the Conservative Government passed the second Reform Bill.

Thus history, in fact, repeated itself with the usual difference. Twenty years earlier Lord John Russell's Edinburgh Letter had forced a Conservative Prime Minister to pass a Liberal measure abolishing the Corn Laws, and now his long agitation for parliamentary reform, in which he had suffered so many rebuffs and disappointments, was at long last successful. But again it was a Conservative Prime Minister who passed the Liberal measure.

It may be that Russell felt he had won in the end. But victory of this equivocal sort over an old friend and opponent

Whig junta of which Russell had been called the last doge. He was seen, recognized, and saluted as a veteran volunteer of the victorious war; and at San Remo three years later a still more pleasant symbol of recognition awaited him.

The principal room of the villa in which the Russells were staying was frescoed with portraits of four national heroes. Cavour, Garibaldi, and Mazzini were there by right of birth, but to the surprise and delight of the tenant, the fourth turned out to be Lord John himself.

The compliment was perhaps excessive. But when you are no longer a national hero at home, it is even better to feel a national hero abroad.

CHAPTER XXX

LAST LAP

AND now the end seemed near; nearer than in fact it was, for Russell still enjoyed life as a spectator, and was in no hurry to go. The town house at Chesham Place was given up, but at Pembroke Lodge there was time and to spare for an old man's hobbies; the writing of reminiscences, a few letters to the newspapers, an occasional little speech, even a projected history of Christianity—with the Pope, of course, as the villain of the piece.

Pio Nono, now officially declared infallible, was still at the Vatican; whereas Russell was only an old gentleman enjoying a long golden autumn in Richmond Park, and quite eclipsed by Gladstone. Strange that the Pope should start as a Liberal and end as a Tory, while Gladstone began as a Tory and ended as a Liberal; but Russell, true to the stock from which he sprang, had been consistent throughout. He was born Whig, and when the time came he would die Whig. In the old schooldays at Sunbury, a mile or so away, he had cheered liberty and damned authority in the person of Mr. Pitt, and the good old creed was good enough for him to the end.

Presently Gladstone fell at Westminster, but Pio Nono still reigned at Rome. Liberty, of course, was right, but in this world authority sometimes has the best of it.

But these things no longer signified very much; life was serene and placid with Lady John by the old man's side. Those who are long past the allotted span are already so old they age but slowly; the years pass and do their unseen work, but leave no outward mark.

Even in 1869 Forster had described Russell as "very old and very deaf, with a velvet cap on his head and a hat in his hand, but in cheery spirits, the plucky old fellow that he is." Disraeli's account at second hand is much

255

the same: a friend told him that Russell was "most agree-able and entertaining because, as he could hear no one talk, he never ceased to talk himself. But when he is exhausted he is bored, and you must go."

So at 77; and at 85 he was still much the same, bar failing memory. But with the year 1878 there came a change. The old man's vitality was now visibly drooping, and by March he had taken to his room, which he was never to leave alive. A month later his old enemy the Pope died. Pio Nono had been born three months before John Russell in 1792, and by an odd coincidence, he died three months before John Russell in 1878. Authority and Liberty had run a very close race, and as usual neither had really won.

Easter was late that year, but Russell lived to see the spring. He knew it was his last.

On Good Friday, April 19, his wife wrote, "I have just been sitting with my dearest husband. He has said precious words such as I did not expect ever to hear from him, for his mind is seldom, very seldom, clear, and I put them down at once as well as I can. We were holding one another's hands. 'I hope I haven't given you much trouble.' 'How, dearest?' 'In watching over me.'

"Then by-and-by he said, 'I have made mistakes, but in all I did my object was the public good.' Again, 'I have sometimes seemed cold to my friends, but it was not in my heart.' He said he had enjoyed his life; at another moment he said, 'I am quite ready to go now.' He so often talked of travelling that I thought he might be planning a journey, although he looked different from usual —grown more like himself—and asked him where to. 'To my grave, to my death.'"

There was no fear, but no longer any hope. The very old die peacefully, as those that have earned their sleep.

On the following day the Gladstones drove out to Pembroke Lodge, and Russell's successor noted briefly in his diary: "For a few moments saw Lord Russell at his desire —a noble wreck. He recognized us and overflowed with feeling."

The sands were nearly out. By May 1 the small body,

which more than seventy years before had seemed too feeble for its brave spirit, alone survived. Still the stout heart beat slowly some weeks longer; but late on the evening of the 28th, while his wife held the hand that had always worked for freedom, John Russell died.

The next day the Queen wrote in her diary: "Heard old Lord Russell was dead, having died last night. He had been ill for the last three weeks, and his memory quite gone. He was nearly 86. A man of much talent, who leaves a name behind him, kind and good, with a great knowledge of the Constitution, who behaved very well on many trying occasions; but he was impulsive, very selfish (as shown on many occasions, especially during Lord Aberdeen's administration), vain, and often reckless and imprudent."

The Queen he served had a long memory. She had not forgotten that Russell defended the Prince Consort in Parliament. But she had not yet forgiven the man who brought down the futile Aberdeen.

The good Lord Shaftesbury, on whose noble life the shadows were now deepening, looked back over fifty years' agreement and disagreement with John Russell, and found nothing here to blame. "To have begun with disapprobation, to have fought through many difficulties, to have announced and acted on principles new to the day in which he lived; to have filled many important offices, to have made many speeches, and written many books; and in his whole course to have done much with credit and nothing with dishonour, and so to have sustained and advanced his reputation to the very end, is a mighty commendation." So one generous soul salutes another when the race is run.

But these things were now over, or almost over; and when a State funeral was offered by the Government, it was found that Lord John Russell had preferred to lie among his own people at Chenies rather than with Pitt and Palmerston in Westminster Abbey.

CHAPTER XXXI

REACTION

LESS than twenty years after Lord John Russell died, the Liberal philosopher John Morley was ruminating over the political changes of the dying nineteenth century. One more Reform Bill had been passed since 1867, but this time with a difference of result; and he noticed "a curious thing, not yet adequately explained." The further extension of the suffrage in 1885 had marked a reversal of "the apparent law of things" that the larger the electorate the larger the Liberal majority.

This unexpected political backwash, suggestive of hidden deeps or shallows in the popular mind, was frankly disconcerting. Was Liberalism after all only a layer of middle-class opinion? If the lower classes, as well as the upper, were inclined to Conservatism, then the future of the party was likely to be sombre. Liberalism, of course, was true. But what if men no longer believed it to be true, at least the whole truth?

Perhaps progress was not, after all, as inevitable as Herbert Spencer thought. There were signs of reaction, impalpable hints of changed values in the air.

Abroad, Bismarck had laughed openly at universal suffrage as the rule of the nursery, yet Bismarck had shown a greater interest in social reform than Bright and many of the English Liberals, and under a new type of benevolent despotism Germany was obviously prosperous. Indeed, this new military Empire, the upstart of Europe, was advancing more rapidly in wealth and population than the French Republic, which seemed barely to maintain itself in unstable equilibrium.

At home, too, there was something of a lull in politics, premonitory signs of a slackening of interest and tension, as though the play had begun to weary and the faith was growing cold. In place of Macaulay's proud boast that the Whigs were always ahead of, and the Tories always behind the times, the pernicious idea was spreading that men and measures were much of a muchness after all.

Even the Radical Grote had lost belief in the ballot, so long the testing-point of Liberal opinion, and had come to think before he died that the reformed House of Commons could not be ahead of public opinion.[1] In that case, then, democracy might defeat itself and "government by good-will," as the Gladstonian phrase had it, was hardly government at all.

That activity and perseverance of mankind on which the excellent Playfair and the enthusiastic Russell had so confidently relied to frustrate the folly and caprice of its governors, seemed less conspicuously exhibited in these latter days than of old; and had not some German philosopher denied the very existence of the will of the people? Absurd, of course, but none the less a portent of the age.

It seemed that the nineteenth century was going out, as it had come in, on reaction. Something, no doubt, had been done. But the fervour and zest had gone; the tide was on the ebb.

In the end Morley came to the dismal conclusion that "Men had ceased either to trust or to distrust liberty, and had come to the mind that it mattered little either way. Men are disenchanted. They have got what they wanted in the days of their youth, yet what of it, they ask?"

The octogenarian Gladstone, discussing the point with his lieutenant as they watched the great Atlantic rollers thundering against the rocks at Biarritz, bravely contended that ideals in politics were never realized. But even that valiant optimist admitted a deterioration in public life, and

---

[1] "Since the wide extension of the voting element, the value of the ballot has sunk in my estimation. I have come to perceive that the choice between one man and another among the English people signifies less than I used formerly to think. The English mind is much of a pattern, take whatsoever class you will. The same favourite prejudices, amiable and otherwise; the same antipathies, coupled with ill-regulated though benevolent efforts to eradicate human evils, are well-nigh universal. A House of Commons cannot afford to be above its own constituencies in intelligence, knowledge, or patriotism."—Grote.

allowed that "democracy had certainly not saved us from a distinct decline in the standard of public men. Interest has moved away from politics and theology towards the vague something which they call social reform; and they won't make much out of that in the way of permanent results."[1]

Was it then to demonstrate this dismal fatuity that Lord John had lived and worked?

Admittedly he made many mistakes, but for fifty years and more he strove to spread the gospel of civil and religious liberty through the world, in season and out of season. If this was to be the harvest, then the best that the best of men can do in politics amounts to little more than waste of time. The reformer is simply delaying—if indeed he is delaying—the swing of the tide back to conservatism. The conservative is merely hindering—if he is not undesignedly helping—the inevitable return to reform.

If that is so, it is easy to push the argument a step further. The Jacobin may promote the cause of religion by plundering the Church, an Oxford Movement promote the cause of secularization by insisting on apostolic succession.

A cynic may believe these things. I cannot.

There was, in fact, a marked reaction against political Liberalism after Russell's death. But better reasons can be found than Morley's chilly dictum of disillusion and disappointment.

I

The problem is confused for us of a later time by the habit of speaking of the Victorian Age as if it were all of a piece. The phrase is convenient, but fallacious. There were in fact two Victorian periods, each contrasted and indeed sharply distinguished from the other in politics, religion, literature, and science.

The dominant note of the first period was conflict, revolt, and the liberation of man from a social order he had out-

---

[1] It is odd that neither Gladstone nor Morley seems to have mentioned the contemporary movement for women's emancipation. (Mill's "Subjection of Women" had been published in 1870.) Perhaps the conversation was not fully reported.

grown. The dominant note of the second period was peace, acquiescence, stability, and the conservation and improvement of the mass.

The first period thought in terms of individual liberty; the second put that liberty to its natural use—the construction of a new social order.

So far as England was concerned, the dividing line between the two periods coincides precisely with the time of Russell's retirement. It is no more than a coincidence, but the fact remains that the old Whig took his hand from the helm at the very moment when the Liberal flood was at the full; and the beginnings of the change, which was invisible to those who were taking part in it, may be dated from the year 1868. Cross-currents and undertow remained to obscure the turn of the tide, but from that critical year the boat swung steadily round on its moorings.

The effect is clearly seen in home politics. For the thirty-six years from 1832, while Russell led the reform movement, Liberalism was the dominant force in the State. It reached its zenith in 1868, when he handed over to Gladstone; and during the next eighteen years it fell, and fell at twice the rate it rose. By 1886 the previous position was reversed.

In the first period the Conservatives under Derby had been merely the temporary occupants of Downing Street when the Whigs were tired. In the second period Liberalism was merely the occasional alternative to a practically permanent Conservative Government, which outlasted the reign and the century.[1]

But it was something more than a coincidence that in the British colonies, as in the nationalist movements in Europe and the unionist movement in the United States, a parallel change of political thought was seen. In each case the Liberalism which emphasized the rights of the

[1] The change is clearly marked in the chronology of successive British Governments. From 1832 to 1868 the Liberals were in office 26 years to the Conservative 10. From 1868 to 1886 the Liberals were in office 11 years to the Conservative 7. From 1886 to 1905 the Conservatives were in office 15 years to the Liberal 3.

individual began to decline, and the Conservatism which insisted on the authority of the mass began to increase.

In the first thirty years of the Victorian period every British colony had emphasized its local individuality as distinct from its immediate neighbour; and these several liberties were warmly fostered by Russell and coldly approved by Grey at the Colonial Office. Autonomy was emphasized almost to the point of independence, and there was some talk of secession and disruption of the Empire in the air. But the prophecy was out.

The separatist tendencies first slackened and then ceased, and they were eventually reversed by local union into Dominion and Commonwealth. The decisive dates are the Canadian Coalition of 1864 and the first Australian Federal Conference in 1880; and from that time the Whig theory of State Rights receded before Tory projects of federation and closer union. Autonomy indeed remained, but it was the autonomy of new nations within the Empire, not of seceding States without.[1]

2

The most casual glance at the Churches shows the same shift over from conflict and liberty in the first period towards unity and peace in the second.

The first half of the Victorian age saw the storm and stress of the Oxford Movement, the Hampden affair, the Newman and Manning secessions, the Presbyterian Disruption, the Gorham Judgment, the No Popery storm, the *Essays and Reviews* hubbub, the Denison and Colenso heresy-hunts. In the second half of the reign, Protestant and Catholic, Churchman and Dissenter still hated each other like good Christians; but the din of battle died down from a war march of the priests to the almost courteous salutations of almost friendly opponents.

For this moderation of the ecclesiastical gale there were

---

[1] The Free Trade movement all over the world suffered a setback at the same time. Before 1867 Cobden's prediction of universal Free Trade seemed possible if not probable. After 1870 it was obviously false.

Russell, a strong Free Trader, thought the delay merely temporary, in his "Reminiscences." But it was not.

indeed special reasons. The Anglican Church steadied itself after the secessions, and gave evidence of vitality abroad in the foundation of new colonial dioceses; while Rome discovered that the conversion of England must be reckoned by geological rather than episcopal time. The papal loss of temporal power might or might not be compensated by the assumption of spiritual infallibility, but the centralizing policy of Pio Nono was in fact defensive rather than offensive, and even zealous Protestants had presently to admit that if the bark of the Vatican was louder the bite was less.

More important still, it became increasingly evident to the thoughtful of every denomination from the middle of the nineteenth century that the situation itself had changed. It was no longer that rival points of doctrine were assailed from within or attacked from without. These things continued, but with diminished force; the new danger was the progress of knowledge inconsistent with the historic foundations of the common faith. Against geology and biology neither anathema nor excommunication could avail, and in the cold clear light of new truth the old contending factions shuddered while they saluted one another as possible allies against a common peril.

The time came when the more unacceptable doctrines were sloughed or symbolized away; and as dogma decayed the mystical element in religion increased. The Church was a standing witness to the existence of the eternal in the midst of the temporal, and if it had fought a losing battle for its own interpretation, it could still remind men that truth is ultimately spiritual and not material. In adversity it began to claim the tolerance and freedom it had once denied, and with the new humility came peace.

3

Politics moves on the medium level of life as the art of the practical. Religion may be either above or below politics, a sublimation of life or a subterfuge from it. But literature, which is both a comment on life and an escape from its tedium, seems independent of the controversies of State and Church, and it is with something of a shock that one realizes how closely the parallel between the two Victorian periods is reflected in English letters.

A great creative impulse in verse and prose had illuminated the first half of the reign. In the second half, genius of this order was rare, and its character had changed. Once again the watershed is in the late sixties and early seventies of the nineteenth century.

The poets are our first witness. By 1872 Tennyson had published all his greatest work; the music remained, but the magic had fled. Browning had little more to say. Swinburne had no more *Songs before Sunrise*; the rest was silence, or prose that was worse than silence. Henceforth there was much minor verse, an occasional lyric that haunts the memory like an echo of a fading past, but no more great poetry for thirty years. The lamp of inspiration had gone out.

It was the same in fiction. In the first half of the reign Dickens and Thackeray had created their immortal characters—grotesque, bizarre, and lovable, but always individual; and Trollope on a smaller scale drew the suave cathedral close and the struggling country clergy. But by 1870 these were done.[1] Meredith carried on the tradition of social comedy in more artificial style, but towards the end there was only Hardy, a titan among the pigmies indeed, but an autumn sunset after a blazing summer sun.

It was the same in history. The first half of the reign saw Macaulay and Froude paint their vast canvases, part fact and part romance, and Carlyle rumble-tumbling over Cromwell and Frederick, part story and part sermon. All these, like Dickens and Thackeray, grouped the stage round the individual hero.

But in the latter half of the reign the historians, like Hardy but without his genius, regarded the individual as a mere unit in the stream of circumstance. Truth was gained by the change from hero-worship to the study of mass-action. But the light and the life had gone out of the past, and only Stubbs remained.

It is something more than a coincidence that American letters showed precisely the same decline. The second and

[1] Trollope published several more novels. But the Barchester series by which he is remembered was finished.

third quarters of the nineteenth century had seen a new English literature spring up across the Atlantic, whose youthful promise suggested that it would presently rival and might some day even surpass the great contribution of the mother country to the thought and happiness of the intellectual world. The poets, the philosophers, the novelists and the historians of New England became as familiar names in Yorkshire and Devon as in Massachusetts and Connecticut; the English-speaking peoples seemed indeed to have dissolved their political partnership only to establish a new literary friendship.

But by 1875 the brilliant American dawn was overcast. Hawthorne, Poe, and Prescott were dead; Emerson had said his say on philosophy, Bancroft and Motley had finished their histories, Longfellow's sweet song was over, and Whitman was lying paralysed, his greater gift hampered and obstructed by a living death. These men had their successors, but in America, as in England, they were of smaller stature, and the note, though fluent, was thin.

The contrast between the two periods is too significant to be accidental. For the fifty years before 1870, in short, English literature had produced masterpieces that will last as long as our language survives. But if the total output of polite letters on both sides of the Atlantic for the following thirty years were destroyed, we should certainly lose some pleasant and profitable work; but apart from Hardy's tragic irony, we should lose nothing that is likely to be of permanent value, or to be read by any but scholars and students a century hence.

4

Oratory is usually on a lower intellectual level than literature, and this for two reasons. The speaker appeals to the mass, and must make his effect at once; whereas the writer appeals only to the individual, and can afford to wait. The average level of the crowd is always lower than that of its better individuals, and since the primary business of an orator is to persuade an audience to follow him, he is bound to appeal rather more to the prejudices of the mass, and rather less to the critical faculty of the individual, than the writer.

It is for this reason that the most effective speeches and sermons generally read so badly after the event, and the least effective speeches sometimes read so well. The opulent phraseology, the fat and often flatulent periods hypnotize for the moment, but rhetoric evaporates under the cool detachment of print, and only the still small voice of reason survives.

Oratory resisted the changing time better than literature, largely because Gladstone carried on the spacious tradition of an older age; but here, too, the lean years followed the fat, and the spring tides of rhetoric gave way to the neap. The vast canvas, the spreading synonyms, the quotations from the past, the perorations about the future, which marked the first Victorian period, shrank in the second like the wild ass's skin in Balzac's story; and the day came when the House of Commons would no longer listen enraptured from the dusk of a summer evening to the dawn of a summer morning while a great politician made the worse appear the better cause. In politics as in physiology, the stimulus and the sedative are near allied, and truth is known by its gait, not its garments.

Something, no doubt, of passionate emotion was lost when the taste for simplicity came in, and the art of speech was transformed into an act of business. But length confuses, brevity clarifies, and precision as well as force was gained by the change. Palmerston's arguments were appeals, Asquith's appeals were arguments.[1]

In part this cult of brevity was due to increased pressure of work, and the consciousness that there were other and perhaps better things to be done in the world than making and listening to speeches which notoriously changed no votes. But it marks none the less a shrinkage of political activity coincident with the fall in religious controversy and literary expression; and closer examination shows that all three derived from the slow but steady change that was

[1] Pulpit oratory also declined during the same period. But the sermon declined in quality as well as quantity; whereas the quality of political argument rather improved as its quantity diminished. Authorities on the eloquence of the pulpit seem agreed that the sermon reached its zenith with Liddon. But that great preacher read from a prepared manuscript.

coming over the whole mental outlook and method of the later Victorian age.

It was usual to attribute this decline to democracy, and to lament the passing of the great days when cultured palates could appreciate the finest vintages of oratory. But the reproach was unjust. The people may have every fault that the Eldon school of Tories debited them with, but they know good speaking from bad, and democracy naturally prefers the personal touch, the emotional approach, the rhetorical and even sentimental appeal to the cold argumentative note. Democracy therefore rather assisted the orator by enlarging his opportunities, and if the current changed it was in spite and not because of democracy.

The truth lies deeper than this.

5

The silent revolution which impressed Gladstone and depressed Morley with a sense of changing values and losing if not lost causes had nothing directly to do with politics or religion or literature.

But indirectly the new scientific and in effect mechanical approach to the problems of life which came in with railways and steamships and sanitation was to influence all three, because the precision and certainty of its methods succeeded where the argumentative, the rhetorical, and the ornamental approach had failed.

It is impossible to dissociate the changing attitude of the public mind in the second Victorian period from the developments of applied science, which revolutionized communications, raised the standard of life, and revealed more wonderful worlds than politician or prophet or poet had ever dreamed of. When the first Reform Bill was passed in 1832 the world still travelled by road at ten miles an hour; the cities were dark and ill-drained, and consumed more life than they produced; typhoid, smallpox, and cholera were common, and anæsthetics and antiseptics were unknown.[1]

---

[1] Jenner introduced vaccination in 1798, but it was not generally used for many years. Simpson introduced anæsthesia in 1846; Lister first practised antisepsis in 1865.

By the time the third Reform Bill was passed, in 1885, all this was changed; and these things were done without eloquence or heat or passion, without any claim to divine right or hierarchical succession, without any dogmatic assumption of the right of minorities to rebel or majorities to rule. But the fact remains that these things achieved more than eloquence or contention or passion had ever done for the advancement of mankind, and were more potent in their results than any Act of Parliament or Order in Council.

While politicians were talking about progress, the engineers and chemists and electricians were actually progressing. While the pulpits were justifying suffering and death as the penalty of sin, the new medicine and the new surgery were relieving pain, and the new sanitation was prolonging life and rendering it more secure. While men of letters were singing the poetry of motion, the men who built locomotives and laid cables were actually achieving it; but their poetry was wrought in action, and their work was cast in the severer and more disciplined mould of mathematics and calculations of gravitational stability, and the strains and stresses of mass multiplied by velocity. There was both beauty and imagination in these things, but it was beauty of a new type.[1] An emotional bridge, a passionate reciprocating engine, and a rhetorical chemical formula would have been as absurd as a *Hymn to the Skylark* by a physiologist or an *Ode to the West Wind* by a meteorologist.

The new science, like the traditional Church and the historic State, appealed to authority. But it was a different authority. Both Church and State, in the last resort, rested on opinion. It is true that both could back their opinion by force, but it was still public opinion that made the force. Newman appealed to the general opinion of the ancient world to prove that Rome was right. Russell appealed to the general opinion of the modern world to prove that Rome was wrong. Each convinced those who wished to be convinced, and exasperated the rest.

[1] The art critics, of course, could not see it. But neither could they see beauty in Whistler or Wagner.

But the engineer, the chemist, and the electrician—the "hodge-podge of scientists" whom Keble had derided[1]—based themselves not on changing opinion but permanent fact and result. There was no need to argue, for the demonstration proved itself, and public opinion was of no consequence one way or the other. The day of the expert and technician had arrived.

A new force had insinuated itself into society, and the old familiar authorities had begun to lose a little of their prestige and their attraction for youthful genius as the new authority made itself felt. Man is after all something more than a political and religious animal. He is also an inventive and mechanical animal who likes doing things even more than discussing things; and if the engineering shop and the laboratory produce results where Parliament fails, he will exalt the scientist and degrade the politician.

The laboratory did produce results where Parliament failed; and its results were often impressively precise and accurate, whereas those of statesmen were always approximate and occasionally the very reverse of what they intended. The new applied science, with its coadjutor and accompaniment statistics, necessitated a higher standard of truth than had hitherto existed in the arts; and since these things were visible to all, it followed as a matter of course that the public readjusted its values. It may be that politics is not susceptible of such exact definition as physics and chemistry; but an uneasy feeling began to prevail that Simpson and Lister and Kelvin had after all done more for the world than Palmerston and Russell and Gladstone.

The Queen herself was not unconscious of the change, as she looked back over fifty years of strife and tumult in State and Church, and contrasted the mighty issues of the time with the petty spite and purely personal ambition shown by some of its leaders. "As I get older," she remarked sadly, "I cannot understand the world. I cannot comprehend its littlenesses. When I look at the

---

[1] The attitude was probably general at that time. Carlyle's almost contemporary "Hero-Worship" lauded prophets, poets, priests, kings, even men of letters, but no scientists. Yet Isaac Newton was not unknown, and as a Scot he might have remembered Napier.

frivolities and littlenesses, it seems to me as if they were all a little mad."

Man himself had shrunk a little in comparison with the new worlds he had discovered; but perhaps the individual ego became more modest as its cosmos increased, and human dust recognized its own insignificance. There was now less reluctance to admit that the questions so confidently asked on the grave problems of fate had been answered wrong, and those strong souls who scanned the new horizon for ultimate reality had to think out the very basis of their philosophy afresh.

This was no mere political reform, but a revolution of the human mind, which distinguished the second Victorian period from the first. The familiar landmarks were vanishing, the recognized authorities were numb, and only the belief in truth survived as the turmoil of the nineteenth century passed from being into history.

6

In the first Victorian period, then, politics were regarded as more important than they are. In the second Victorian period Morley noted the first faint flush of doubt whether politics could solve the problems of life. And in the post-Victorian period the reasonable doubt has become an exaggerated conviction, and politics are now regarded as less important than they are.

Some part of this reaction was manifestly inevitable. The "government of the people, by the people, for the people" obviously presupposes that all men are interested in politics all the time; and all men know this is not true. The result is that any democratic government is at best a compromise, and at worst a sham.[1]

The status of the trade has declined; it is more doubtful whether the quality of the tradesman has deteriorated, for the politicians of the eighteenth century were hardly angels

---

Cf. Morley's famous "Essay on Compromise"; and Colonel House on the advantage of being the power behind the President rather than the President. Under aristocracy or oligarchy the actual leaders are the acknowledged leaders; under despotism or democracy, the real power is concealed behind a nominee.

of light. And democracy, though its incompetence to solve its own problems makes it an easy target, is not entirely to blame for the decay in politics; circumstance has played its part here as in other fields.

It happened that in the Palmerston-Russell period the problems of the State took on a predominantly political aspect, because there was a shift in the social structure from rural to urban; and here Parliament was supreme, because on the essentially political matters of franchise and the constitution politicians are their own experts.

But presently things began to take a different turn.

In the first place, the new scientific discoveries made civilization more complex, and fresh departments of the State were required to deal with them. But here Parliament was less sure of its ground, and more in the hands of independent experts, whose advice it could only accept or reject.[1] On the whole it accepted, with the result that an unseen and anonymous executive grew up in the Civil Service; and it was found that most men are willing to pay an adequate price for a reasonably efficient administration, so long as it leaves them fairly free to run their private affairs as they will. Parliament remained the grand inquest of the nation, but outside purely political matters its competence was no longer beyond question,[2] and with the decline of political interest its supreme importance in the national life diminished.

In the early Victorian period the House of Commons had dominated the executive. In the late Victorian period the executive dominated the House of Commons. Here, again, the change is first noticeable in the critical year 1868, when the influence of political groups declined, and a Government with an impregnable and docile majority

[1] The tendency can be traced in the increased number of Royal Commissions and purely departmental Bills, in some of which the Secretary of State at Westminster was obviously no more than the mouthpiece of Whitehall. The Electricity Act of 1927 was the most conspicuous case in point.

[2] *Cf.* the bungling and timidity shown over Vaccination, Vivisection, and Divorce.

Morley held that Parliament is more efficient than bureaucracy. It may possibly be so; on the other hand, bureaucracy is certainly more efficient than the crass incompetence of ordinary local government.

controlled Parliament for the first time in thirty years. From that time the strength of the executive grew, Government measures and Supply occupied the bulk of the session, and the private members began to lament the loss of their old liberties under Palmerston and John Russell. Mass action had encroached on individual right in the very temple of liberty.

In the second place, social reform presently began to displace political reform as the urgent question of the time.

It became clear after a time that a perfect political constitution is no guarantee of industrial equity, that equality of franchise does not necessarily mean social freedom, and that even the unattainable "free Church in a free State" may only give orthodox answers to questions which science has already answered differently. The Whigs thought in terms of political liberty, and we owe them thanks for that. But they were inclined, in their consequent restrictions of the functions of the State, to forget equity, which is at least as important to society as freedom.

The liberty which the Whigs insisted on helped the strong, but they were rather scandalized when the Tories suggested that equity should protect the weak. Even John Russell, the kindest of men in his own household, could not see the need for protecting the wretched little chimney-sweeps, whose case became a classic of philanthropy and literature; and many of his colleagues worshipped at the altar of liberty, unconscious that Mr. Gradgrind and his kind were also among the congregation.[1]

It is the fact, however, that equity can only be attained, as Shaftesbury and the social reformers maintained against Bright and the Manchester School, by an apparent abridgement of liberty; and in the second Victorian period men became increasingly conscious of the claims of the mass against the individual man who was exploiting them. A

---

[1] When Macaulay read Dickens's "Hard Times," he dismissed it as pure Socialism.

Similarly John Bright, in a famous set piece of oratory, lamented the death of British officers in the Crimea. Lamentable indeed, but the great orator had no indignant eloquence to spare for the greater toll of life in the slums and factories at home.

more humane economic theory was developed as the trade unions and co-operative societies struggled into being, and these naturally combined with philanthropic effort and scientific discovery to strengthen the foundation of labour on which the whole social structure rested.

The limitation of factory hours, compulsory education, and compulsory notification of infectious diseases, were all gross interferences with the liberty of the subject. But it is no paradox that social liberty was increased by these restrictions on the liberty of the individual. After all, every tyranny in history has been established by men who enlarged their own liberty at the price of equity, and the first Victorian period was not very far from the establishment of another such tyranny in the name of freedom and progress. From that attitude there was certain to be a revulsion, and it was certain that some would regard it as reaction.

7

The time came, then, when the nation tolerated an enlargement of the administrative side of government and paid more attention to social than political reform; and these things naturally and perhaps necessarily coincided with the decline of Liberal individualism and the revival of that Conservative nationalism which is more concerned with the State as a whole than with its several units.

It seemed to those who thought on purely political lines that men had lost their love of liberty; and it is true that men care less for liberty than they should, seeing that there is so little of it, and that little so unevenly distributed. But the idea that men, and more particularly Englishmen, will ever cease to value liberty seems to me absurd. They had not lost their love of liberty when Gladstone and Morley lamented the changing values of this difficult world; they were merely using it after their own fashion, and not as their mentors had expected.

Russell had been mortified in 1850 to find that Catholic Emancipation was used to restore the Catholic hierarchy. Morley was mortified to find in 1890 that a Liberal franchise was used to return a Conservative Government.

But these things were in effect liberty in action; for in the last analysis liberty is not an end but a means, and unless it is used it is nothing. But the only use to which men ever put liberty is to build up a new authority, and when that fails they assert their liberty again. There is no final solution of the problem of politics, or if there is, men have not found it.

The pendulum swings from left to right, and so the clock goes round.

INDEX

An asterisk after a page number indicates that the subject is dealt with in a note.

Printed in Great Britain by Butler & Tanner Ltd., Frome and London

F.20.730